SEX AND HORROR

THE ART OF EMANUELE TAGLIETTI

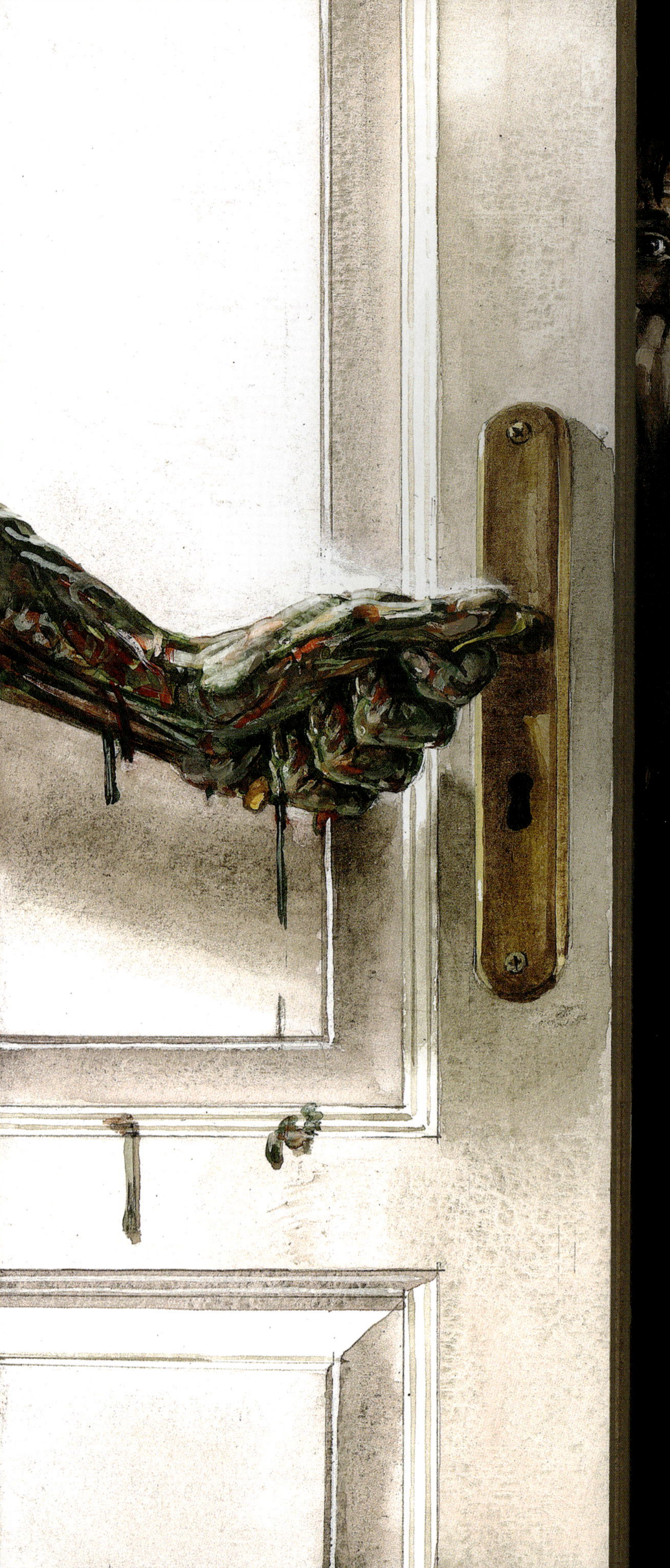

First published in 2015 by Korero Press Ltd,
157 Mornington Road, London, E11 3DT, UK

www.koreropress.com

© Korero Press Limited
© Emanuele Taglietti
© Eredi Barbieri/Edizioni If.

A CIP catalogue record for this book is available from
the British Library

ISBN-13: 9780957664944

Printed in China

SEX AND HORROR

THE ART OF EMANUELE TAGLIETTI

KORERO PRESS

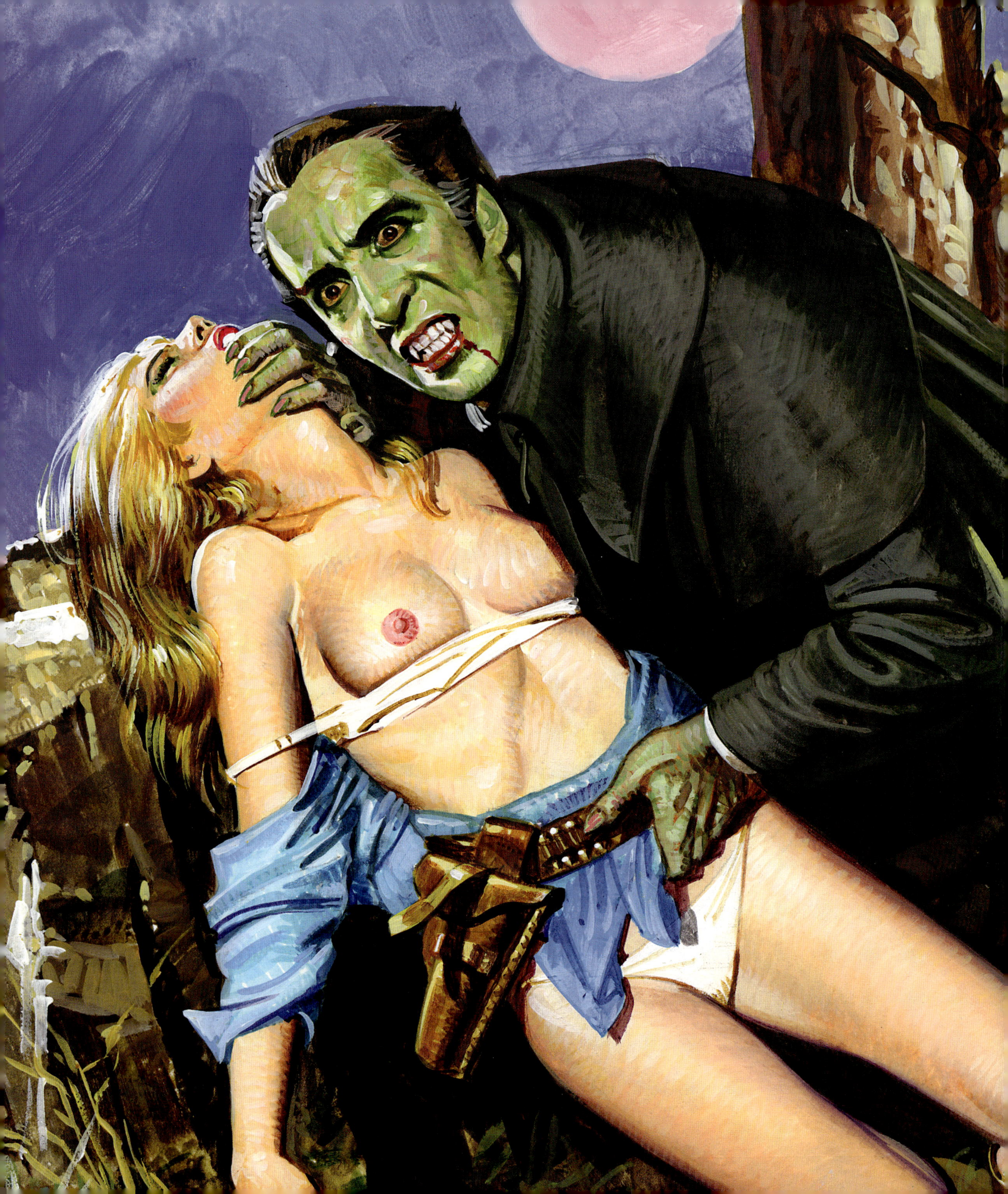

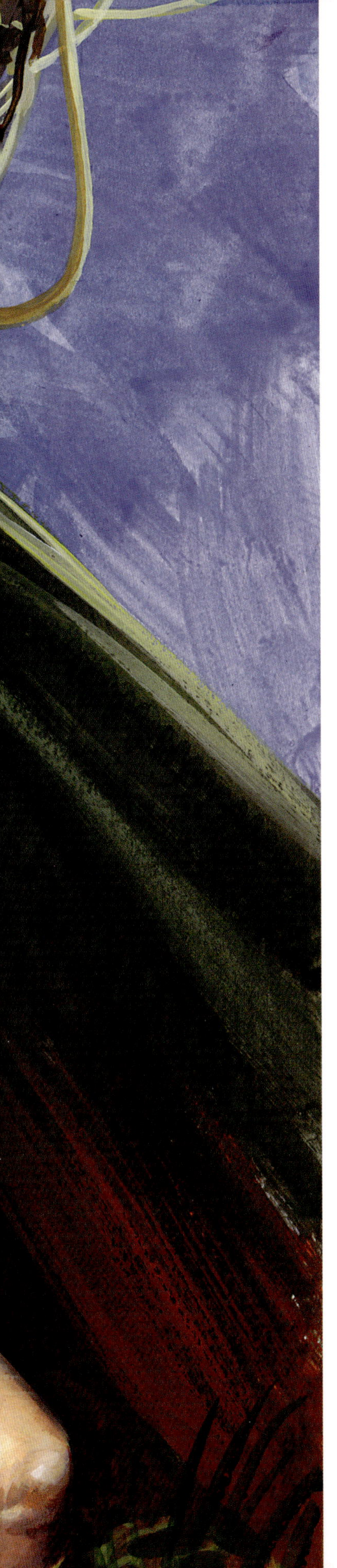

CONTENTS

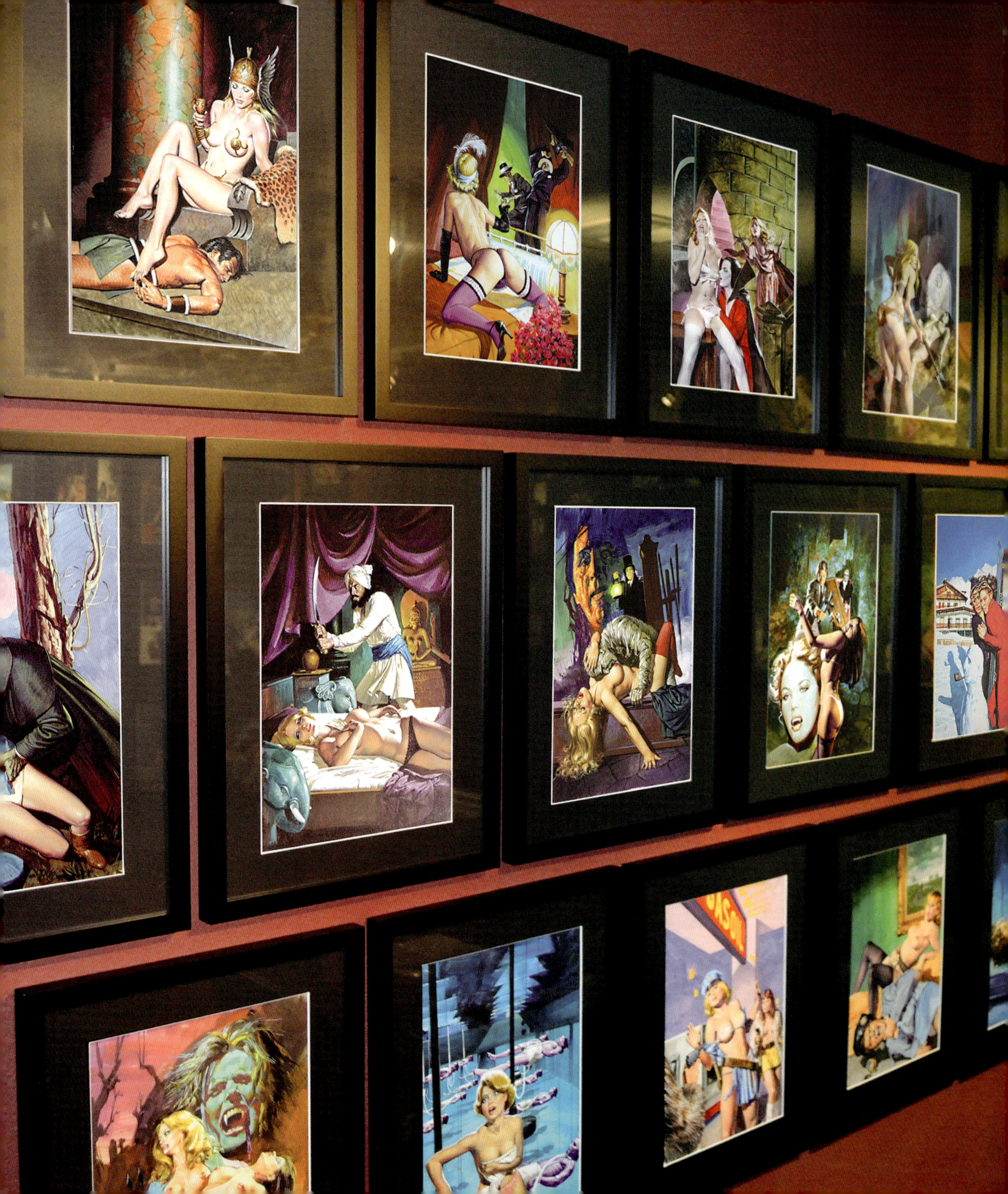

FOREWORD

NEVER JUDGE A COVER by its book. That's what comes to mind when I think of the erotic pulp comics of 1970s Italy. Like their American counterparts, Italian pulp comics are remembered not for their content but for their cover art. I've always been a fan of American pulp art, both pre-war and post-war, but when I discovered the Italian pulps of the '70s it was like discovering a new color in the spectrum! I knew I had found the most exciting pulps ever produced.

Among the very best of this era are the works of Emanuele Taglietti. His covers are the most detailed and refined, and his women are luscious and gorgeous – his Sukia may be the most beautiful character of the genre. These qualities are especially impressive given the speed at which these covers were produced. In fact, this may be a clue to their greatness. There was no time to second guess; no time for the energy to diminish. His covers won't allow themselves to be viewed casually. Once his imagery meets your eye it captures your gaze like the power of Dracula. You savor it and want to see more. You can't look at five or ten covers, say, and feel you've seen them all. Every cover is a new exploration of color, drama, whimsy, beauty, fetish, humor, horror. These layered elements converge to arouse the viewer like no other art form.

When I began collecting these cover paintings I did not know the name "Taglietti". As my collection began to grow I researched every bit of information I could find about the genre and cover artists. I soon concluded that the covers which most impressed me were associated with two names: Allesandro Biffignandi and Giuseppe D'angelico. One day I acquired a cover that was identified as a Taglietti. I studied the piece and compared it to other covers in my collection. That's when I began to realize a terrible injustice was occurring. Some trick of fate was wiping away the name of Taglietti from comic art history and crediting his accomplishments to another artist.

I discovered that a dozen pieces in my collection that had been sold to me as works of the master Biffignandi were actually those of the master Taglietti! As a professional artist myself I know how this can occur with unsigned works, and I felt compelled to undo the damage occurring to this man's legacy. On blogs and websites I found Taglietti cover paintings credited to Biffignandi and would post comments crediting Taglietti. I communicated with Italian collectors and dealers and told them which of their pieces were the works of Taglietti. Some of them doubted me; some told

Right: Mark Alfrey's framed collection of Emanuele Taglietti's paintings.

me I was wrong. After all, I'm just some ignorant American. How could I possibly know anything about Italian comic art? Later I decided to track down the master himself and report these injustices to him personally. Unlike most people of his age Taglietti embraces the internet and has created a web page to show some of his more recent work – scenes of Italy rendered in watercolor. Up to that point he was not displaying his comic cover art or even making mention of it. Feeling uncertain I had the right guy, I emailed him.

There's an old saying that goes, "Never meet your heroes." If I had believed in such wisdom I'd never have had the pleasure of making the acquaintance of Emanuele Taglietti. His extraordinary talent speaks for itself, but it's when you speak with the man that you realize this talent resides in the heart of a kind, friendly and generous being. For a non-traveling, non-Italian speaking American such as myself it seems almost impossible that I should be able to communicate with an Italian master. Our meeting could not have occurred in any previous time in history. We are separated by continents, cultures and most of all, language. But the blessed internet dissolved those barriers. Now I find myself contributing to this awesome document of the master's work. And to see, with its publication, that justice has been served.

Mark Alfrey

Right: Wallestein il Mostro, 2014.

FOLLOWING SPREAD
Left: Mondo Corrotto, n. 21, *La 24 Ore della Morte*, The 24 Hours of Death, 1986.

Right: Telefilm Proibiti, n. 6, *Il Caso di Alex Barringer*, The Case of Alex Barringer, 1986.

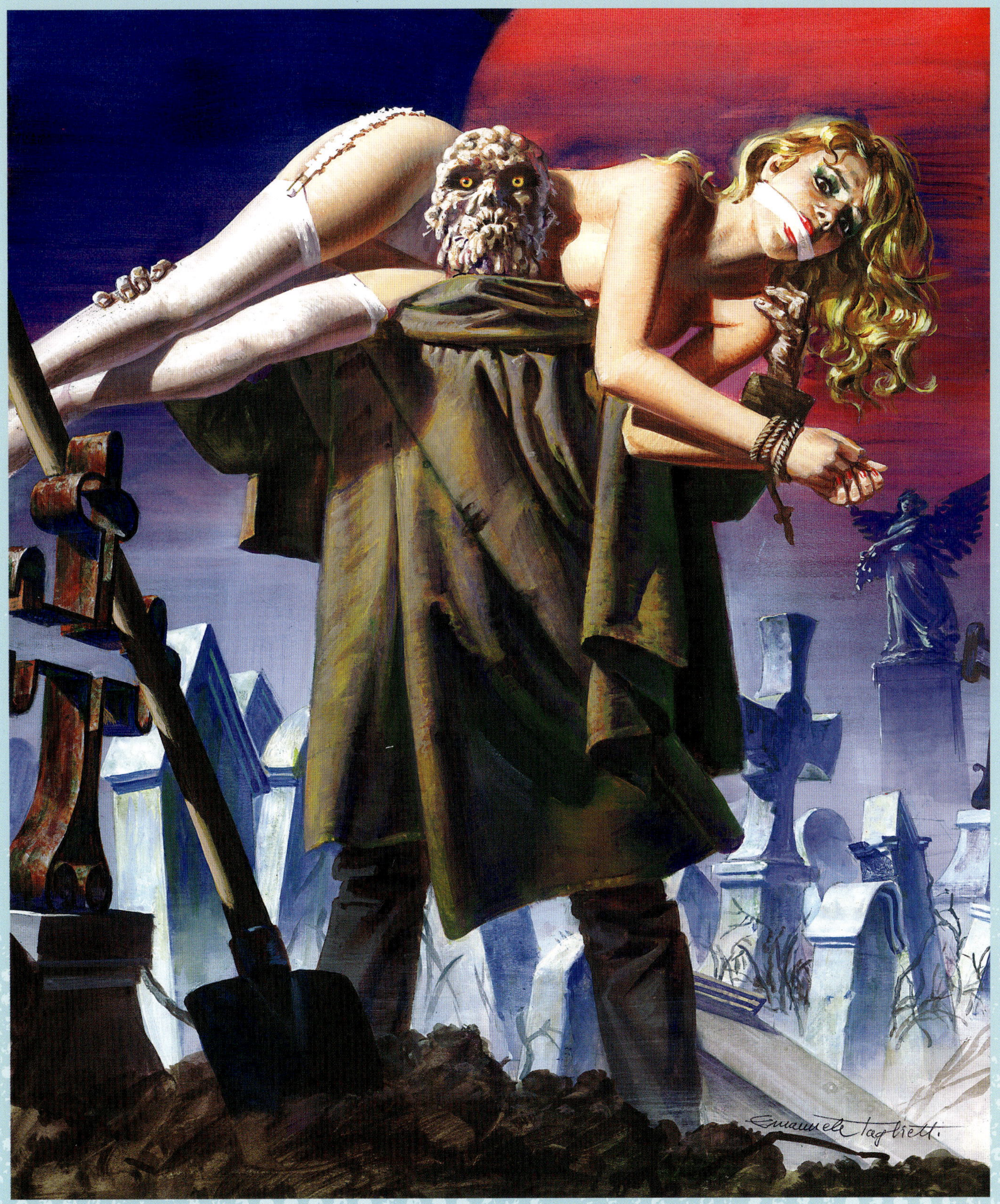

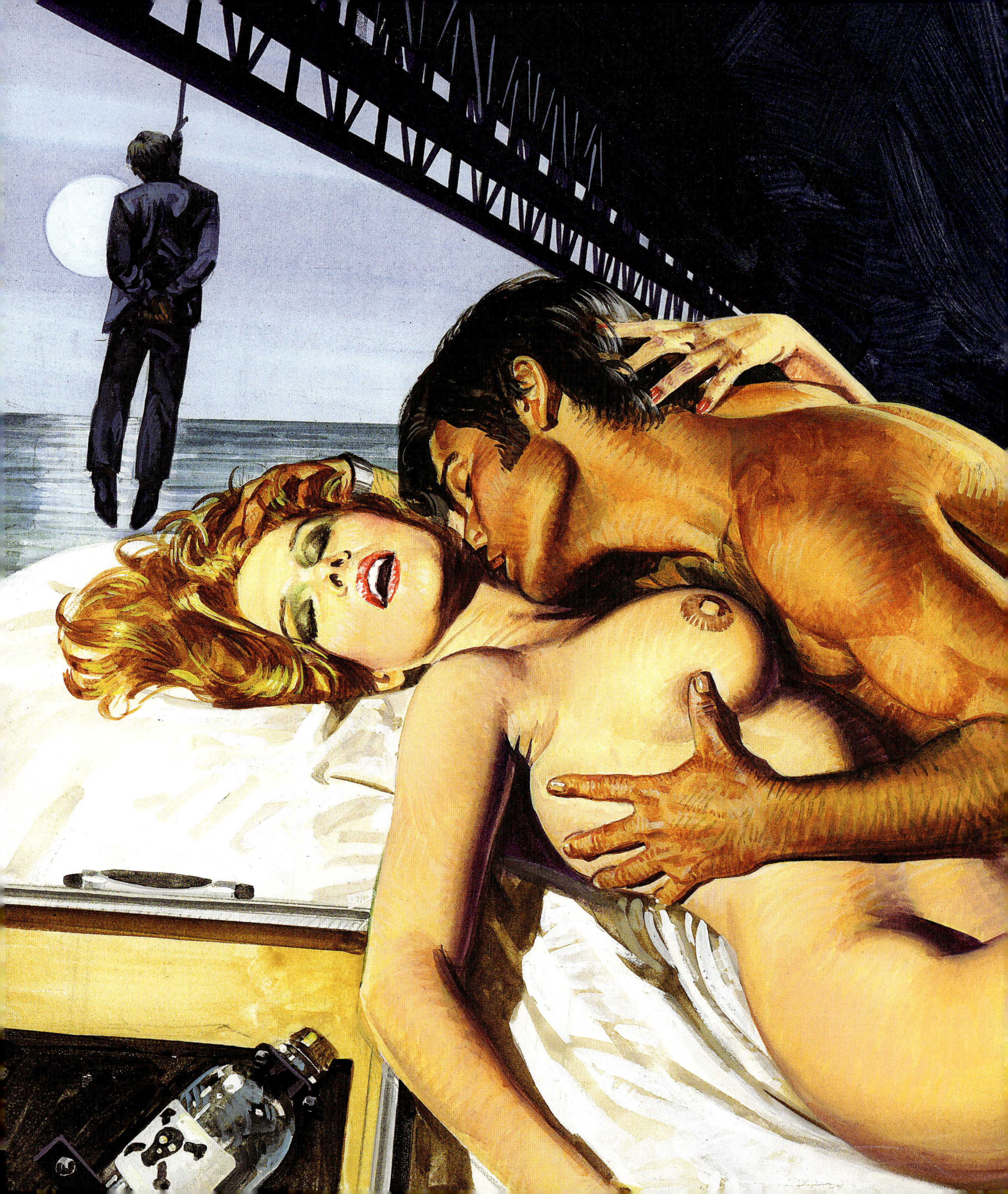

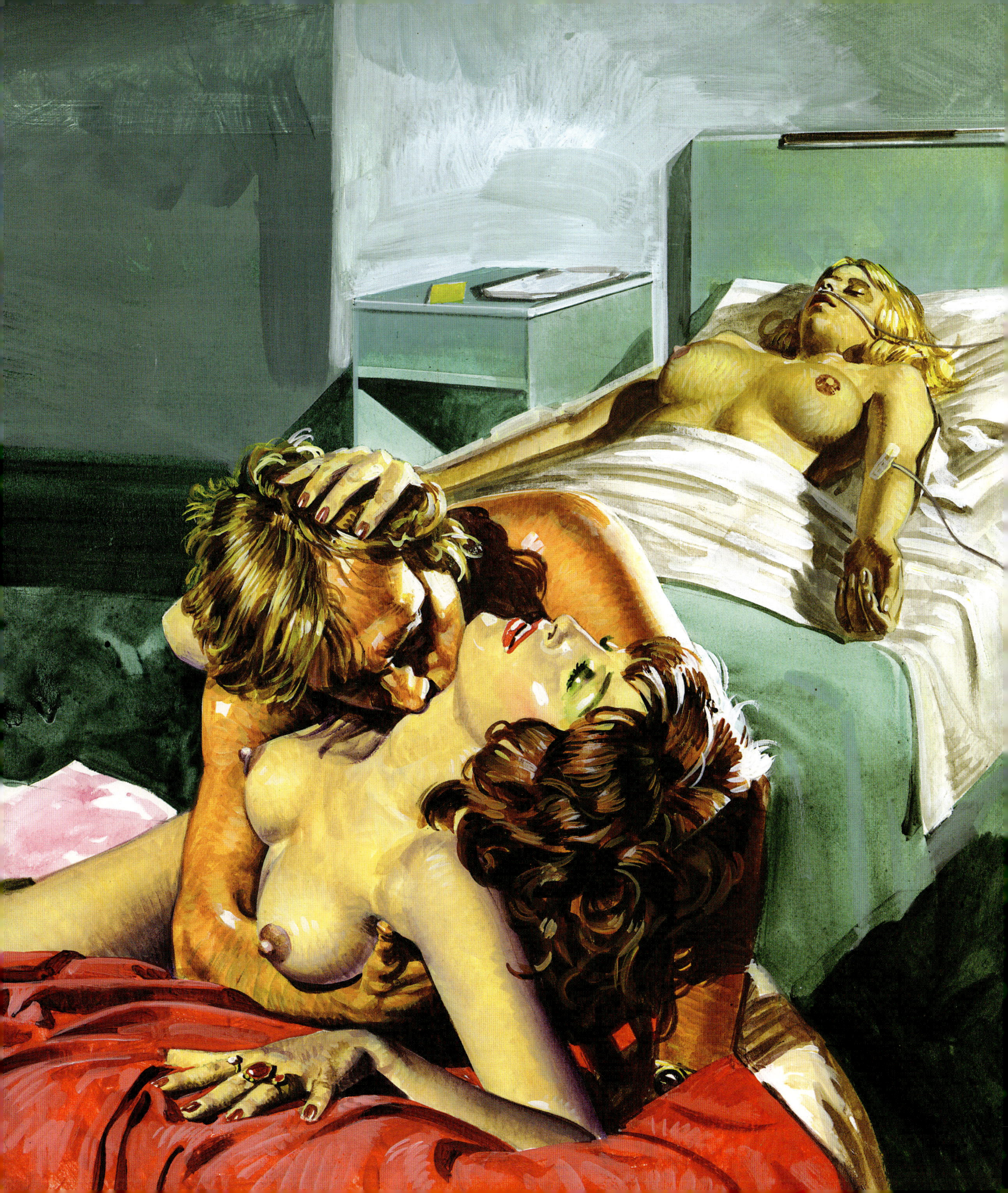

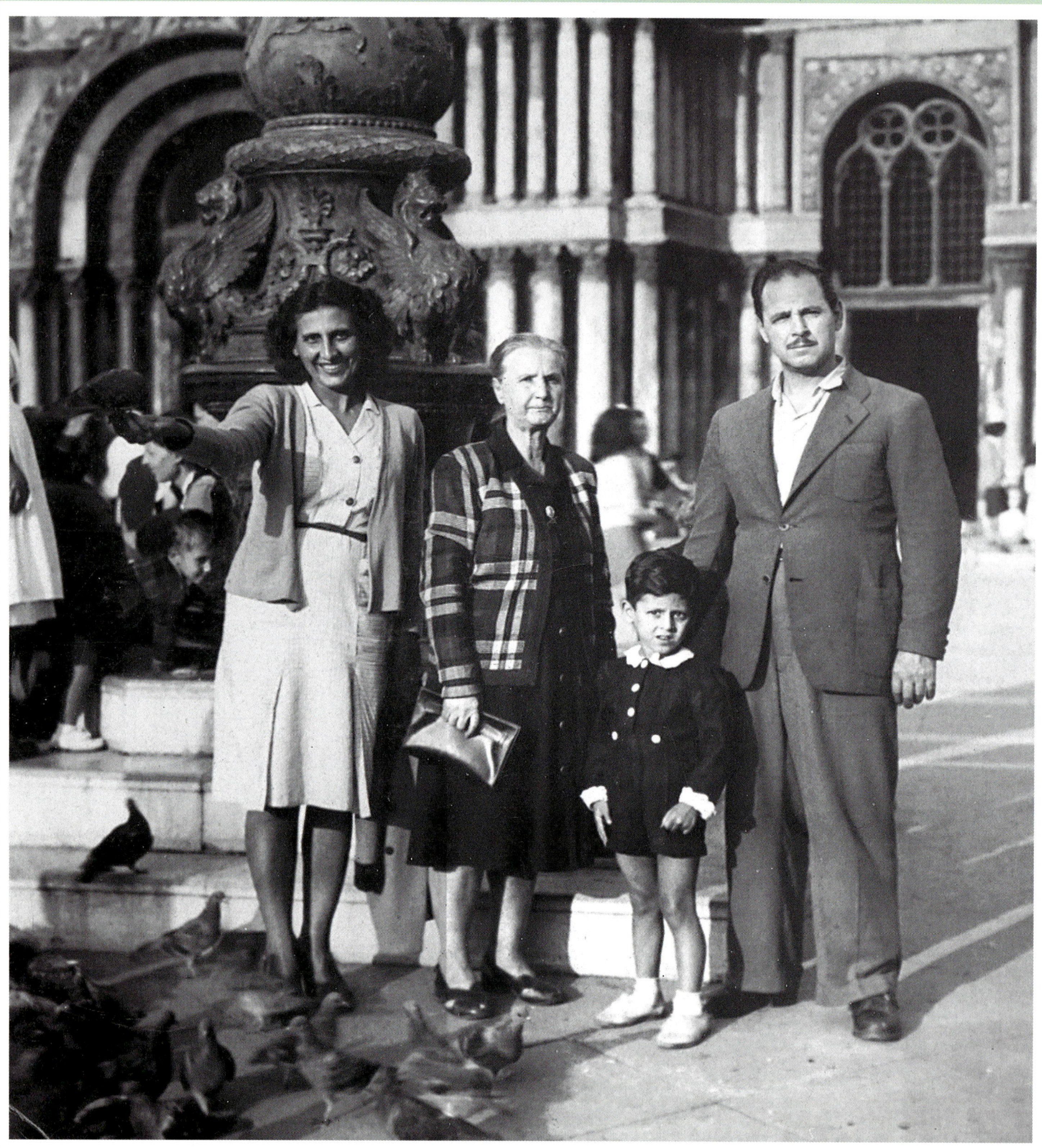

A PORTRAIT OF THE MAESTRO

EMANUELE TAGLIETTI was born in northern Italy, in the city of Ferrara, Emilia-Romagna, on January 6, 1943. His father, Othello, was a painter and decorator and as a child, Emanuele would sometimes help him carry his materials to work, so he became familiar with the use of colour and paintbrushes. In the 1960s, Othello worked as a set designer on several movies made by his cousin, the director and screenwriter Michelangelo Antonioni, and Emanuele joined him on the film sets several times, sparking an early interest in the world of movie-making.

After leaving school, Emanuele attended the local art college and then, at the age of 18 he moved to Rome to study set design at the Experimental Centre of Cinematography, the oldest film school in Western Europe. After graduating, Emanuele became involved in Italian cinema and worked on around 30 films – including Federico Fellini's *Juliet of the Spirits* (1965) and Marco Ferreri's *The Harem* (1967) – as an assistant art director and later as an interior decorator. On the movie set, he'd often draw detailed and realistic concept sketches to help the director visualize particular scenes – a skill that he'd later draw on in his second career.

By 1973, Emanuele had grown tired of the world of cinema; he also wanted to leave Rome with his family. He started to look at more flexible career options that would allow him to work where and how he pleased. "The idea of working from home and sending jobs to the client once they were completed appealed to me," he recalls. With these aims in mind, Emanuele wondered whether he could become a freelance illustrator producing cover art for the Italian publishing phenomenon of the day: *fumetti*, or comic books.

The word *fumetti* literally means "small puffs of smoke", which suggests the speech balloons common to most comic strips. *Fumetti* had a long tradition in Italy, dating back to the early 20th century. Originally they were marketed for a mostly young and male readership and were quite often based on historical events, but by the mid-1960s they had developed into a new type of entertainment, strictly for adults, with most titles now covering crime, horror or sexual themes. The comics' content and imagery became increasingly graphic as the sexual revolution wore on and attitudes about what was offensive or obscene shifted. In the early 1960s a naked female breast was seen as outrageous but by the early '70s it was viewed as almost chaste and innocent.

Left: Emanuele in Venice in 1948, with his parents Othello and Flora, and his grandmother Pauline Antonioni, aunt of the Italian film director Michelangelo Antonioni.

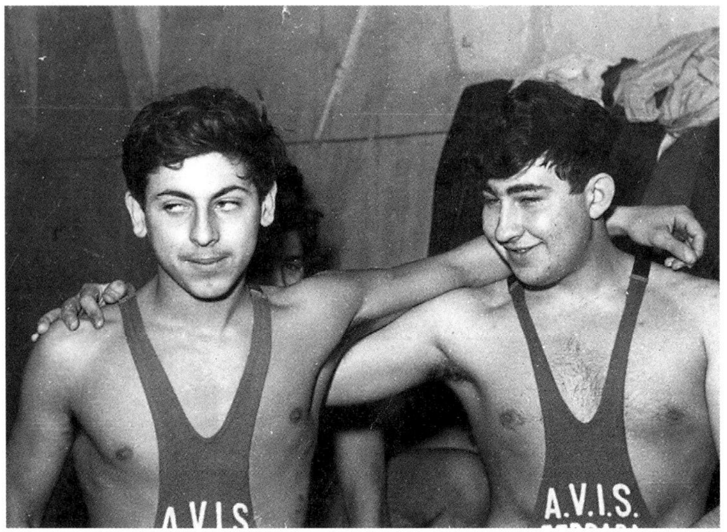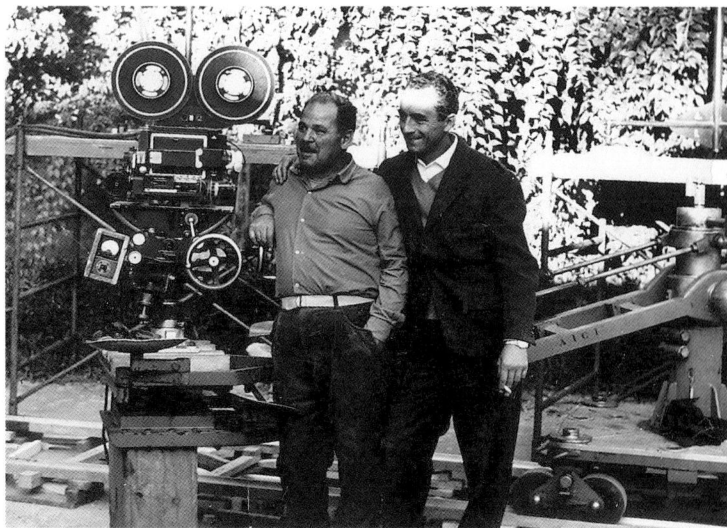

The sales of these comic series relied heavily on the impression their covers made on the newsstands: buyers were lucky if the inside art was just as good and the story exciting and well plotted. Often the comics were purchased solely for their cover art, and today this is their main attraction for collectors. Emanuele believed that he possessed the right skills to produce this type of work. His good friend Dino Leonetti – a production designer whom he'd met on the set of a Federico Fellini film – was now working as a comic book artist and he encouraged Emanuele's interest, giving him the contact details for three prominent comic book publishers in Milan. Emanuele knocked up some test boards and then made an appointment with all three.

The first publisher on the list was Edifumetto, which had been founded by Renzo Barbieri in the early 1970s. They had a big share of the market for erotic, fantasy, and horror-themed comics. "That meeting was decisive for my professional life," Emanuele recalls. He was aware that Edifumetto gave work to a lot of artistic people: "It was almost a school where people could hone their art," he says. "When you entered their offices there was a lounge full of painters and designers clutching their work." Emanuele met with Renzo Barbieri and his art director, Giuseppe Pederiali, as well as the company's administrator. The team looked at Emanuele's samples and asked him how many covers he thought he could produce in a month. Emanuele said that he reckoned he could probably manage six or seven, as he was new to it and would be a bit slow at first. His response must have been the right one, because he was immediately offered a 12-month contract as a cover artist; he didn't need to keep the appointments with the other publishers.

With his first commission from Edifumetto in the bag, Emanuele made arrangements to leave his job in the movie industry and he and his family relocated to his home town of Ferrera. Once there, he set up a studio and launched his new career as a comic cover artist. The work for Edifumetto began straight away. However, it was a steep learning curve for Emanuele – although he was able to draw on his past experience as a set designer, his first few covers were a little rough and naïve. He'd had little experience of drawing human anatomy – especially female anatomy – which, given the highly realistic, figurative style of the covers, was something of a drawback. But Edifumetto had confidence that he'd succeed, and patiently waited the few months it took for him to bring his figure drawing up to scratch. The publishers' production and commissioning process was fast and furious,

Top left: Emanuele (on the left) and a fellow competitior in Italy's Greco-Roman Wrestling Regional Championships, 1957.

Top right: Emanuele's father with his cousin, Michelangelo Antonioni, during a break in filming the movie *Eclipse*, which was nominated for the *Palme d'Or* in 1962.

with the writers producing 30–35 stories per month. It was a race against time, and the work was backbreaking for the cover artists. Initially, Emanuele had to paint about 12 covers a month, but when he became more confident, he was able to turn some work down, and reduced the number to 10. He'd be given a verbal brief over the phone, or, for the more complex covers, he'd receive a written brief containing just one or two lines of direction on a sheet of paper. Today, he says that he believes the best cover designs were born from the ideas and imagination of those who had to implement them – him and the other artists employed by Edifumetto. "The Zora la Vampira, Cimiteria, Wallestein, Karzan, Belzeba, and Playcolt characters had been created before I arrived so I had to adhere to the guidelines already set by other artists and the writers of the comics,' he says. "But those covers where I could just let my imagination run riot were often the best."

"My sources of inspiration for the covers were always the same: the masters of painting and of illustration, as well as books, films, photographic and current affairs magazines. A big contribution also came from the cinema, especially its scenic and photographic aspects. I studied the stills from movies, the characters and the costumes... and topped it all off with beautiful busty girls."

"It was important for my work to have to hand a wealth of inspirational source material. I created a small image reference library feauring weapons, military uniforms, motorcycles, animals, furniture, and so on. I could then use this to deal with any request and work within the brief. The workload was hectic, but the diverse subject matter involved – from fairy tales to horror, and from comedy to police action – always made it varied and interesting. I remember that I drew five or six covers at the same time, possibly in the same genre; it was easier to get organized, working in blocks like that. I worked on many different characters and series, sometimes alternating issues with the other cover artists. I realized some series from beginning to end, though, including

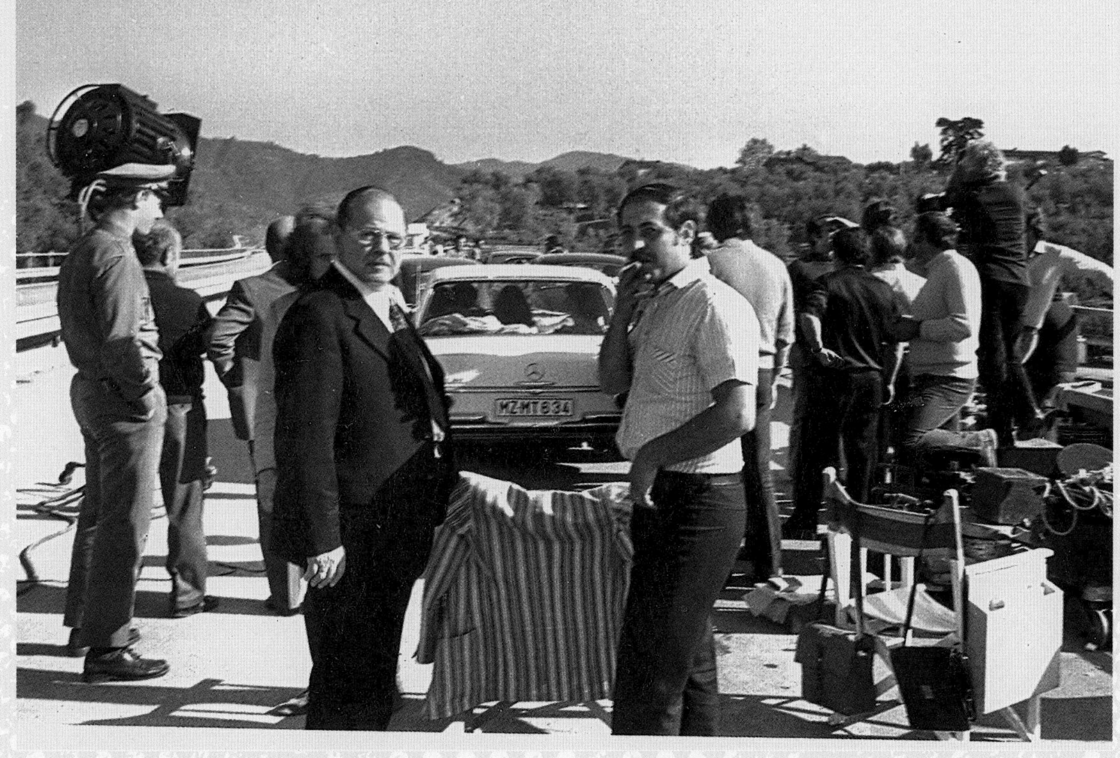

Left: Emanuele (right) and his father on the set of *Hit and Run* (1973), directed by Dino Risi and starring Marcello Mastroianni and Oliver Reed.

Sukia, Fata Turchina, Vipera Bionda, Fox, 44 Magnum, and Moschiettiera." Dino Leonetti had opened Emanuele's horizons to the world of illustration. "In Dino's study, for the first time, I had the opportunity to see the work of illustrators, both Italian and international artists. Among these were the Italian erotic illustrator and cover artist Averardo Ciriello, with his painted movie posters, and US fantasy artist legend Frank Frazetta, with his heroes skillfully rendered in oils." Emanuele went on to create a unique style of his own – influenced by masters such as these – and his work for Edifumetto demonstrate remarkable skill in portraiture and in scenic backgrounds.

Emanuele was familiar with several painting techniques: "From an early age, helping my father with murals, I learned to use tempera, and as a teenager I learned the technique of oil painting," he says. "While studying set design in Rome I'd often sell my oil paintings of Venetian scenes to help my rather poor finances." At Edifumetto he started out using acrylic paint for his illustration work. He'd choose suitable images from his reference library, start painting in acrylic and then add the finishing touches in tempura. The finished paintings measured 25 cm x 36 cm (10 x 14 inches).

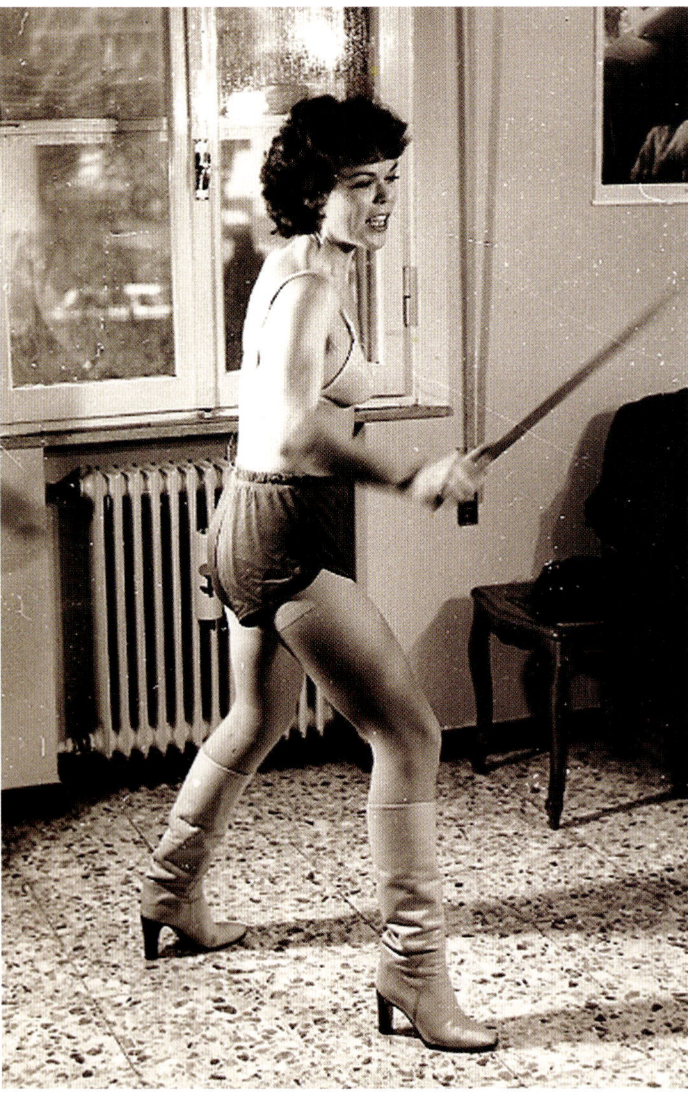

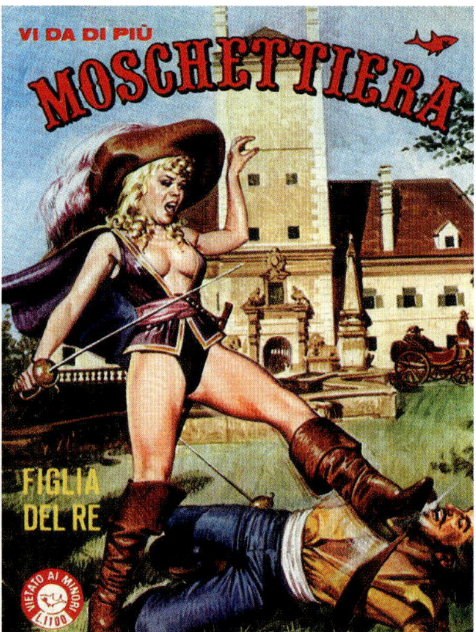

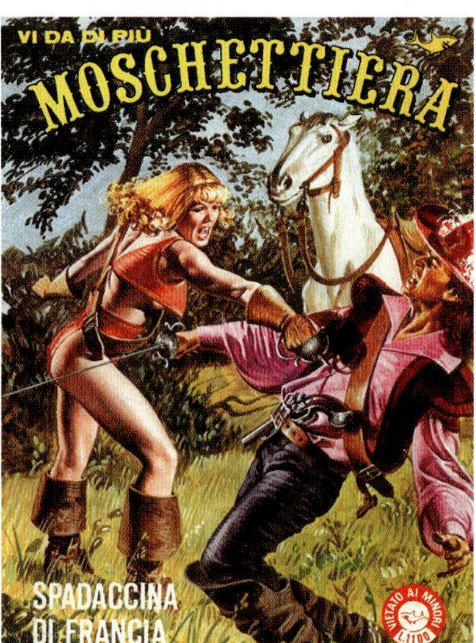

Far left: Fiorella Bonazzi, sister of comic book artist Germano Bonazzi, was Emanuele's model for the heroine in the series Moschettiera.

Top left: Moschettiera, n. 1, *Figlia del Re*, Daughter of the King, February 1982.

Bottom left: Moschettiera, n. 2, *Spadaccina di Francia*, Swordswoman of France, March 1982.

Right: Santa Claus, 2013.

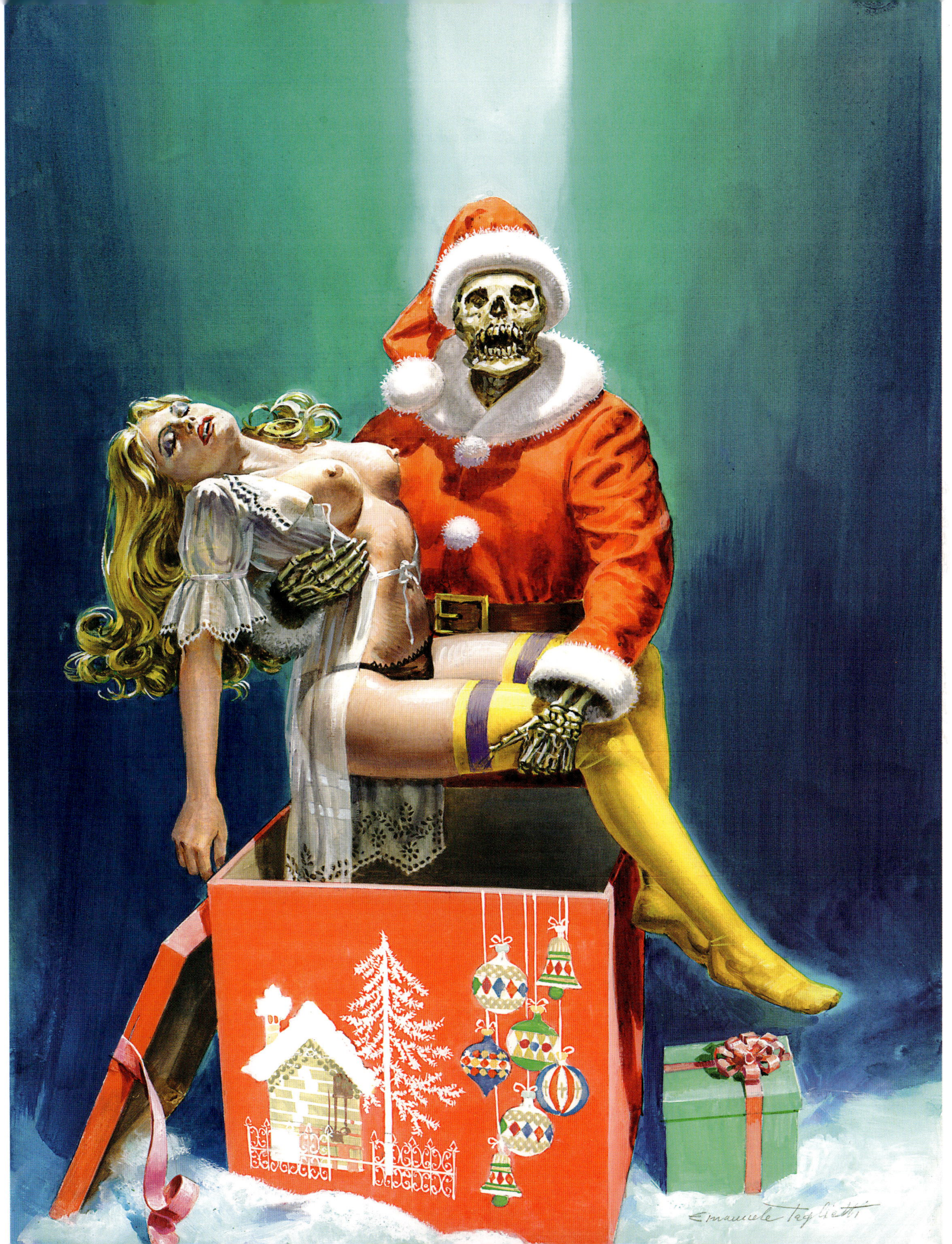
Emanuele Taglietti

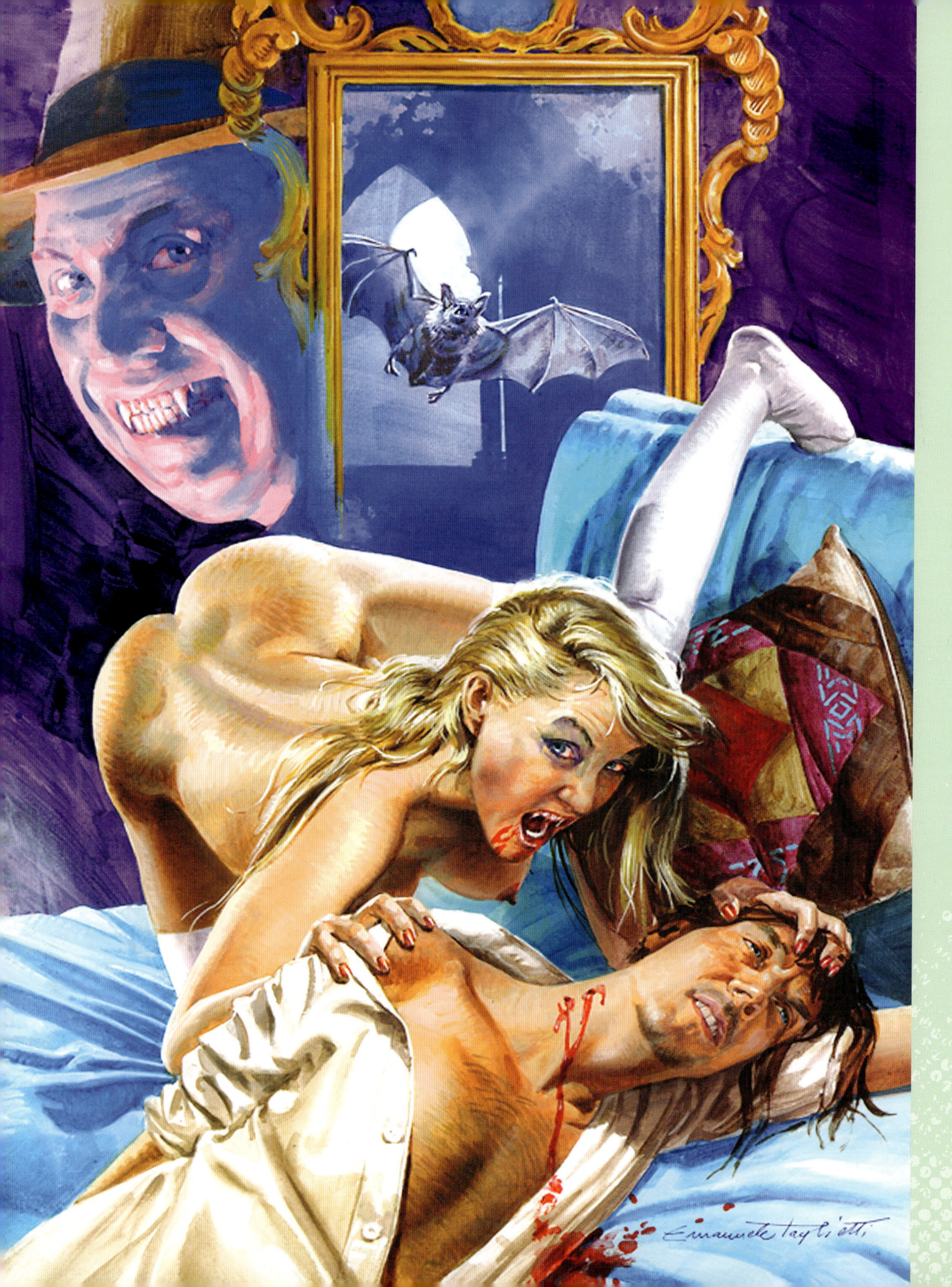

The trademark female nudity and erotic content of Edifumetto's comic series sparked a period of censorship, both in Italy and in other markets, such as Spain. "Censorship was a problem," Emanuele admits. "A number of books were seized on the newsstands, but the big overseas market meant there was plenty of work." In the 1970s, *fumetti* publishers had to face down legal opposition to their sexually explicit covers, and they started self-censoring them in the hope of appeasing the censors, as collector and fan Mark Alfrey explains: "An in-house artist would lay a piece of acetate over the finished art, paint a ridiculous-looking white bra and panties over it, cut out the underwear and glue it onto the painting. Voila! Another masterpiece ruined. Once the artists who'd created the covers were informed this was happening they started designing them to hide the nudity in a more creative manner. The censorship took place over only about two months or so, but dozens of covers were affected by it. Finally the publishers won the case, and the underwear came off."

By the end of the 1970s censorship had slackened even further, and the content and imagery of *fumetti* publishers' output became much more explicit, with many titles crossing over into full-on pornography. "By the end of the decade the words best used to describe this genre would be rape, torture, homosexuality, incest, cannibalism, bestiality, necrophilia and morally ambiguous heroes – and they rarely left out castration," Alfrey says. "They covered every known fetish and perversion and even invented some!" But not every series that Emanuele worked on was like this – there were a few that were comparatively tame, such as Playcolt, Karzan and Sexy Favole." By the mid-1980s Edifumetto was publishing more than 100 titles, but by the end of the decade its market had collapsed, due in part to the changing tastes of the public, the rising cost of printing paper, and the emergence of a competing media – home video.

Emanuele left Edifumetto in 1988 and began to focus on oil painting; he also started teaching an evening class in the decoration and conservation of mural painting. In 2000 he retired from teaching and widened his artistic interests, devoting himself painting murals and watercolours. "Today I have some people in my studio who come to learn the art of painting," he says, "and when I spot quality in someone I follow it with a passion. Over the years, I've taught talented people in the early stages of their career and today many of these are professionals working in various disciplines, such as cartoons, interior decoration and restoration. For me this is a big satisfaction. Working as a hobby is a good thing – it helps me stay in contact with young people and up-to-date on things in the art world. My interests are still related to colour and brushes, as they were at the beginning of my life. I'm unable to have too many different interests these days, so I stick to the ones that best suit my lifestyle. When I travel, which I love to do, instead of taking photographs to record my journey, I paint watercolours in the open air, capturing the character of the places I visit.

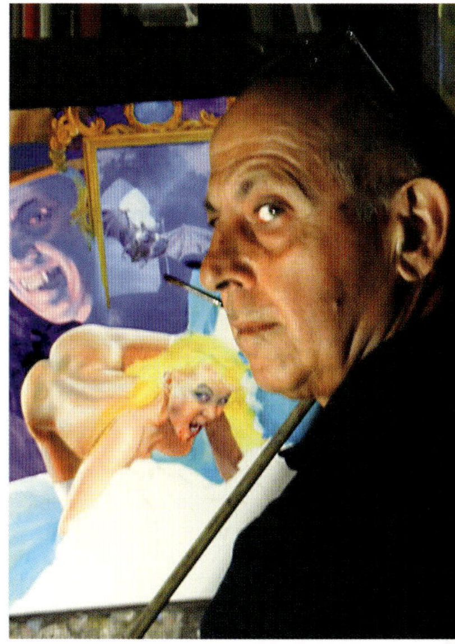

Above: Emanuele Taglietti in his studio in Ferrerra, with his brush in hand.

Left: Blayne, Vampire of Las Vegas, 2014.

FOLLOWING SPREAD
Left: Rosa & Nero, n. 4, *Selezione*, Selection, September 1984.

Right: Fiabe Proibite, n. 18, *Il Meglio delle Mille e Una Note*,
The Best of the Thousand and One Nights, December 1974.

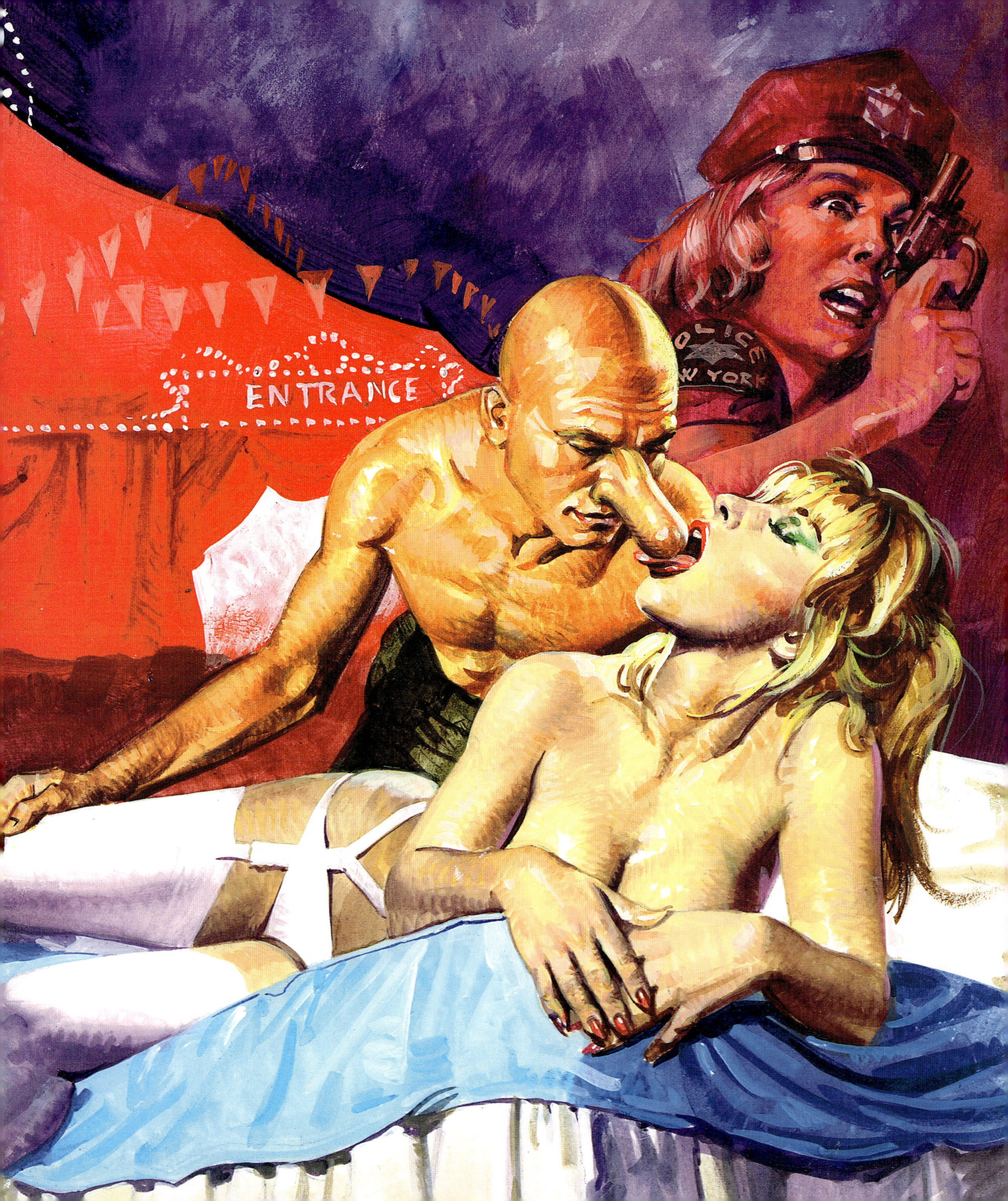

ENTRANCE
POLICE
NEW YORK

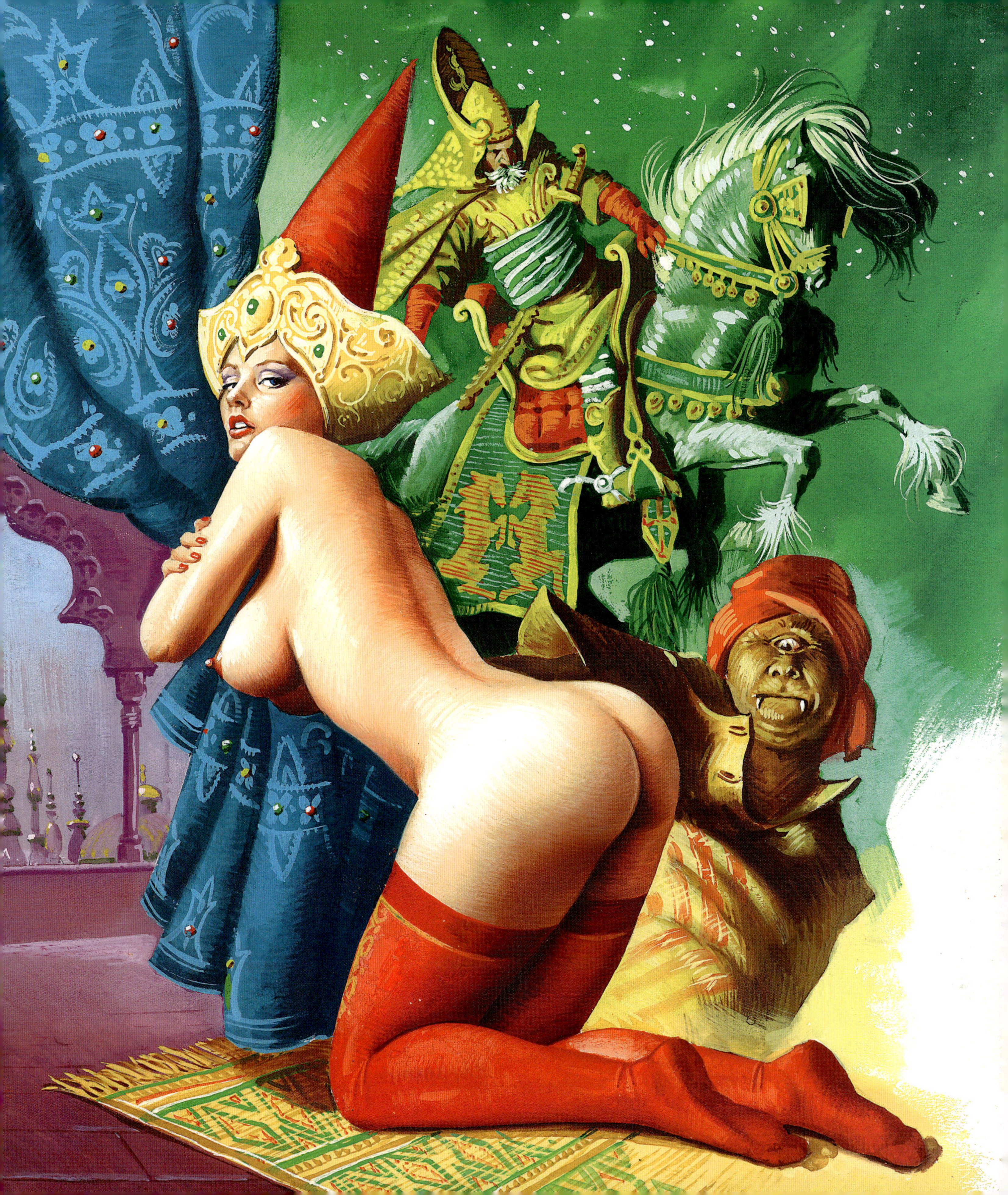

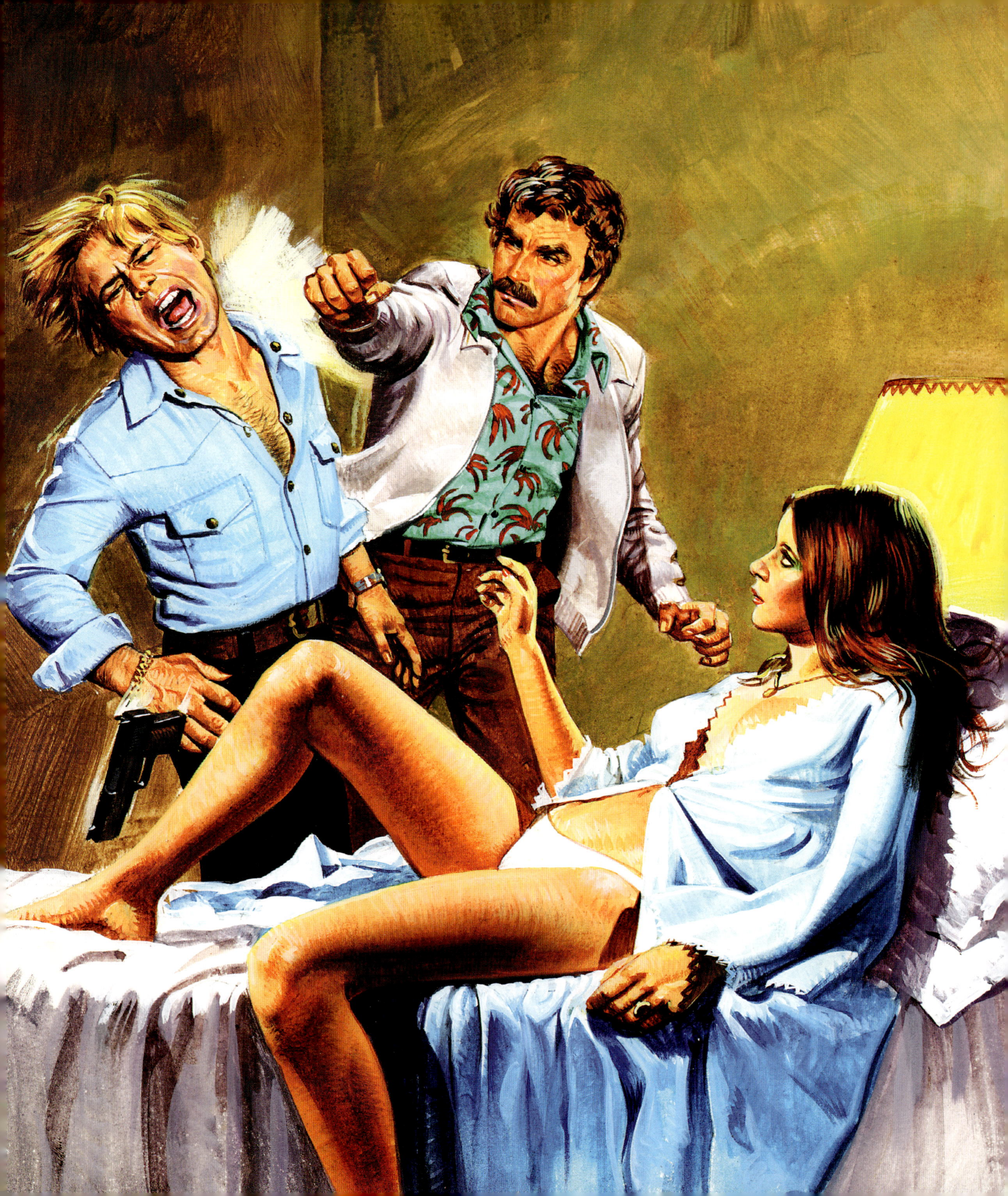

44 MAGNUM

PUBLISHED JANUARY–OCTOBER 1984; 10 ISSUES

The team at Edifumetto were always attuned to what was hot in the Italian media and quick to incorporate it into their comics. This series, in which a former CIA agent becomes a private investigator, was clearly inspired by the hugely popular 1980s US TV show *Magnum, P.I.* starring Tom Selleck, but with the publisher's signature dose of eroticism and nudity livening up the action. Emanuele was briefed to create a Selleck look-alike character for the covers, but recalls having some difficulty finding suitable reference for his artwork: "In these days of the internet, it's easy to find hundreds of images of celebrities, but back then, these weren't readily available, especially for non-Italian stars – I had to browse through dozens of magazines to find photographs of Tom Selleck."

Left: 44 Magnum, n. 2, *Fuochi d'Artificio,* Fireworks, February 1984.

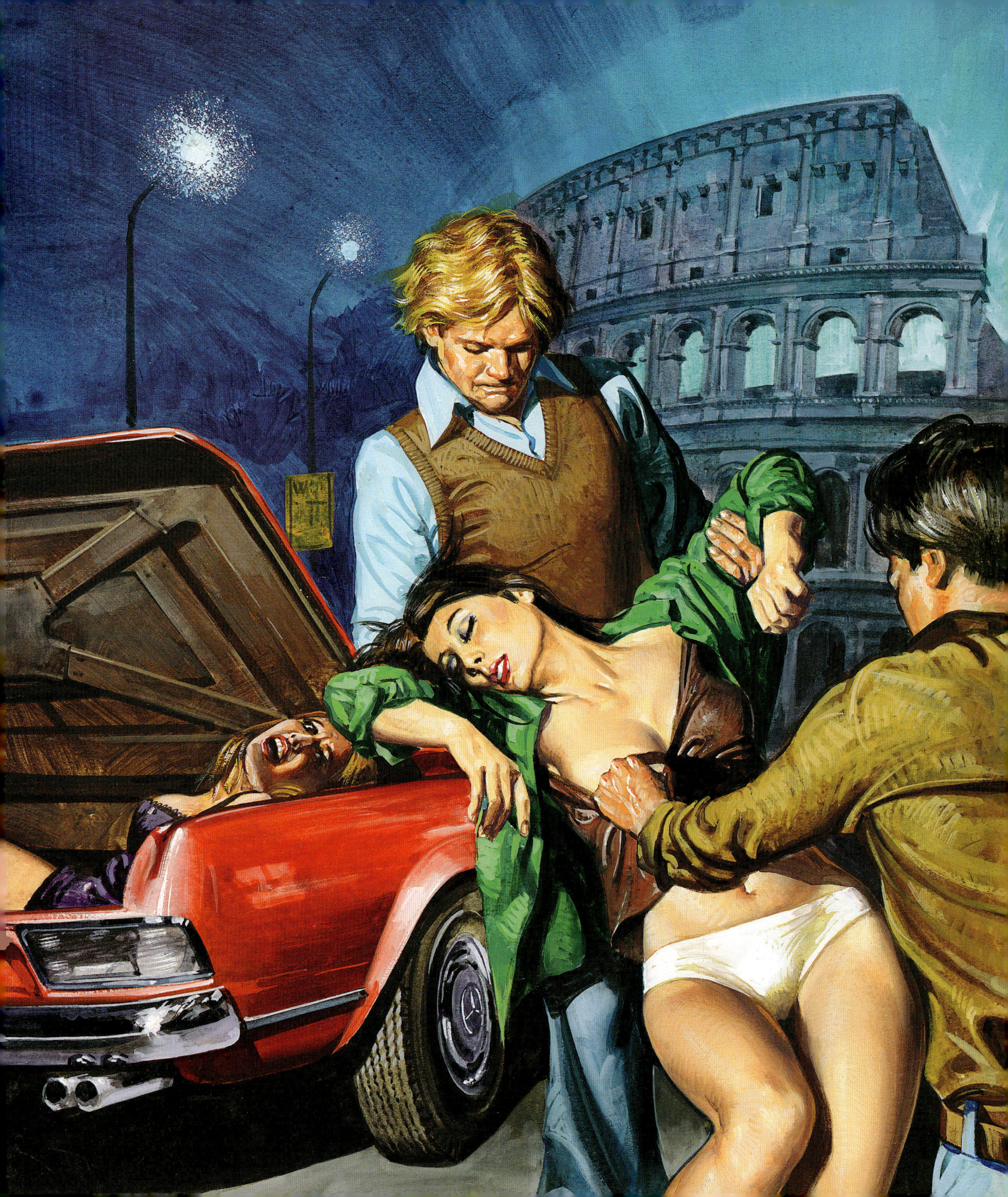

ATTUALITÀ NERA

PUBLISHED 1978–1989; 210 ISSUES

This long-running series, which translates into English as Black Current Affairs, was very succesful for Edifumetto. The stories were inspired by real-life events and topics of the day, and were spiced up in the usual way to satisfy readers' appetites for sex and violence.

Left: Attualità Nera, n. 3, *Il Delitto dei Ragazzi-bene*, Crime of the Well-Bred Boys, July 1978.

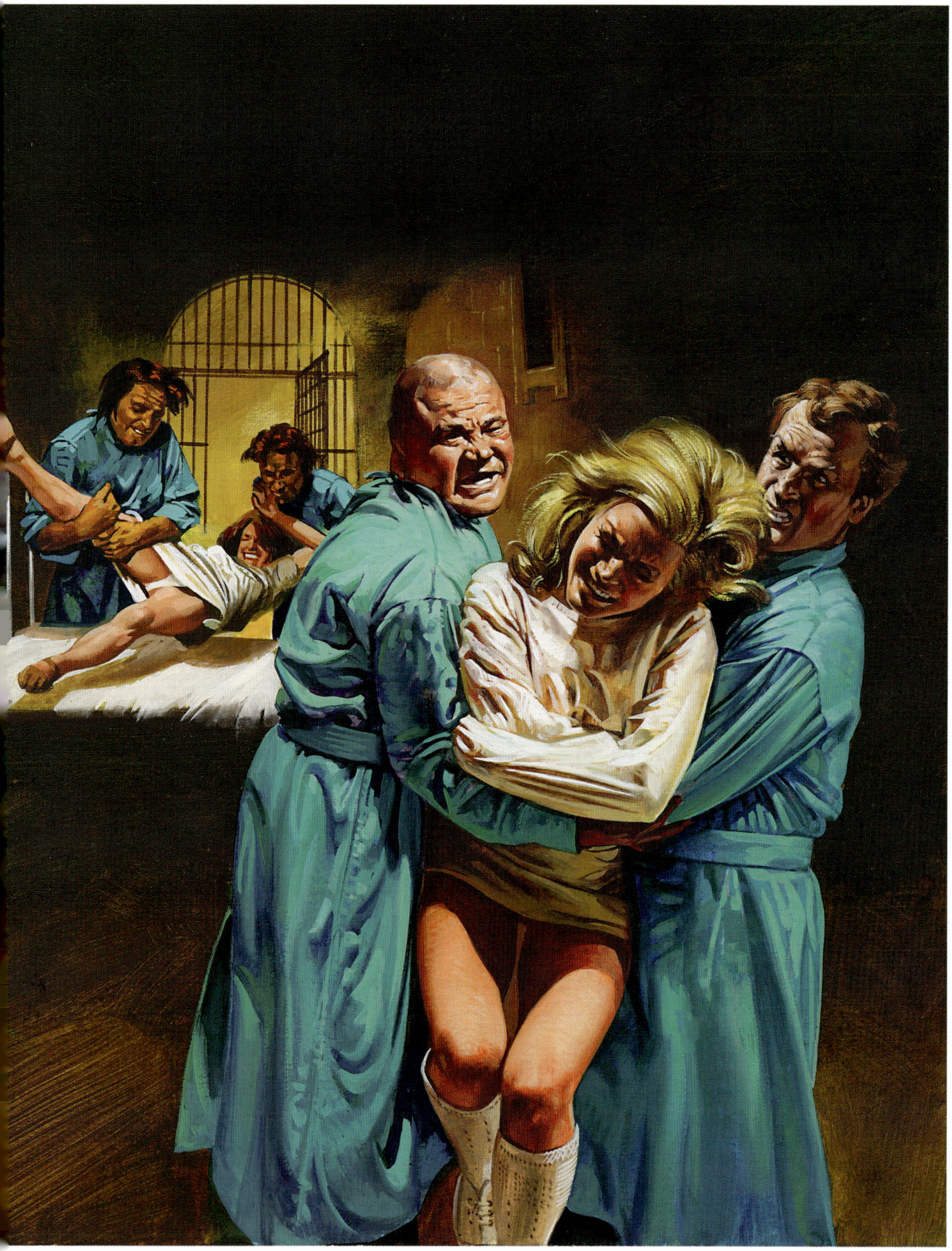

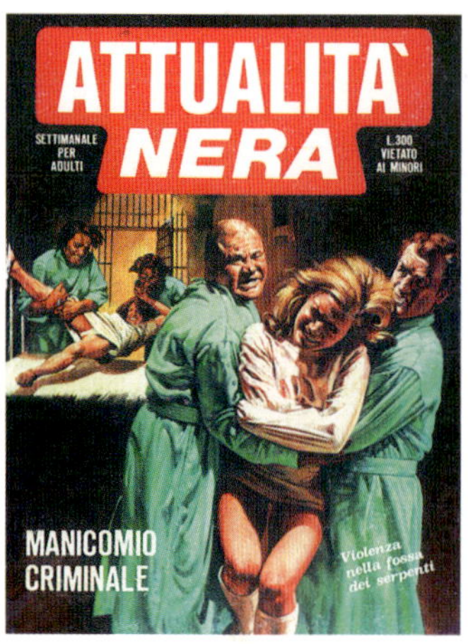

Left: Attualità Nera,
n. 10, *Manicomio Criminale*,
Criminal Lunatic Asylum,
August 1978.

Right: Attualità Nera Extra,
n. 83, *Sesso Diabolico*,
Sex Demon, February 1987.

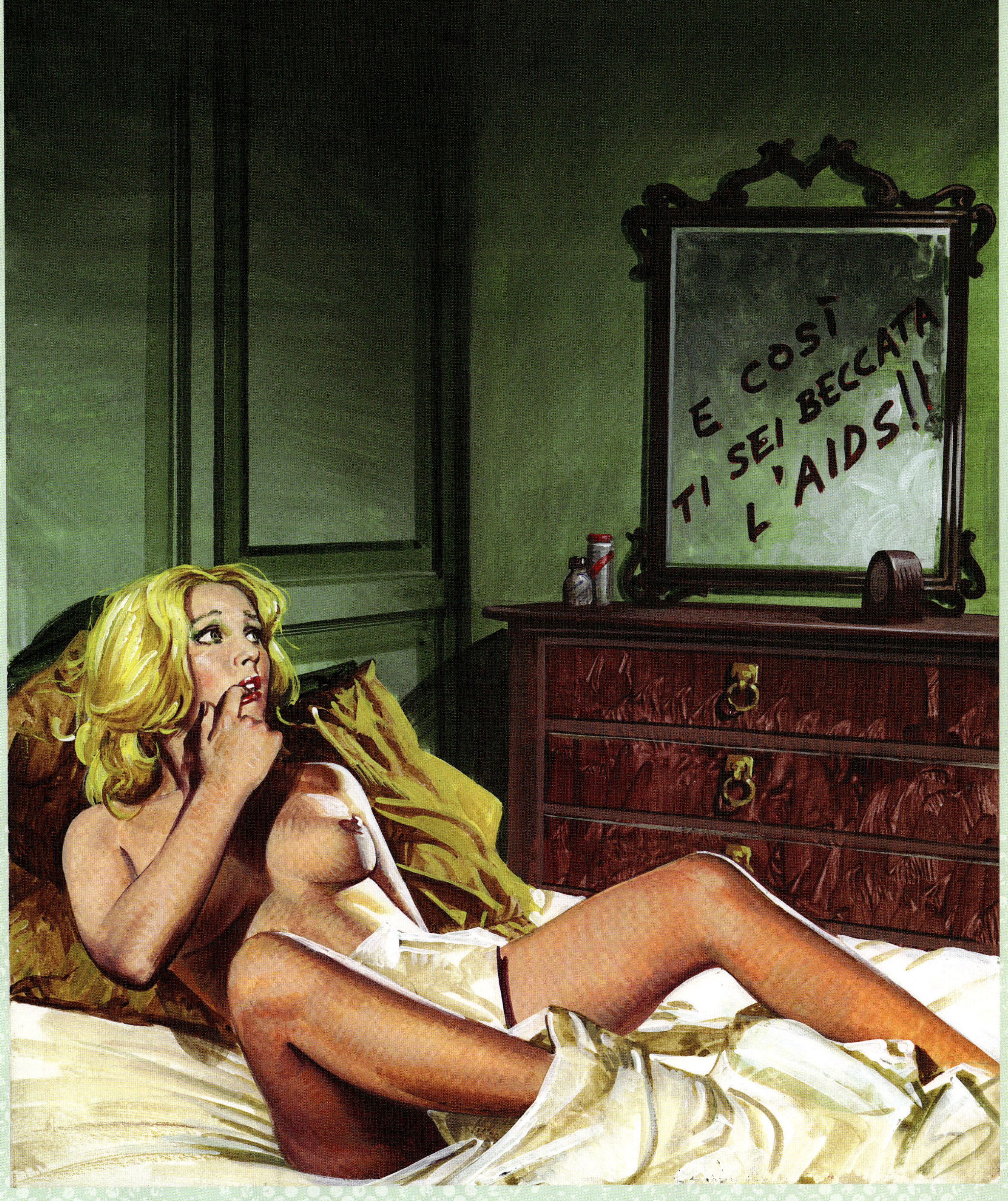

E COSÌ TI SEI BECCATA L'AIDS!!

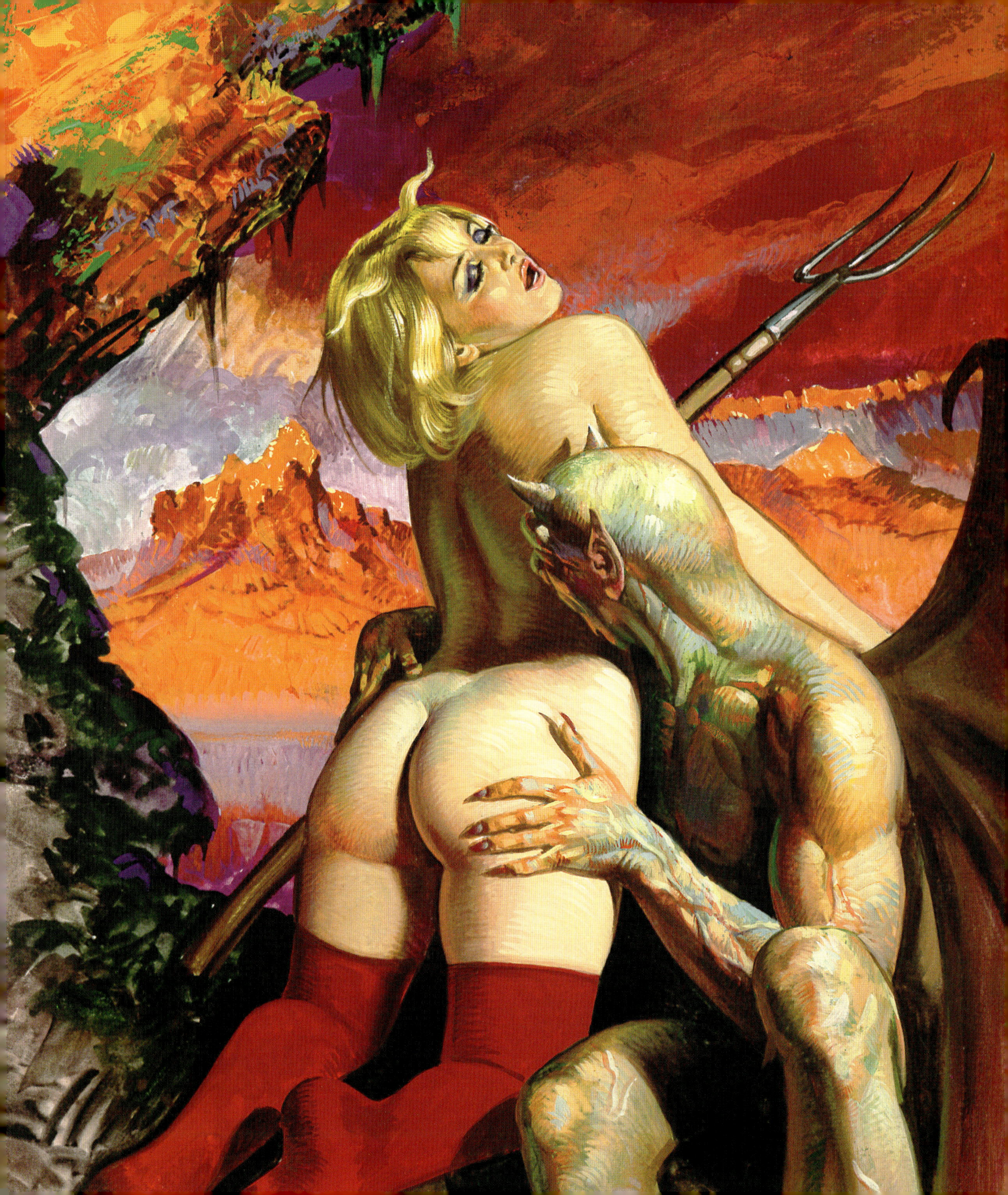

BELZEBA

Belzeba is set in 15th-century Spain, during the era of the Inquisition – the tribunal court system used by both the Catholic Church and some Catholic monarchs to root out, suppress and punish heretics. It's a period associated with horrific methods of torture and execution, so it's unsurprising that Edifumetto chose it as a story backdrop. Belzeba is the daughter of the Devil, who sends her down to Earth to thwart the cruel and sadistic plans of Tomas de Torquemada, Inquisitor General of Aragon and Castile during the reign of the Catholic monarchs King Ferdinand of Aragon and Isabelle of Castille. The "Princess of Hell" herself is described as a hermaphrodite, but she's pictured as all woman: a beautiful blonde whose head is crowned with two horn-like tufts of hair. Belzeba is a saga swimming with blood, violence and horror, and steeped in the blackest humour, with each episode depicting confrontations between the amoral, perverse and sexually insatiable Belzeba and the outwardly moral and sexually repressed, yet secretly kinky, Inquisitor General.

Left: Belzeba, n. 11, *Abacuc il Mago*, Habakkuk the Magician, November 1977.

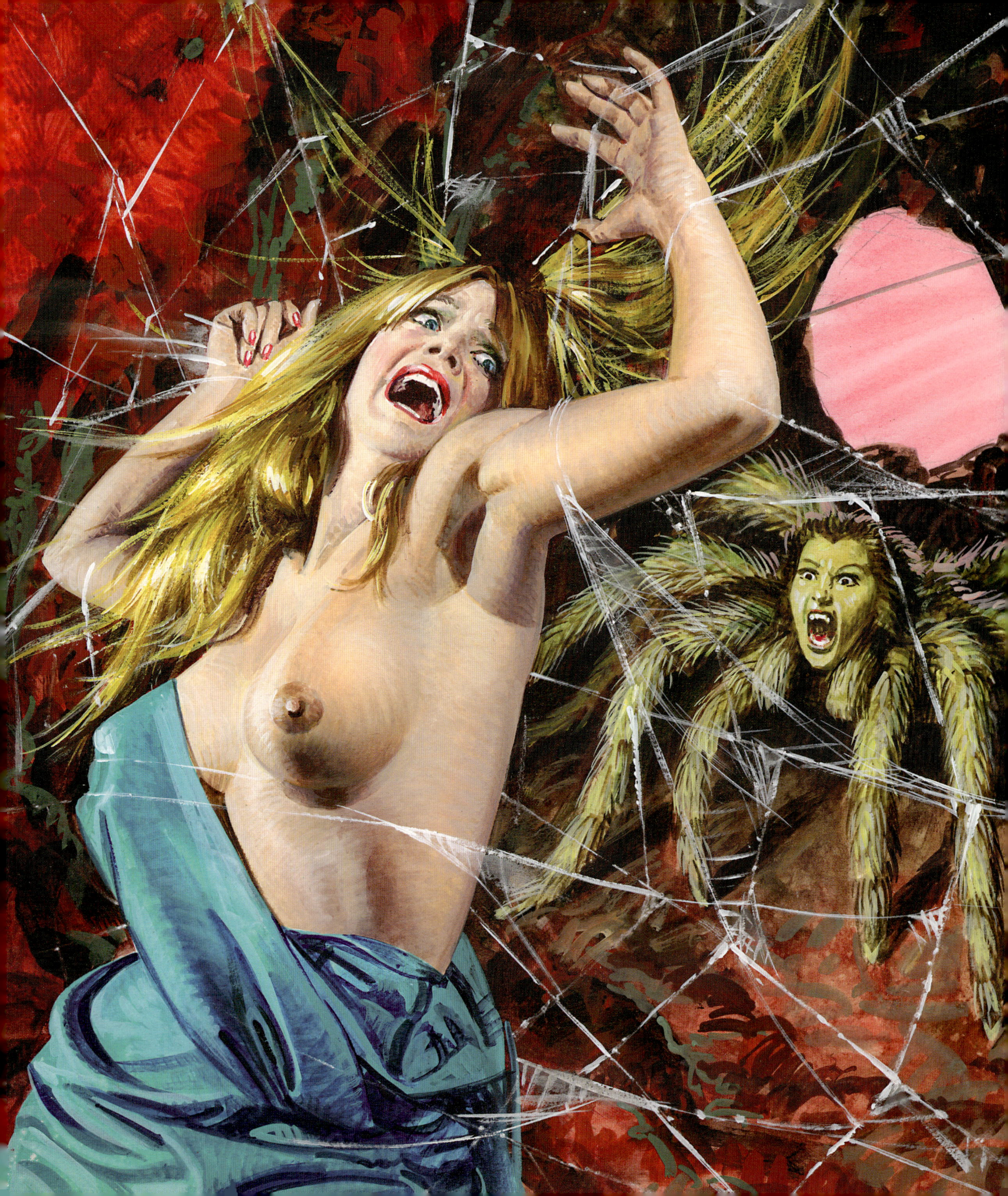

CIMITERIA

PUBLISHED 1977–1984; 119 ISSUES

Emanuele produced 21 of the covers for this outrageous, taboo-busting, London-set horror series. Cimitera ("Cemetery") appeared after Zora la Vampira, and was less successful, but its later debut enabled the tone and imagery to be a lot darker and more pornographic – the violence, torture and necrophilia are cranked up to the max. Cimiteria is the revived corpse of a beautiful young woman, raised from the dead by a sorcerer using black magic and electricity; he's helped in this feat by the cemetery's caretaker, a hunchback called Quasimodo. The latter is sexually attracted to Cimiteria, but unfortunately she carries inside her an enormous electrical charge that kills or maims all the unfortunates who try to have sex with her. Cimiteria falls in love with Lord James and kills his bride-to-be at the altar; out of jealousy Quasimodo frames the lord for the murder. Later in the series Cimiteria's sexual problem is resolved and she and on-off lover Quasimodo enjoy many bizarre adventures: they fight robots and monsters, get kidnapped and go on sex and killing sprees.

Left: Cimiteria, n. 9, *Gli Orrori di Aracne*, Spider Horrors, July 1985.

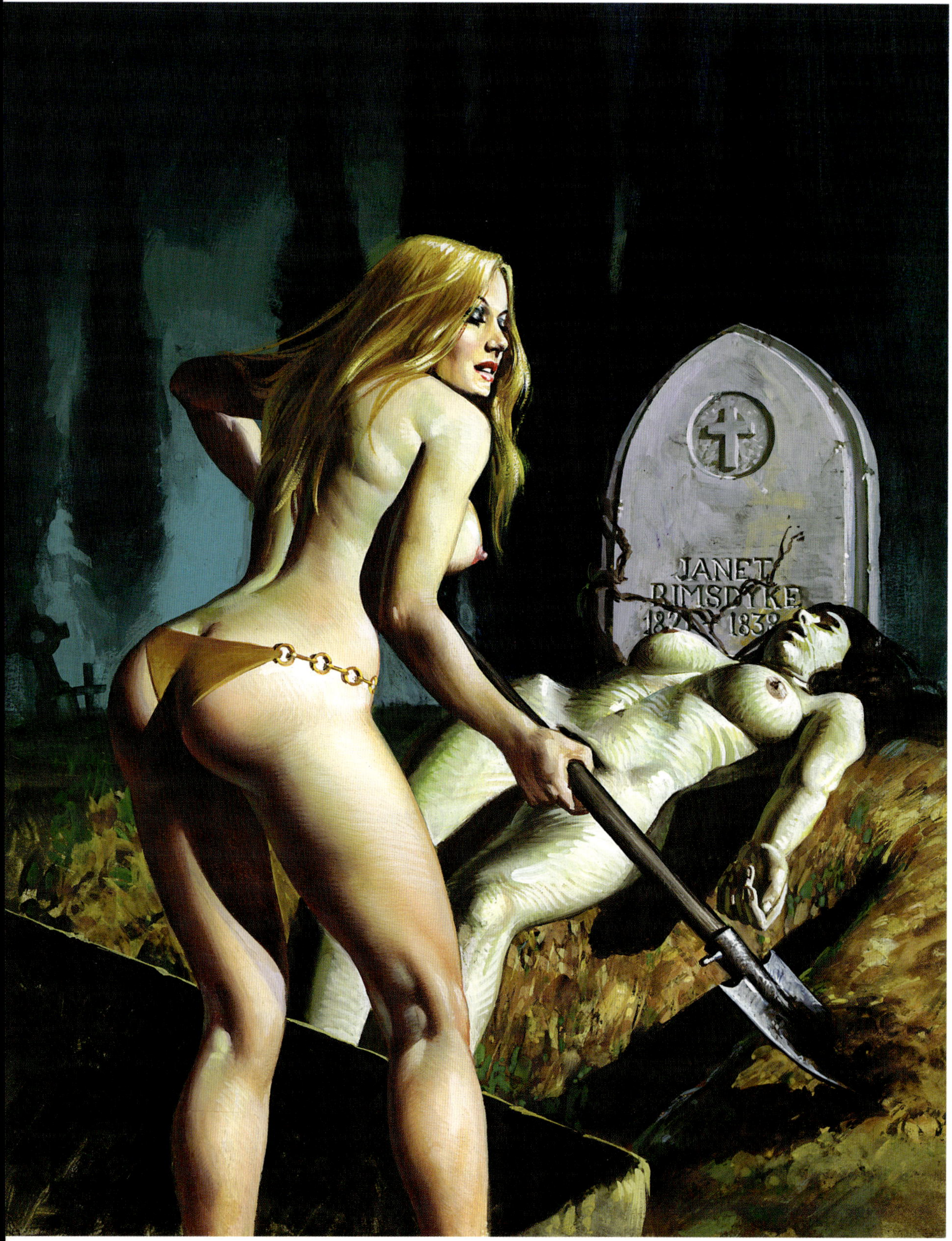

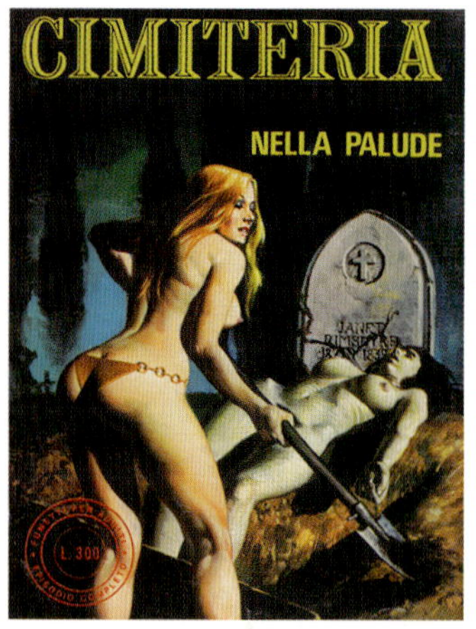

Left: Cimiteria, n. 21, *Nella Palude,* In the Swamp, February 1978.

Right: Cimiteria, n. 26, *Le Macchine per l'Amore,* The Machines for Love, April 1978.

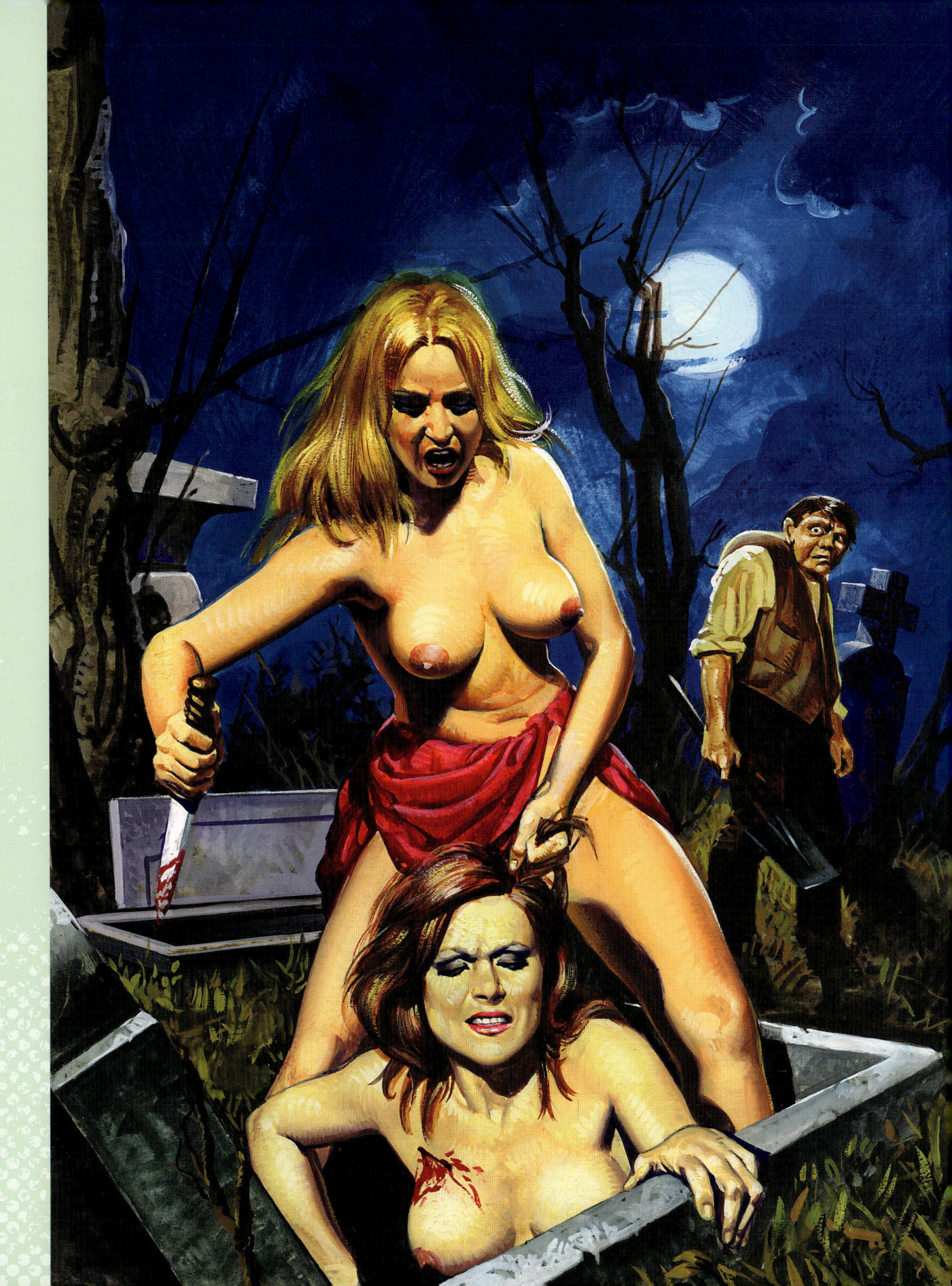

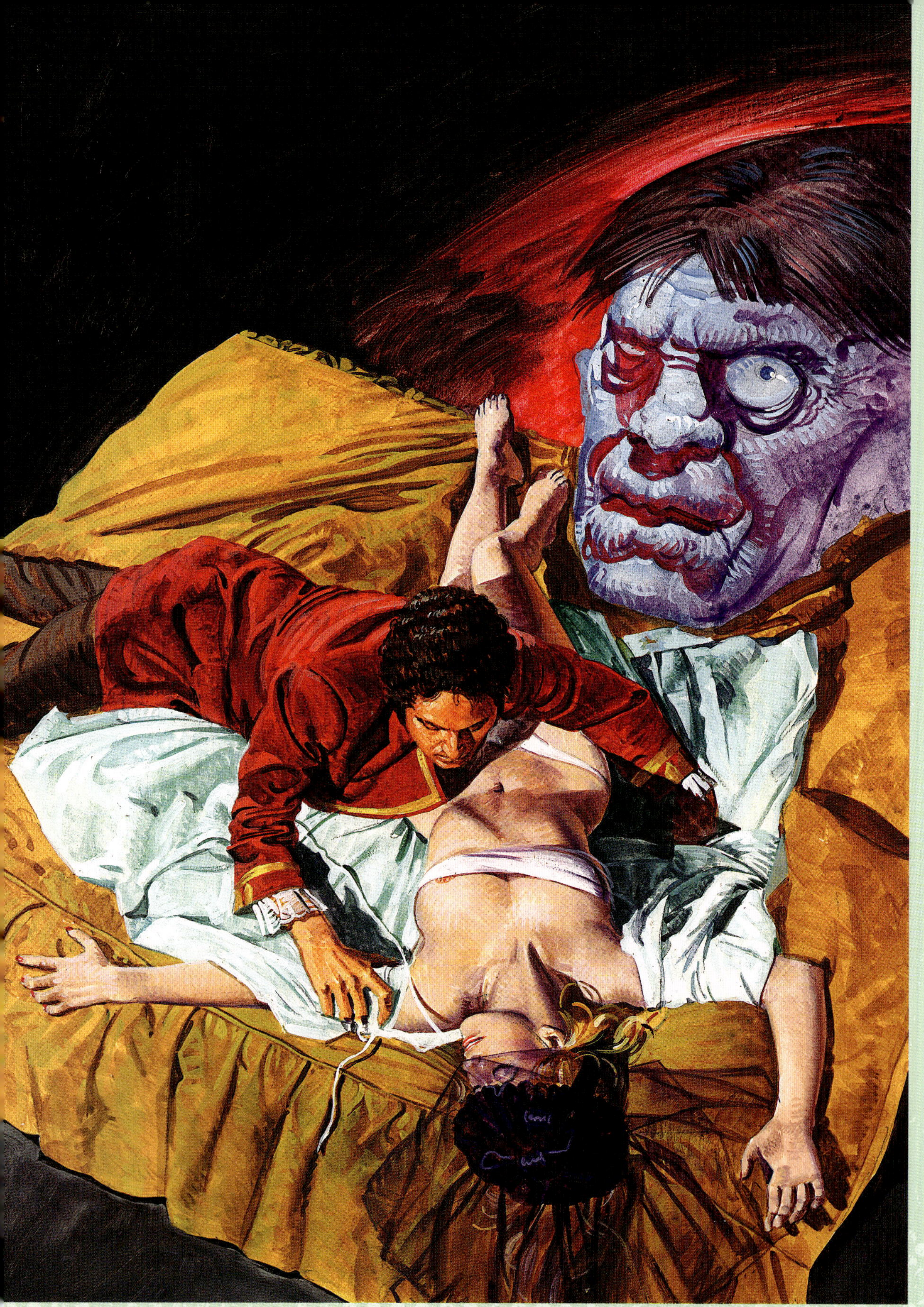

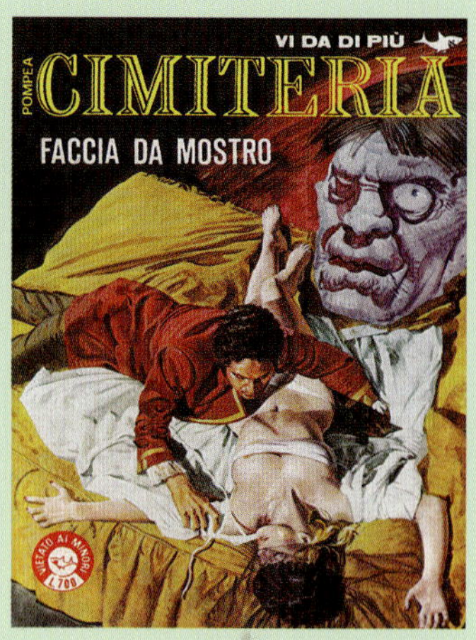

Left: Cimiteria, n. 99, *Faccia da Mostro,* Face of the Monster, October 1982.

Right: Cimiteria, n. 15, *La Mano dell'Assassino,* The Hand of the Assassin, April 1983.

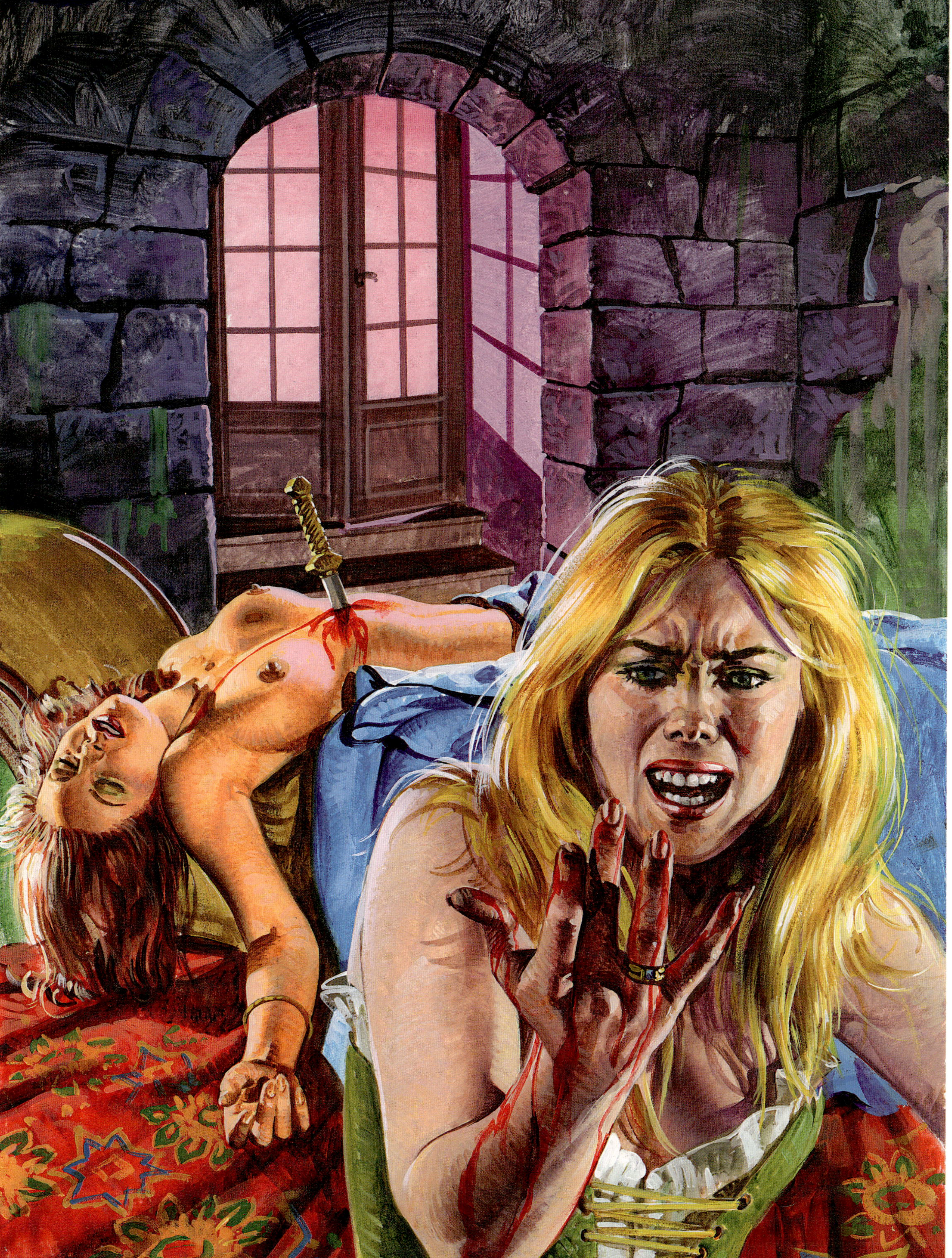

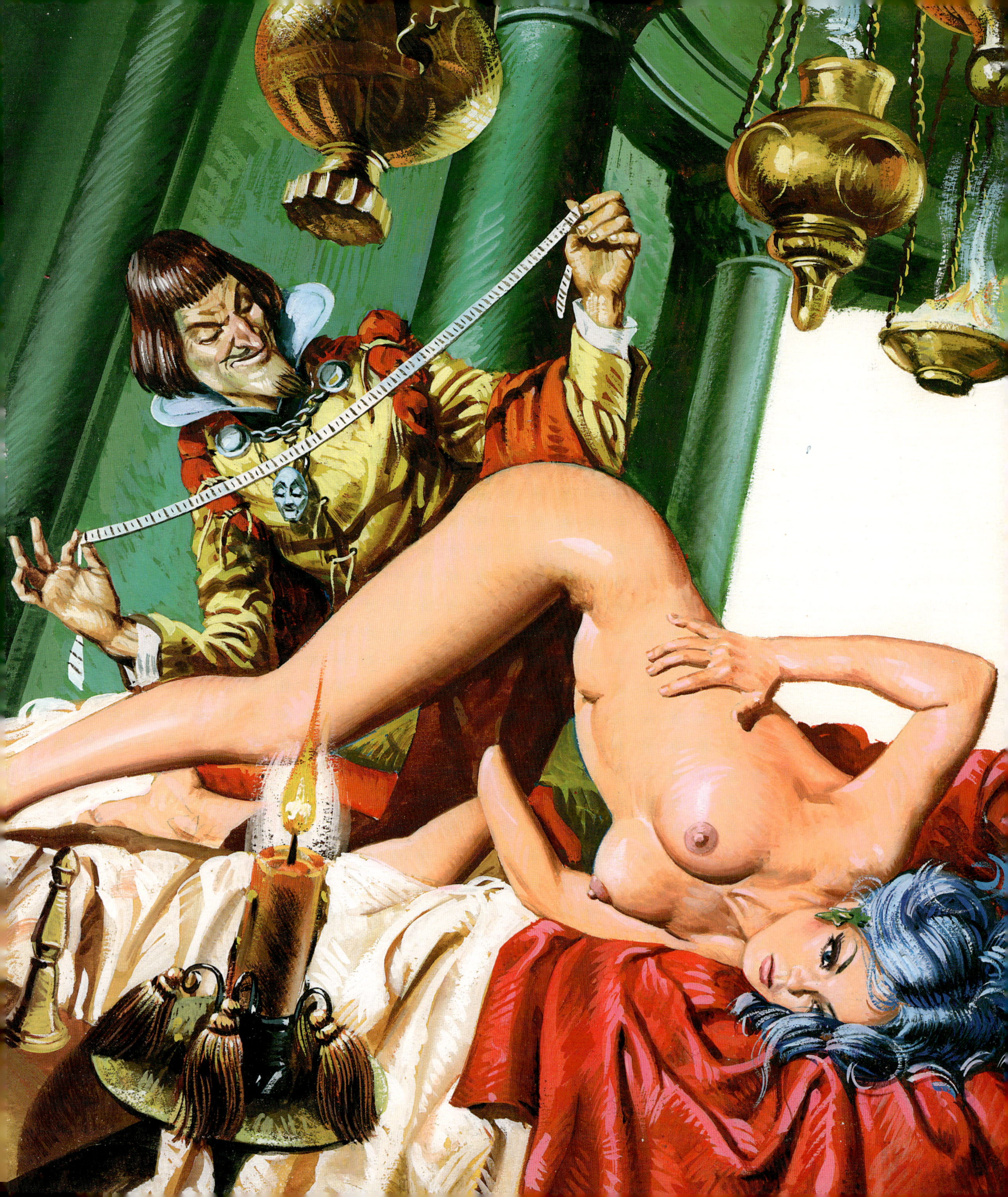

FATA TURCHINA

PUBLISHED 1975; 8 ISSUES

The inspiration here is *La Fata dai Capelli Turchini* – the Fairy With Turquoise Hair – a key character in Carlo Collodi's 1883 book *The Adventures of Pinocchio*. In the original story, the Fairy is a spirit of the forest who rescues Pinnochio and eventually turns him into a real boy. The long-nosed puppet doesn't feature in Edifumetto's series, and while their black-eyed Fairy is beautiful and good, like the original, her dress sense and behaviour are considerably sexier! Fata Turchina hit the newssands around the same time as another Edifumetto series called Sexy Favole (Sexy Fairy Tales), which featured deliciously naughty and funny erotic parodies of children's classics, including Cinderella, Alice in Wonderland, Little Red Riding Hood, Sleeping Beauty, Peter Pan and The Little Mermaid.

Left: Fata Turchina, n. 5, *Prigioniera nell Harem*, Prisoner in the Harem, April 1975.

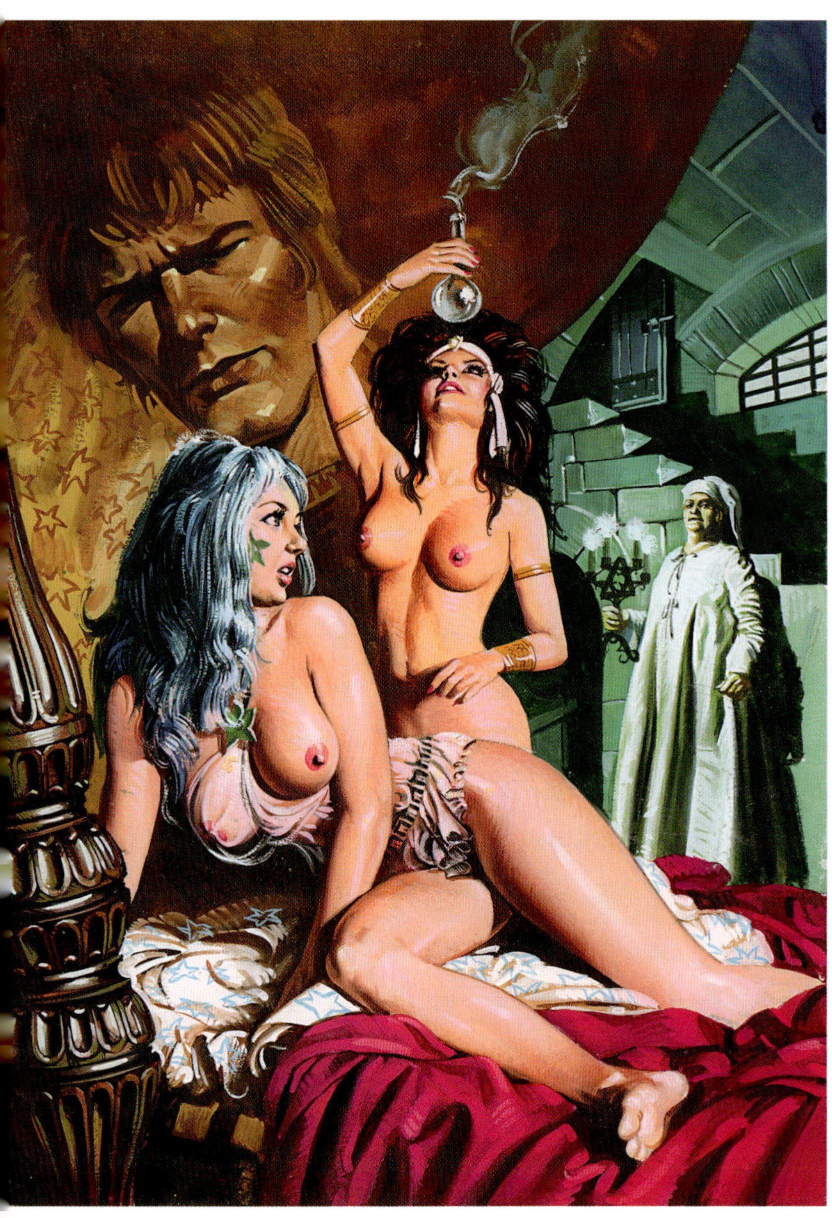

Above: Fata Turchina, n. 4, *Nelle Mani dei Pirati*,
In the Hands of Pirates, March 1975.

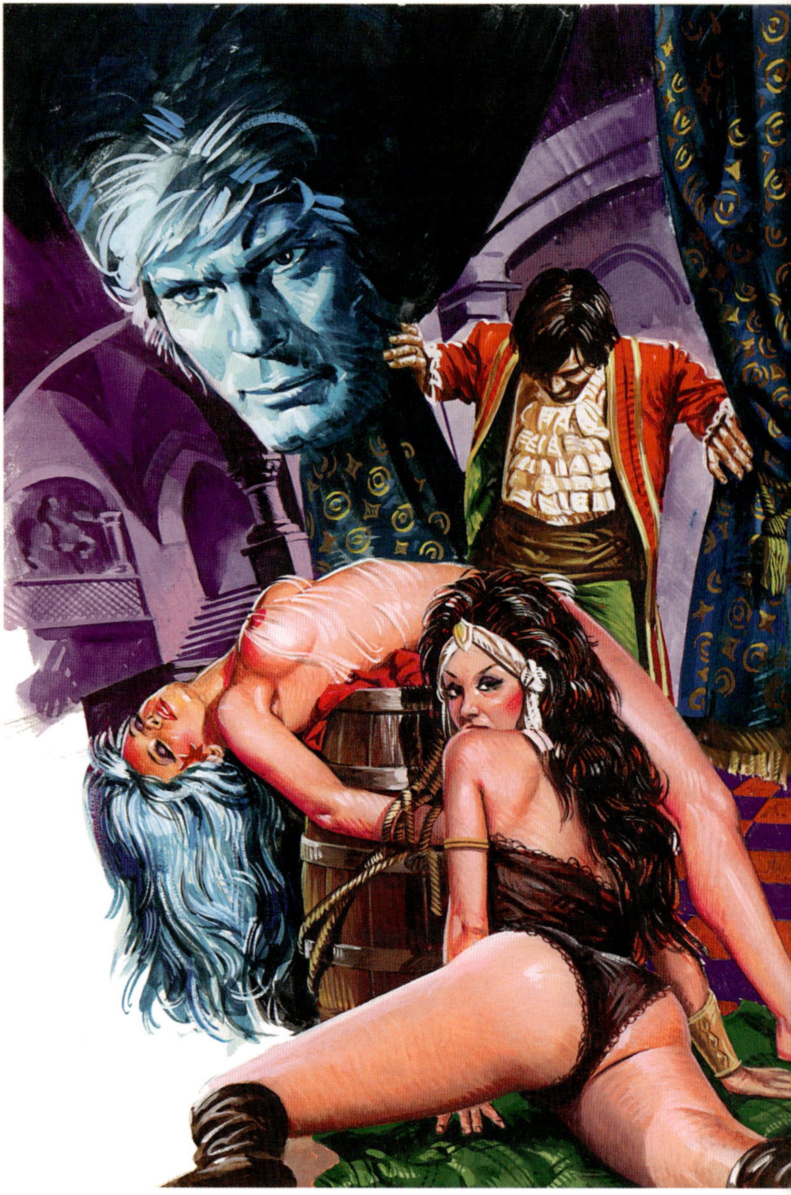

Above: Fata Turchina, n. 6, *Il Letto del Piacere*,
The Bed of Pleasure, May 1975.

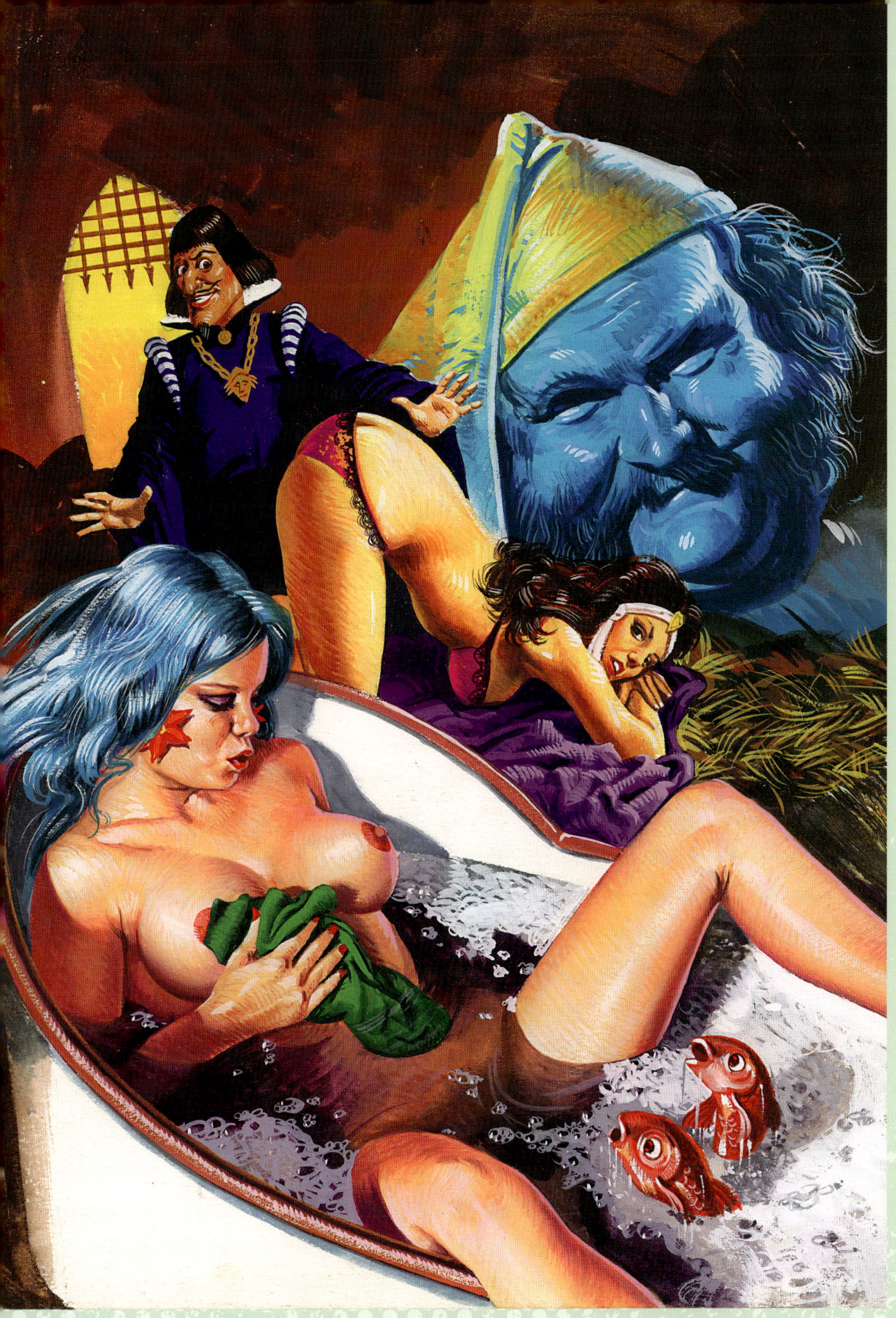

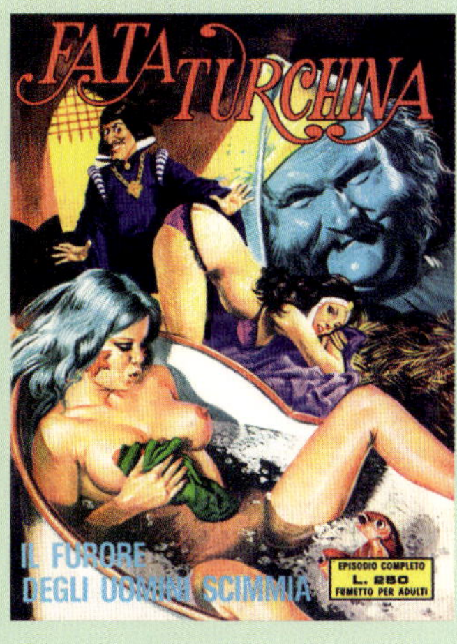

Left: Fata Turchina, n. 8,
Il Furore degli Uomini Scimmia,
Rage of the Ape Men,
July 1975.

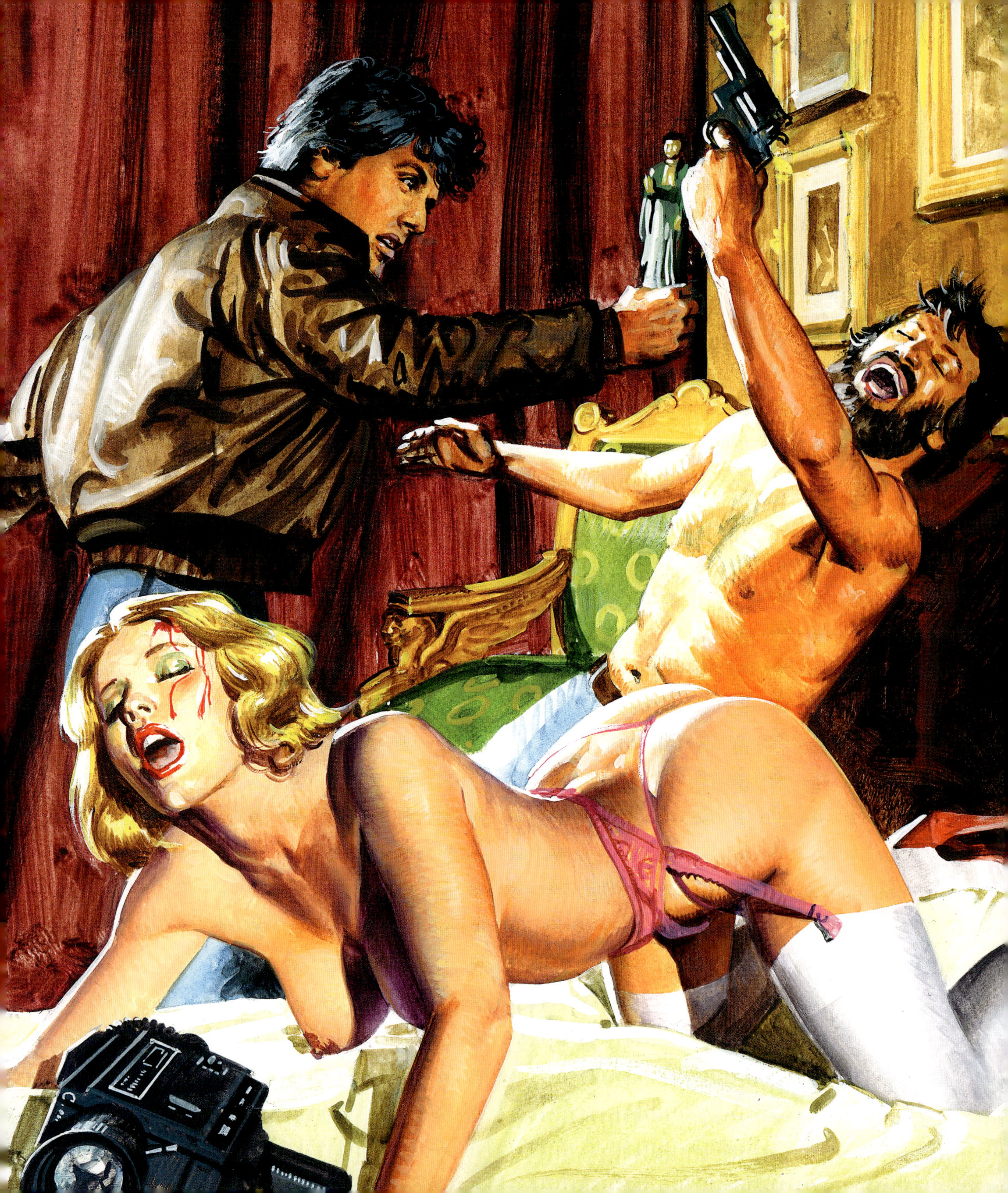

FOX

PUBLISHED 1986–1987; 11 ISSUES

In the mid-1980s Edifumetto decided to cash-in on the massive popularity of US actor Sylvester Stallone – who'd recently appeared in the violent action film series *Rambo* – with the creation of a series called Fox. It's set in the suburbs of New York City, and the main character is Paul A. Fox, a journalist who is renowned for his ability to solve crimes. Fox, who is a dead ringer for Stallone, is accompanied on his adventures in the seedy criminal underworld by his loyal cameramen Rick-Rick and Marlon, and secretary Elly, who always manages to defuse her boss's more fiery actions. Among the other supporting characters are journalist Barbara "Baby" Barrell, Fox's lover, who tends to cover criminal cases of a sexual nature. And in a mutually beneficial "you scratch my back and I'll scratch yours" arrangement with local police sergeant Mullivan, Fox is frequently given scoops on the hottest cases of the moment. Emanuele created all the covers for this series.

Left: Fox, n. 10, *La Trappola*, The Trap, March 1987.

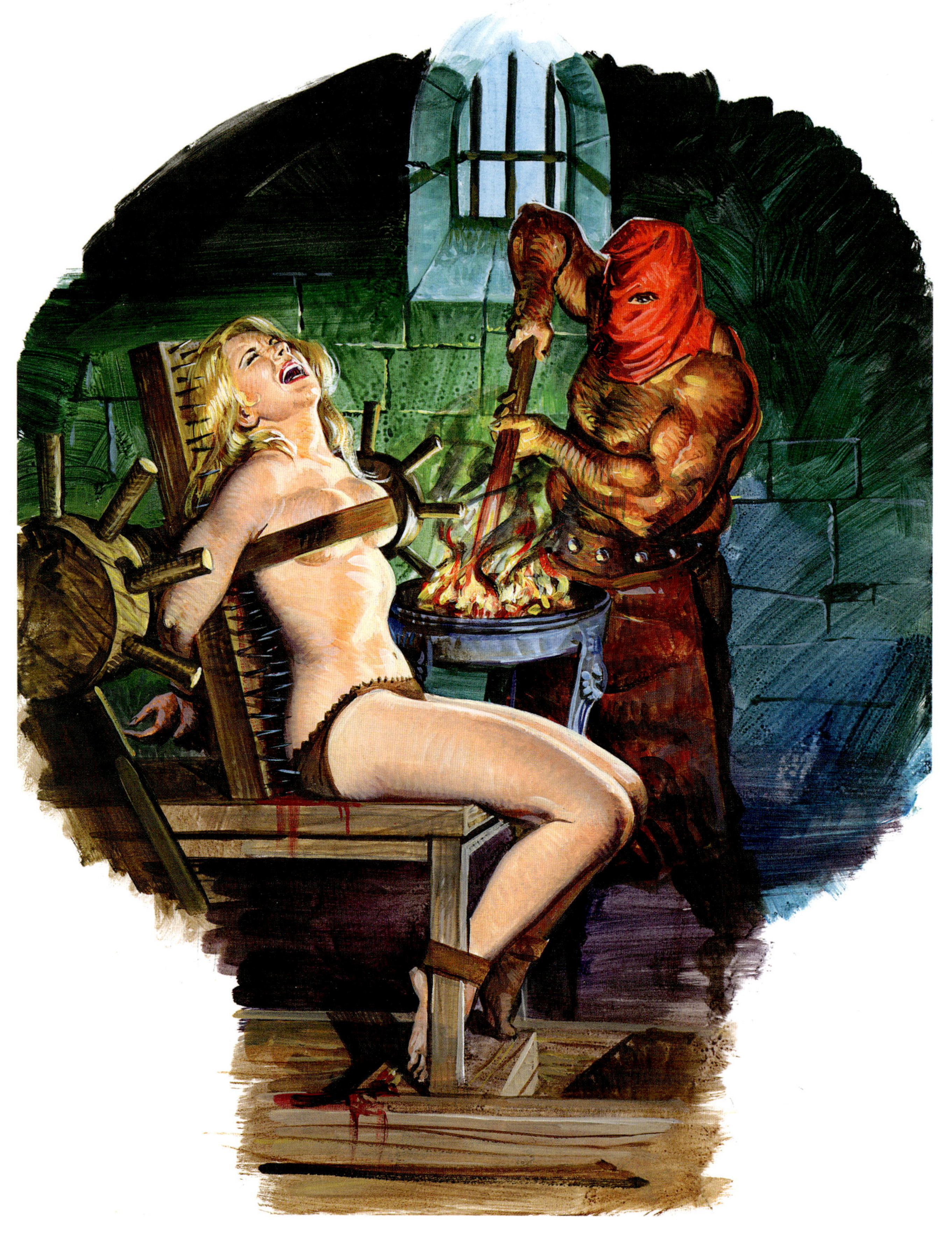

I LIBRI DELLA LUCE ROSSA

PUBLISHED 1981–1985; 53 ISSUES

The Red Light Books is an erotic series stuffed with lurid stories of vice, torture and perversion through the ages – its authors all wrote under false names. It is difficult for fans to collect the issues in this series today because they are very rare.

Left: I Libri della Luce Rossa, n. 9 *La Tortura nei Secoli*, Torture through the Ages, September 1981.

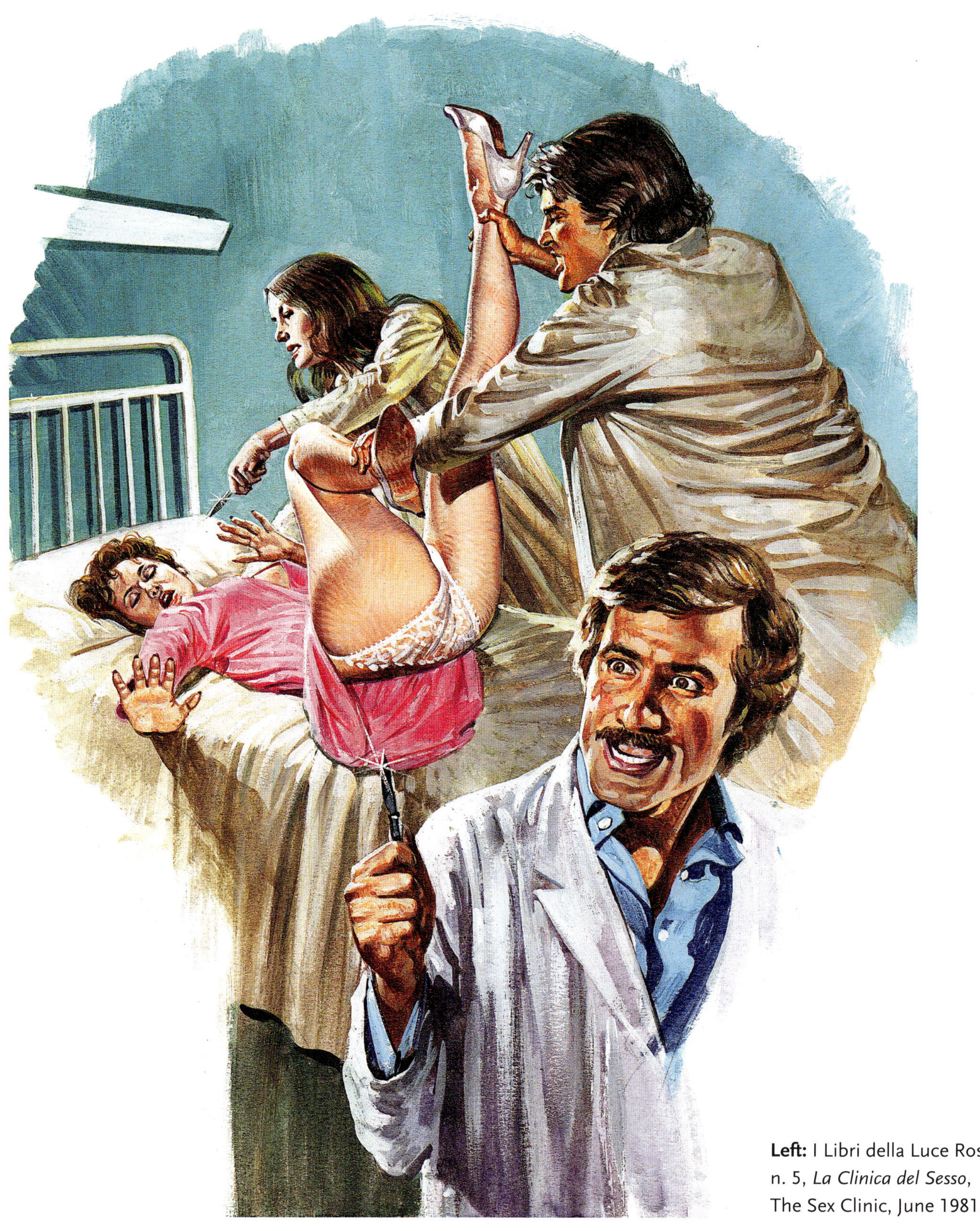

Left: I Libri della Luce Rossa,
n. 5, *La Clinica del Sesso*,
The Sex Clinic, June 1981.

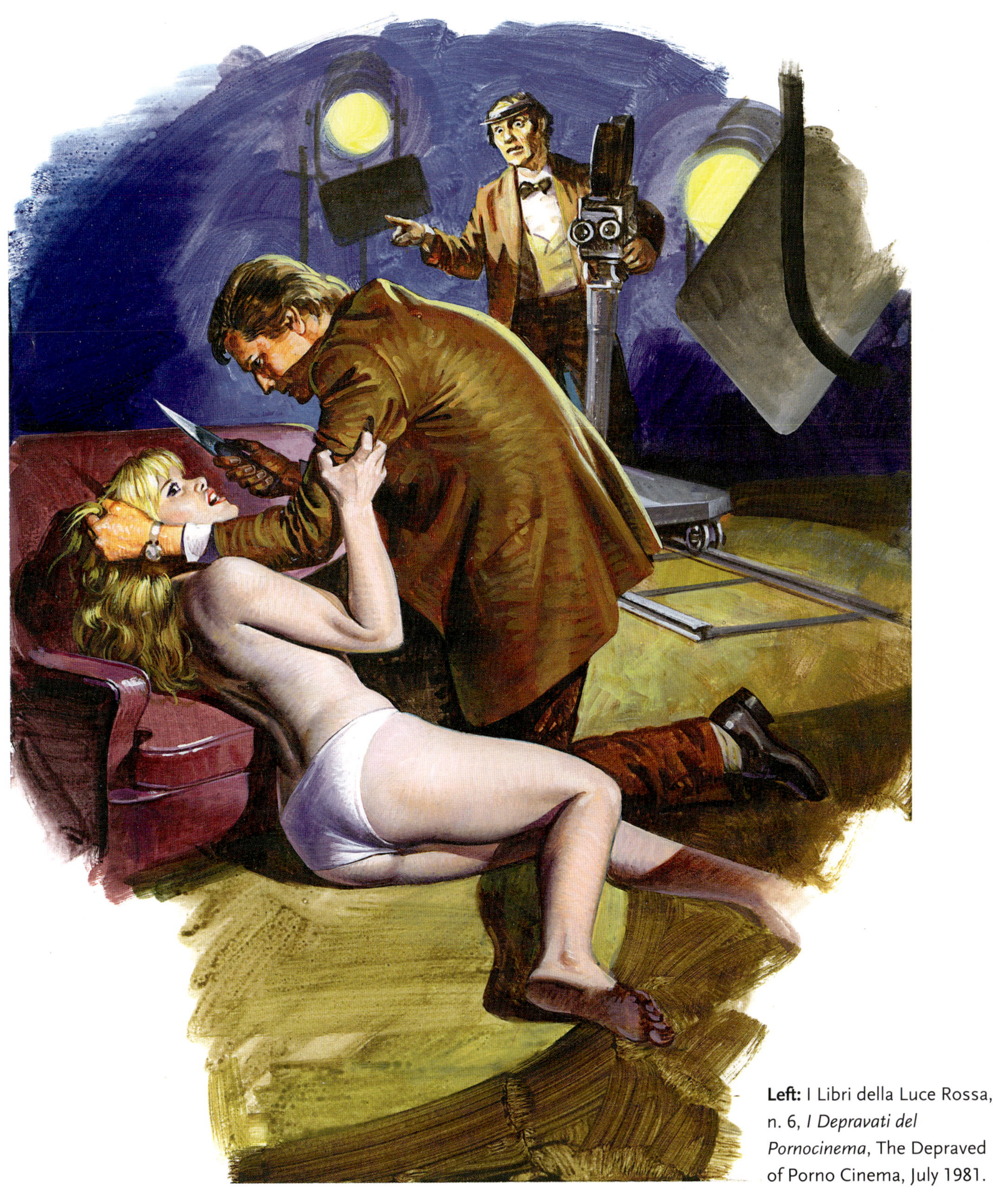

Left: I Libri della Luce Rossa,
n. 6, *I Depravati del
Pornocinema*, The Depraved
of Porno Cinema, July 1981.

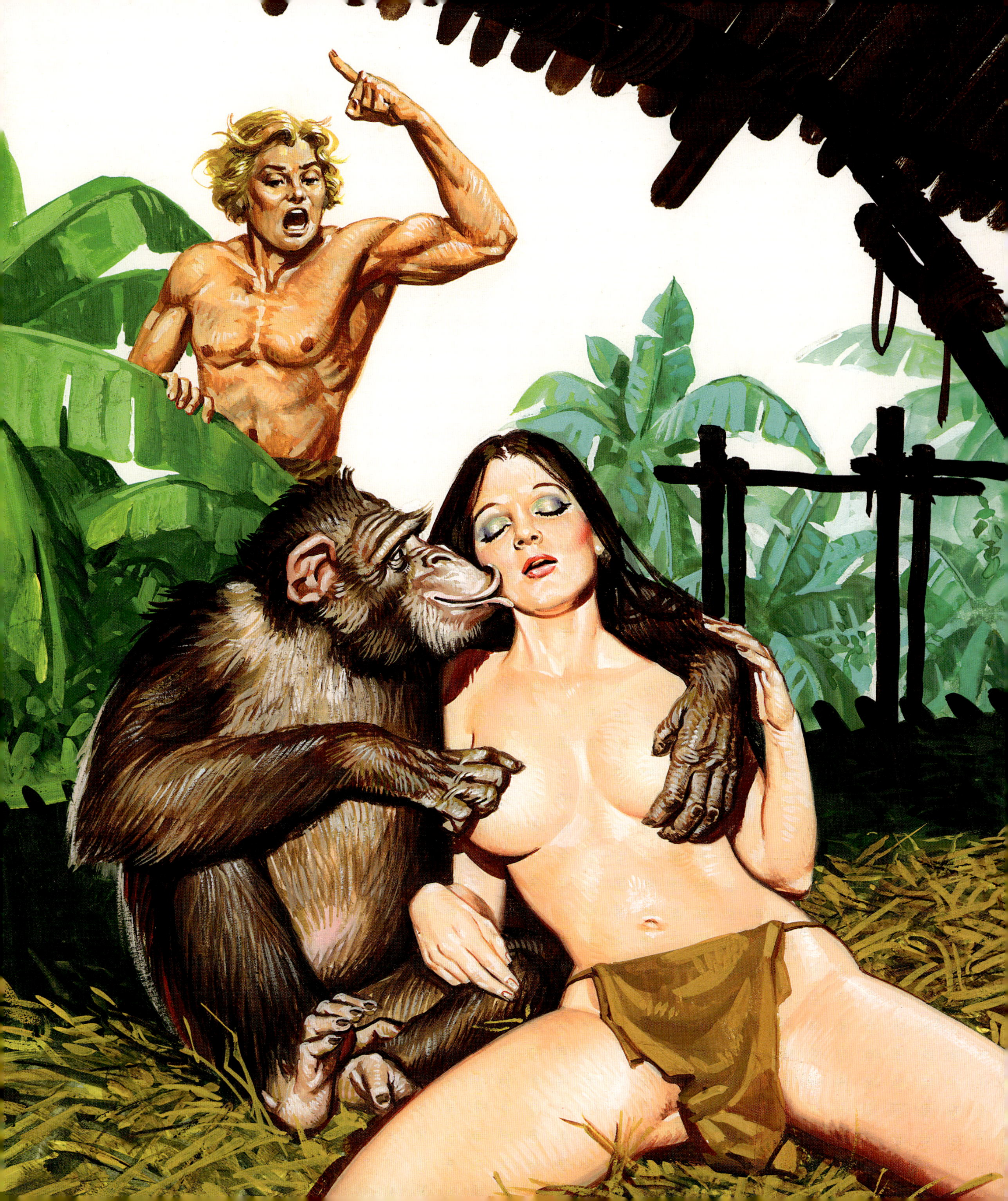

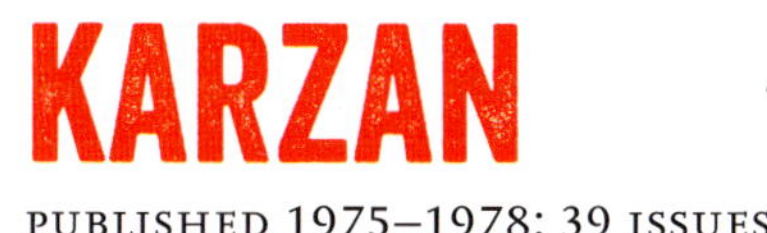

KARZAN

PUBLISHED 1975–1978; 39 ISSUES

This raunchy series was clearly a parody of the story of Tarzan, the feral child raised in an African jungle by apes, created in 1912 by Edgar Rice Burroughs. In Karzan, a plane bound for Nairobi in East Africa is diverted and crashes. A lone survivor is later found among the twisted metal: a baby boy, lying in the arms of his dead mother. Little Karzan is adopted by gorilla couple Gongo and Kut, who raise him as their own. One day a small plane lands in the jungle – it's carrying Professor Frank Finimore and his daughter Jane, along with a dodgy character called Bob Mitchell, who've come to undertake some scientific research. Karzan gets to know Jane pretty intimately and discovers, to his delight, that sex with her is far more pleasurable than with the gorilla prostitute Magog.

Left: Karzan, n. 30, *Gli Uomini Talpa*, The Mole Men, January 1978.

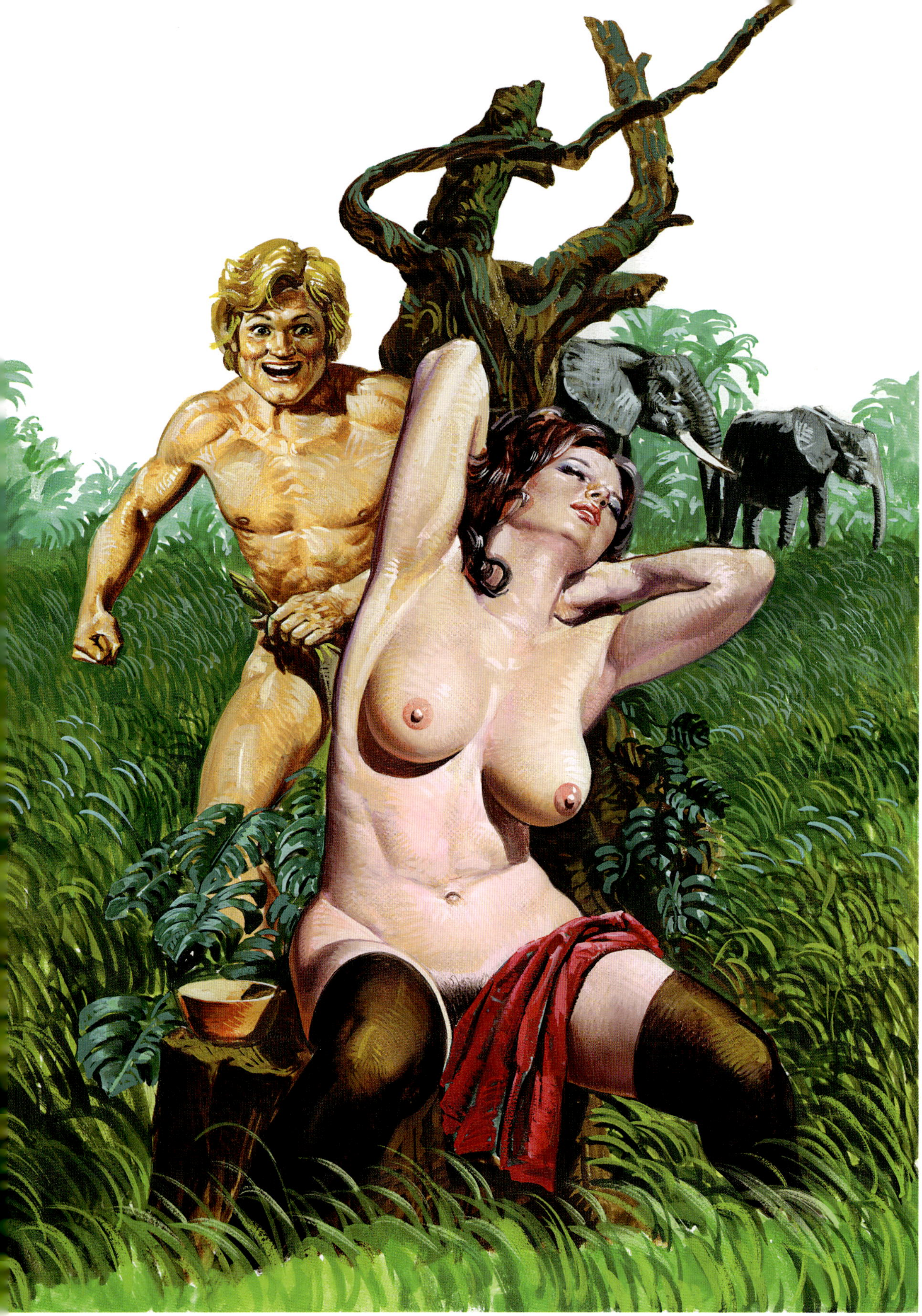

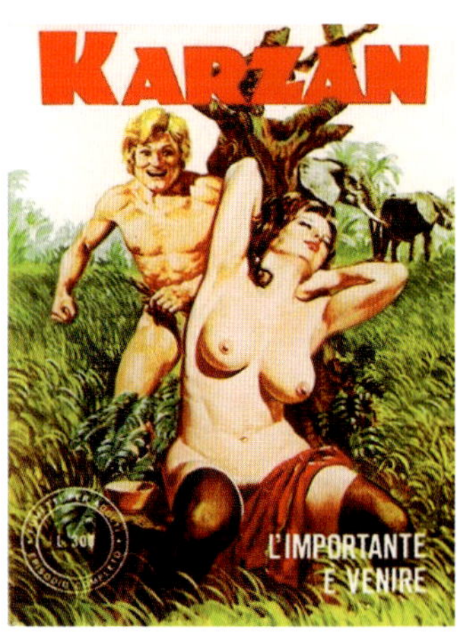

Left: Karzan, n. 26, *L'Importante e' Venire*, Coming is Essential, September 1977.

Right: Karzan, n. 27, *Una Bella Bestia*, A Beautiful Beast, October 1977.

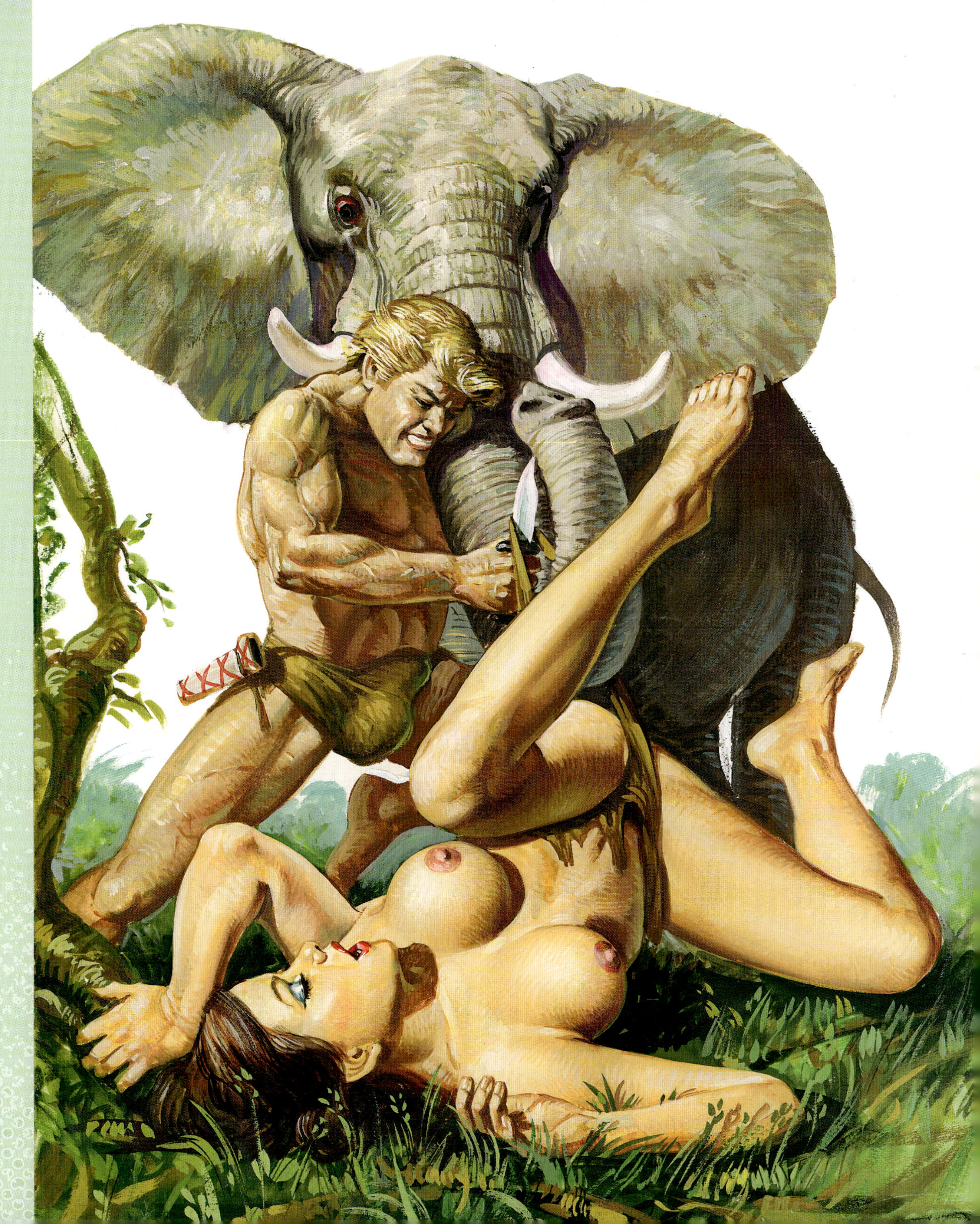

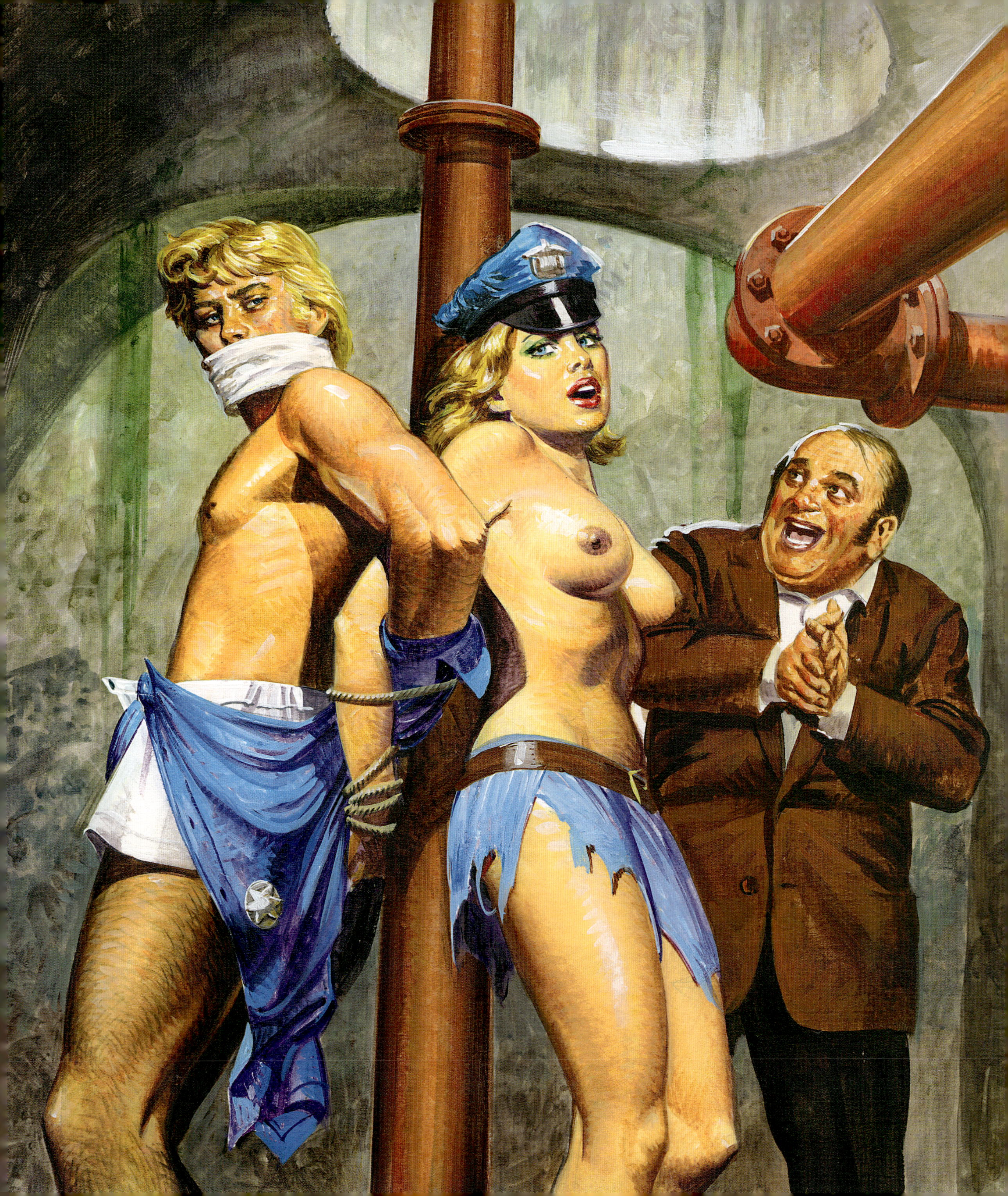

LA POLIZIOTTA

PUBLISHED 1980–1988; 88 ISSUES

Emanuele painted the covers for the first 80 issues of "The Policewoman". The protagonists are a male and female cop duo called Star Winder and Silver Bird, whose activities take place in a small American town called Marysville. By the 1980s the so-called "escalation of the naked" had moved most of Edifumetto's output into no holds barred porn. "In the last period of the comics, the storylines started to feature things like sadomasochism and borderline paedophilia, so the illustrators were asked to create some really heavy things," Emanuele recalls. "Those who later became respectable artists are not pleased that their earlier work is now being dug up."

Left: La Poliziotta, n. 61, *Vendetta Porno*, Revenge Porn, June 1981.

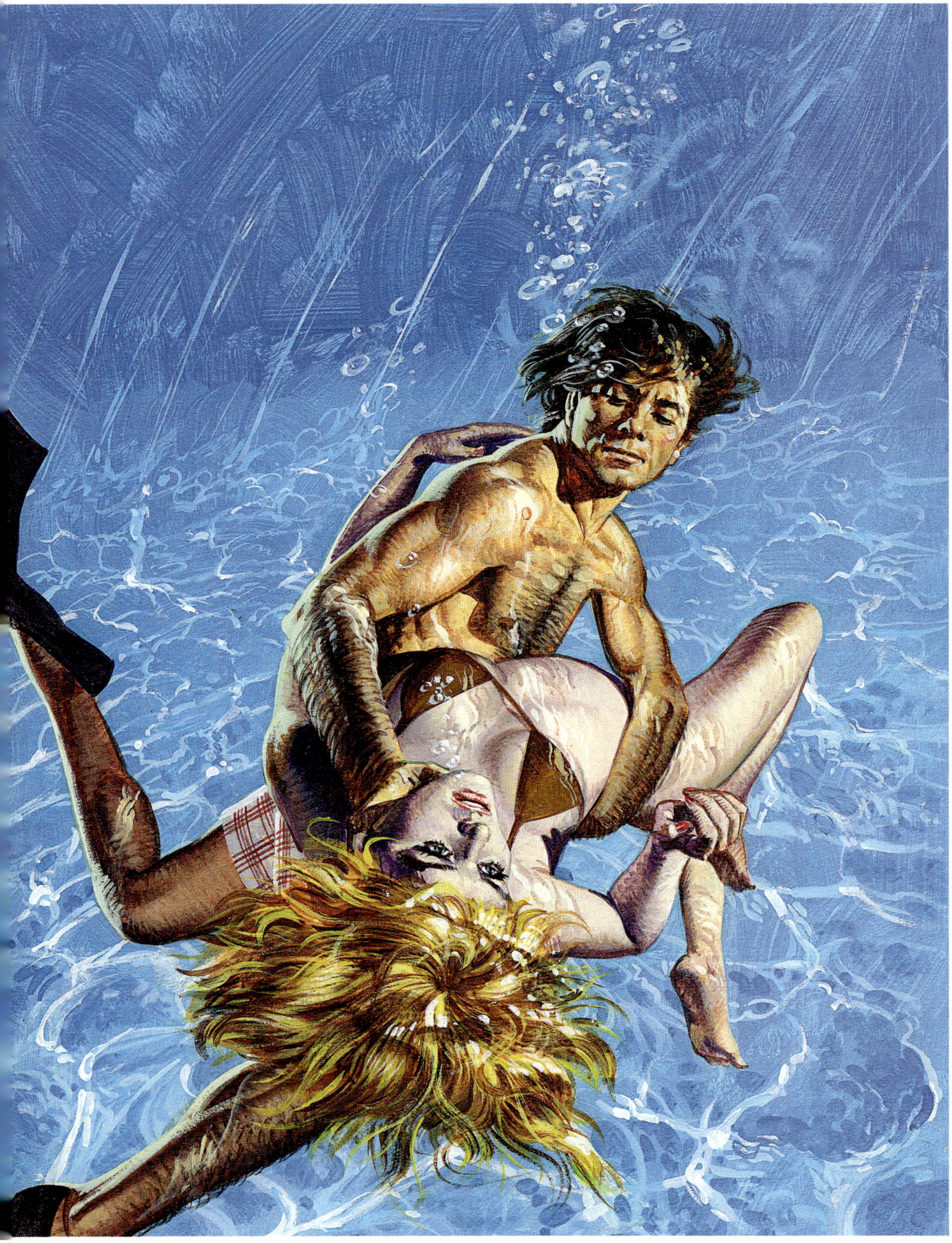

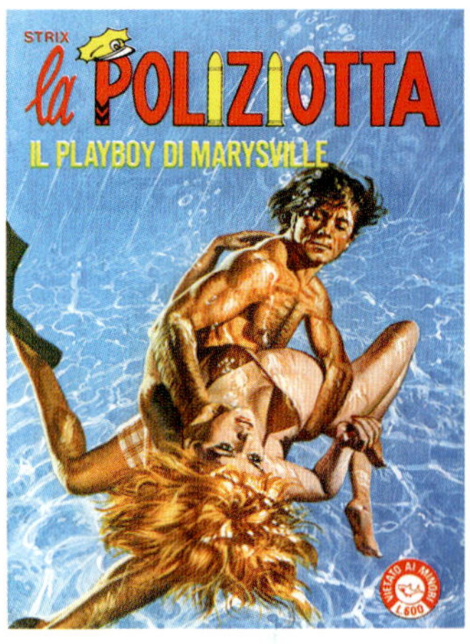

Left: La Poliziotta, n. 8,
Il Playboy di Marysville,
The Playboy of Marysville,
January 1981.

Right: La Poliziotta, n. 25,
Il Sadico di Marysville,
The Sadist of Marysville,
January 1982.

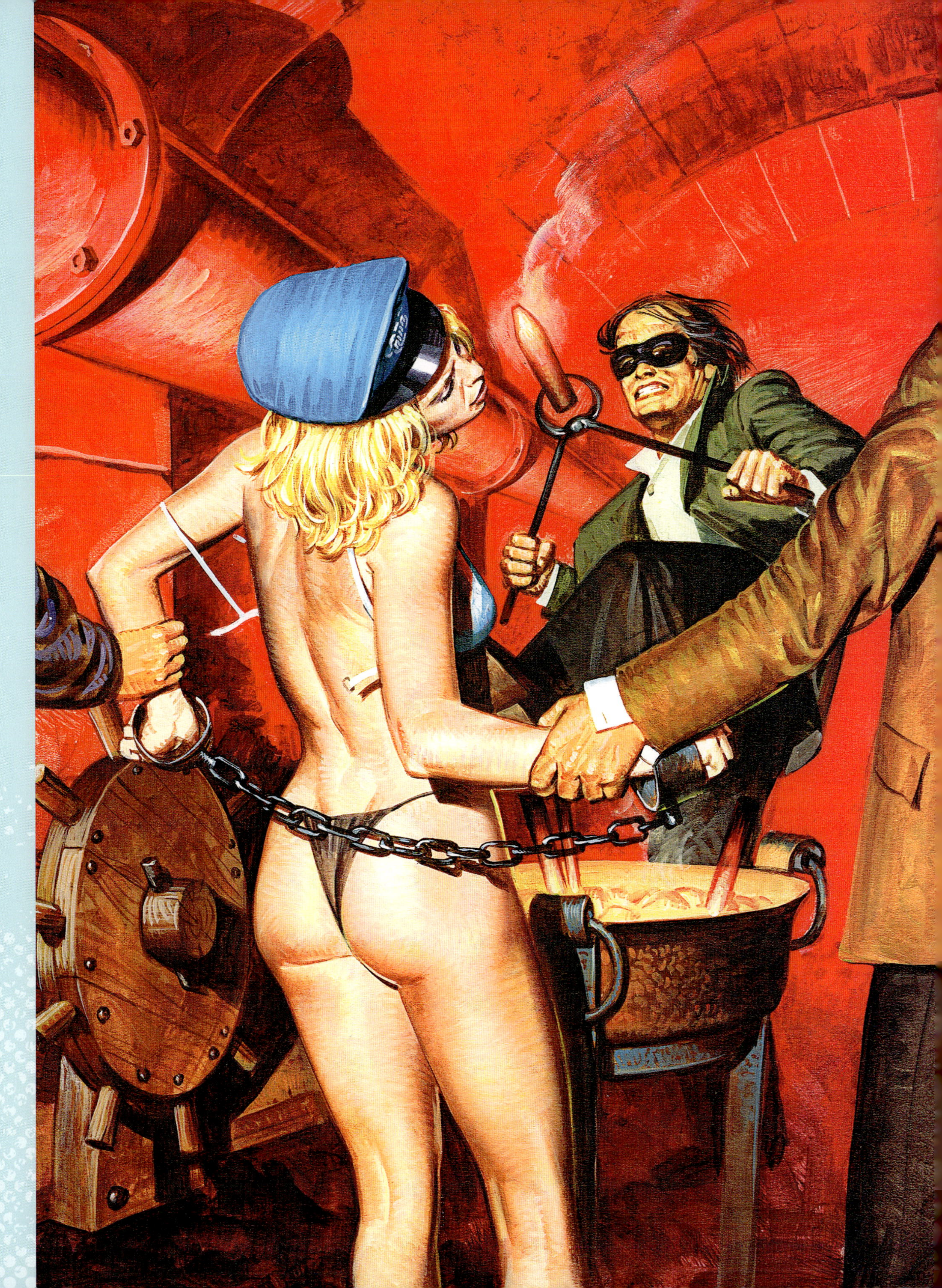

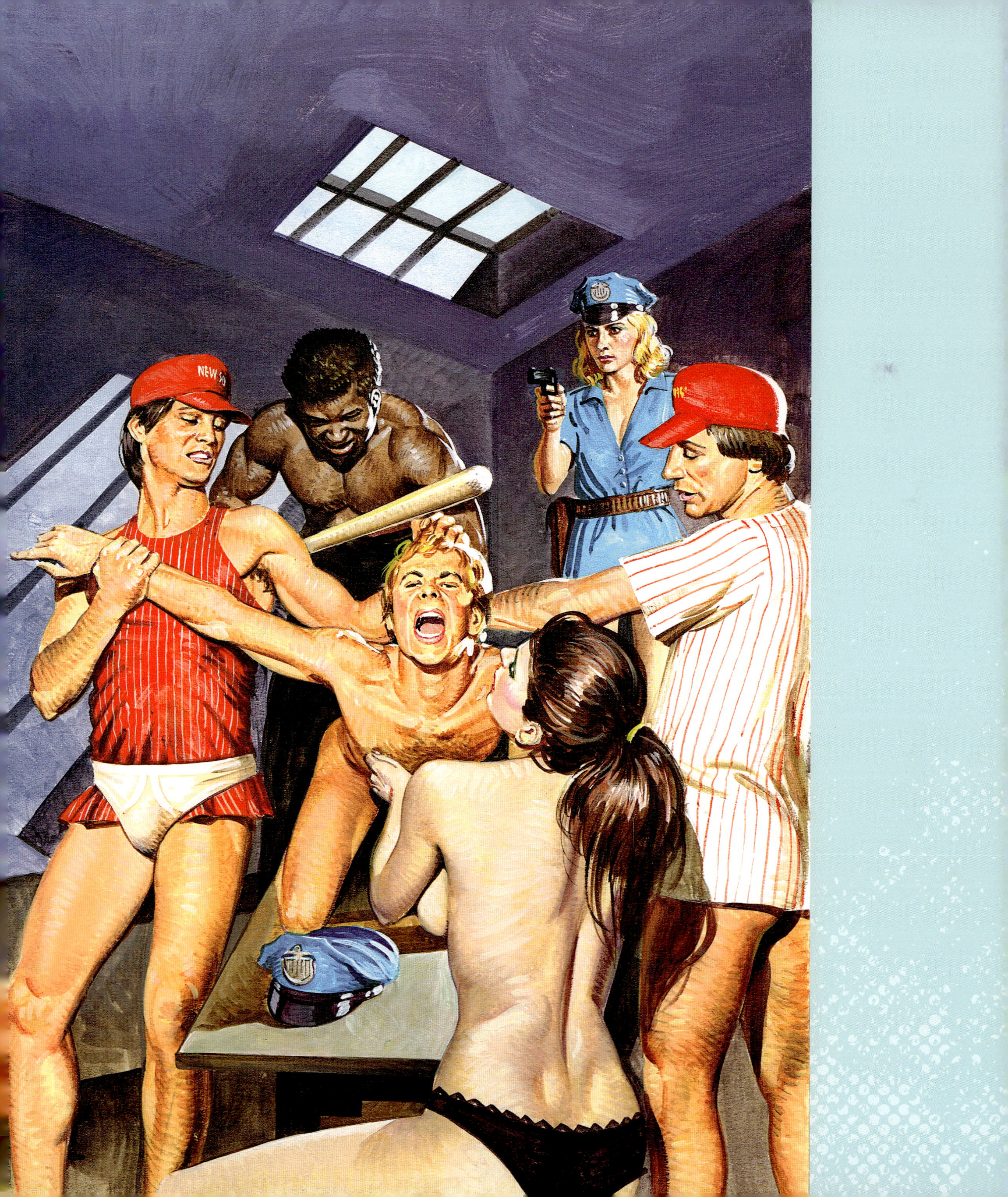

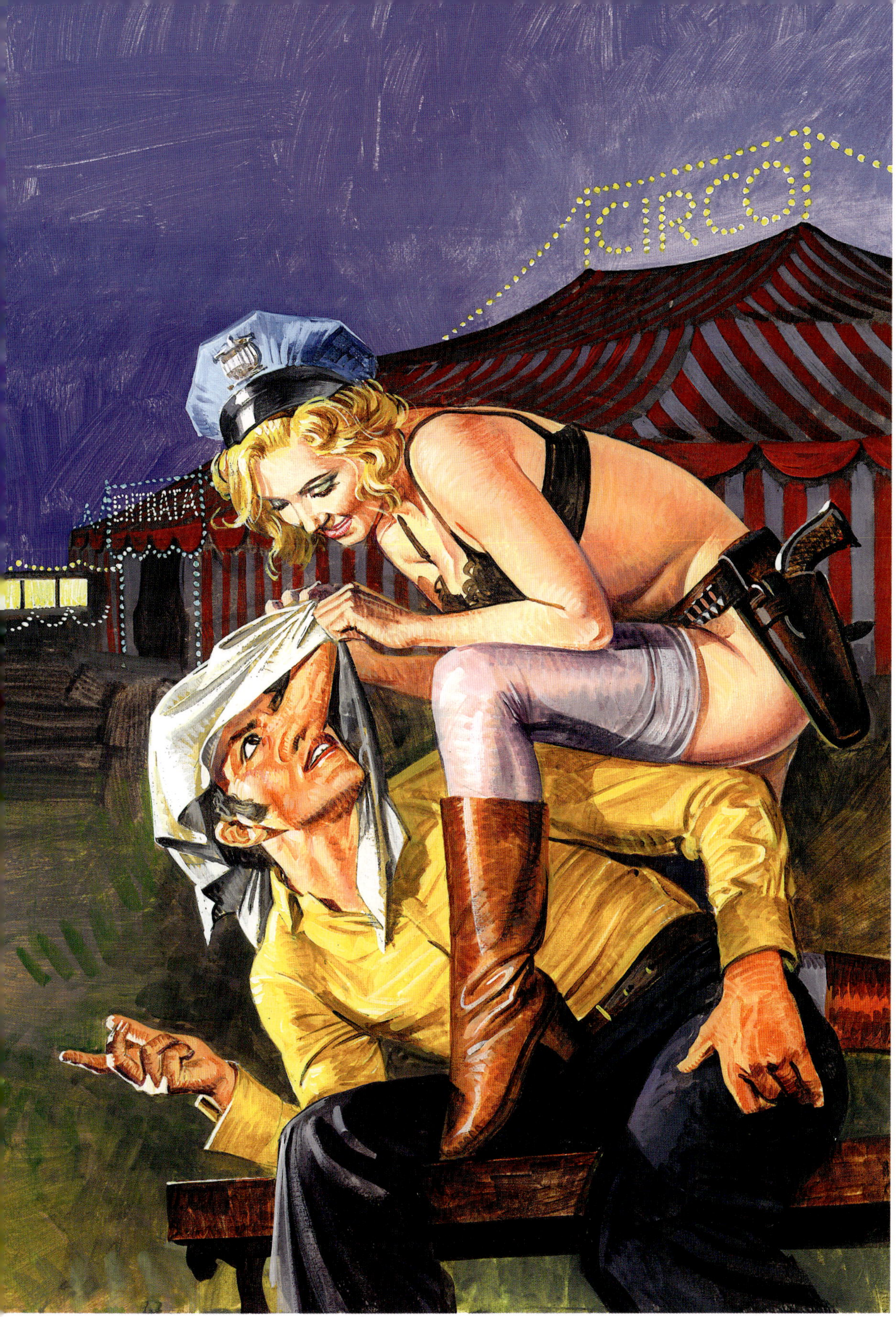

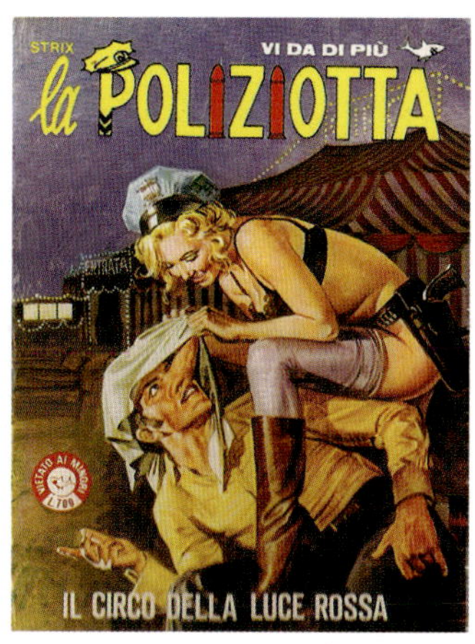

Left: La Poliziotta, n. 28,
Il Circo della Luce Rossa,
The Red Light Circus,
September 1982.

Far left: La Poliziotta, n. 26,
Due Palle e una Mazza, Two
Balls and a Bat, July 1982.

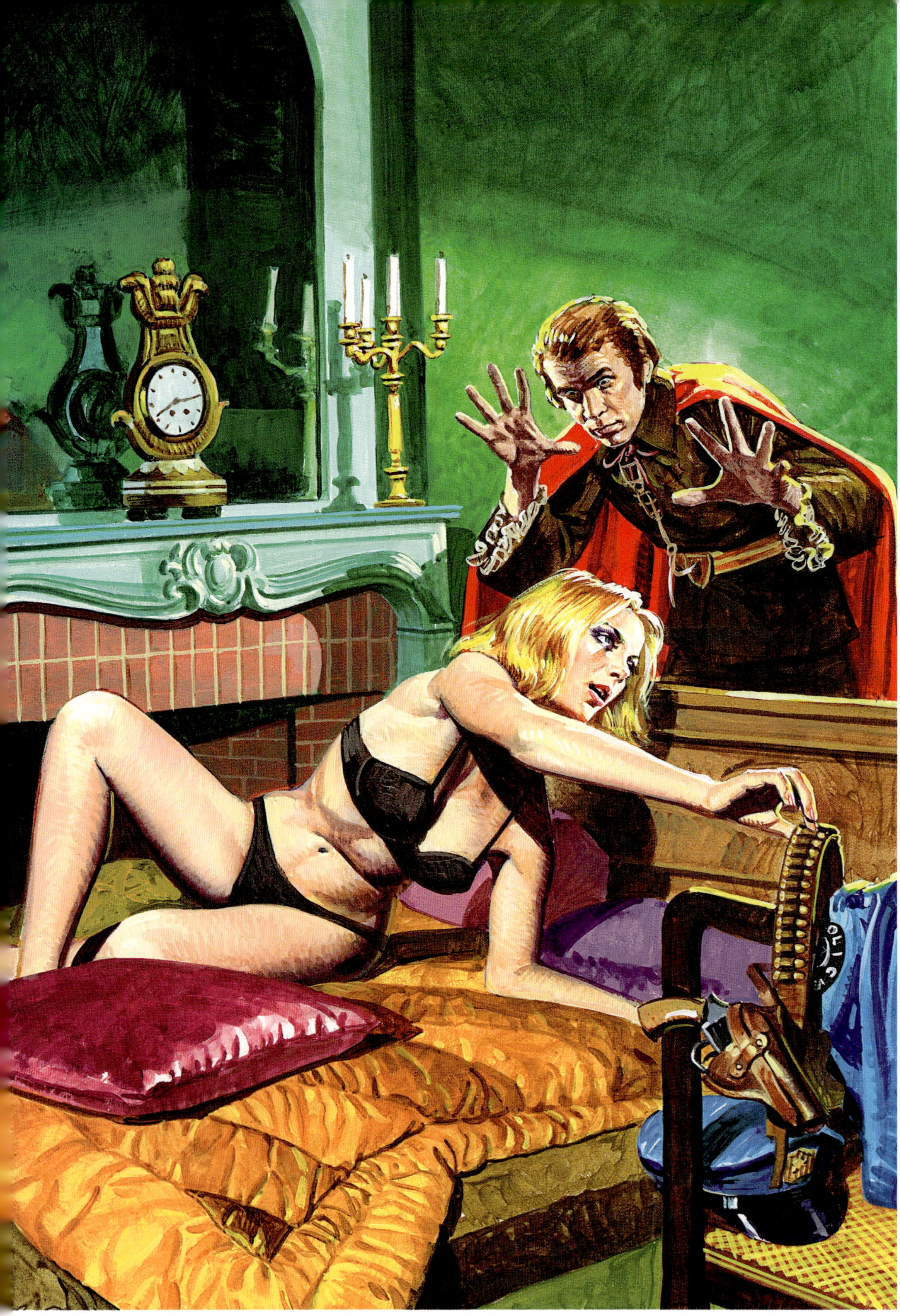

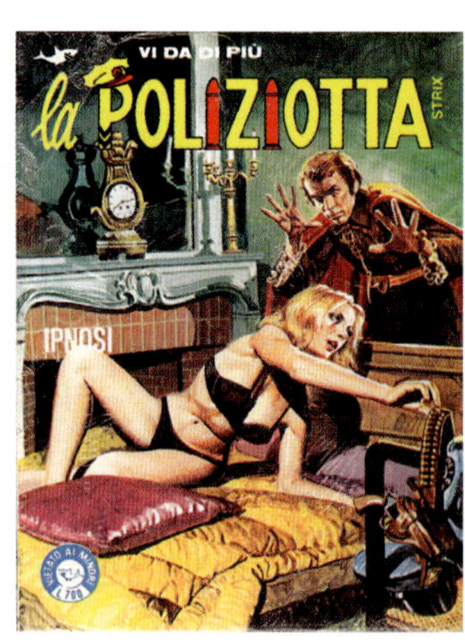

Left: La Poliziotta, n. 33,
Ipnosi, Hypnosis,
February 1983.

Right: La Poliziotta, n. 35,
Il Bruto, The Brute,
April 1983.

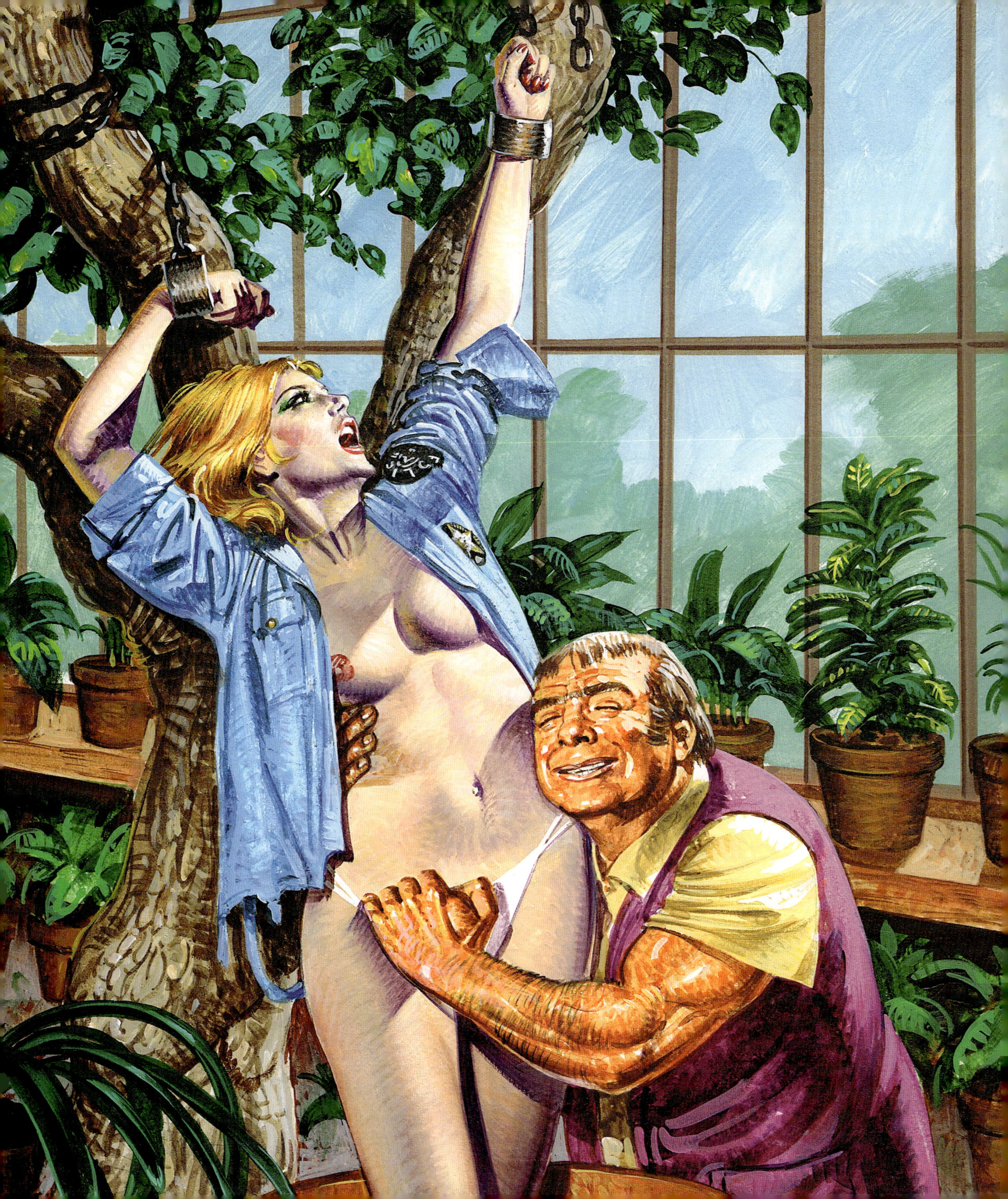

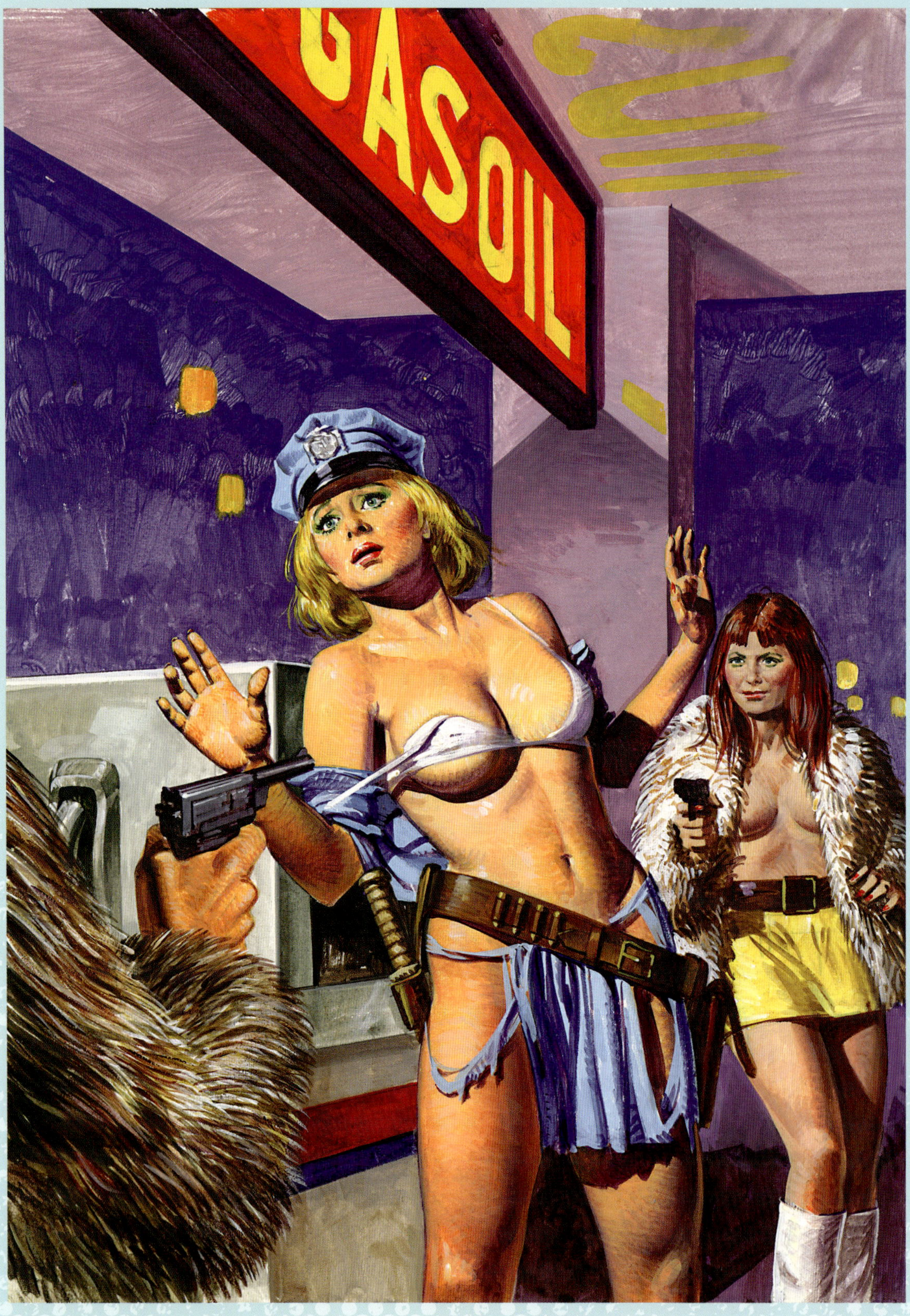

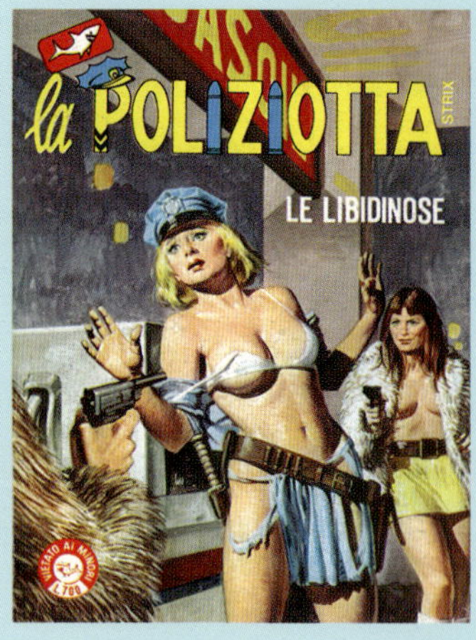

Left: La Poliziotta, n. 36,
Le Libidinoes, The Lustful,
May 1983.

Right: La Poliziotta, n. 40,
Il Travestito, The Transvestite,
September 1983.

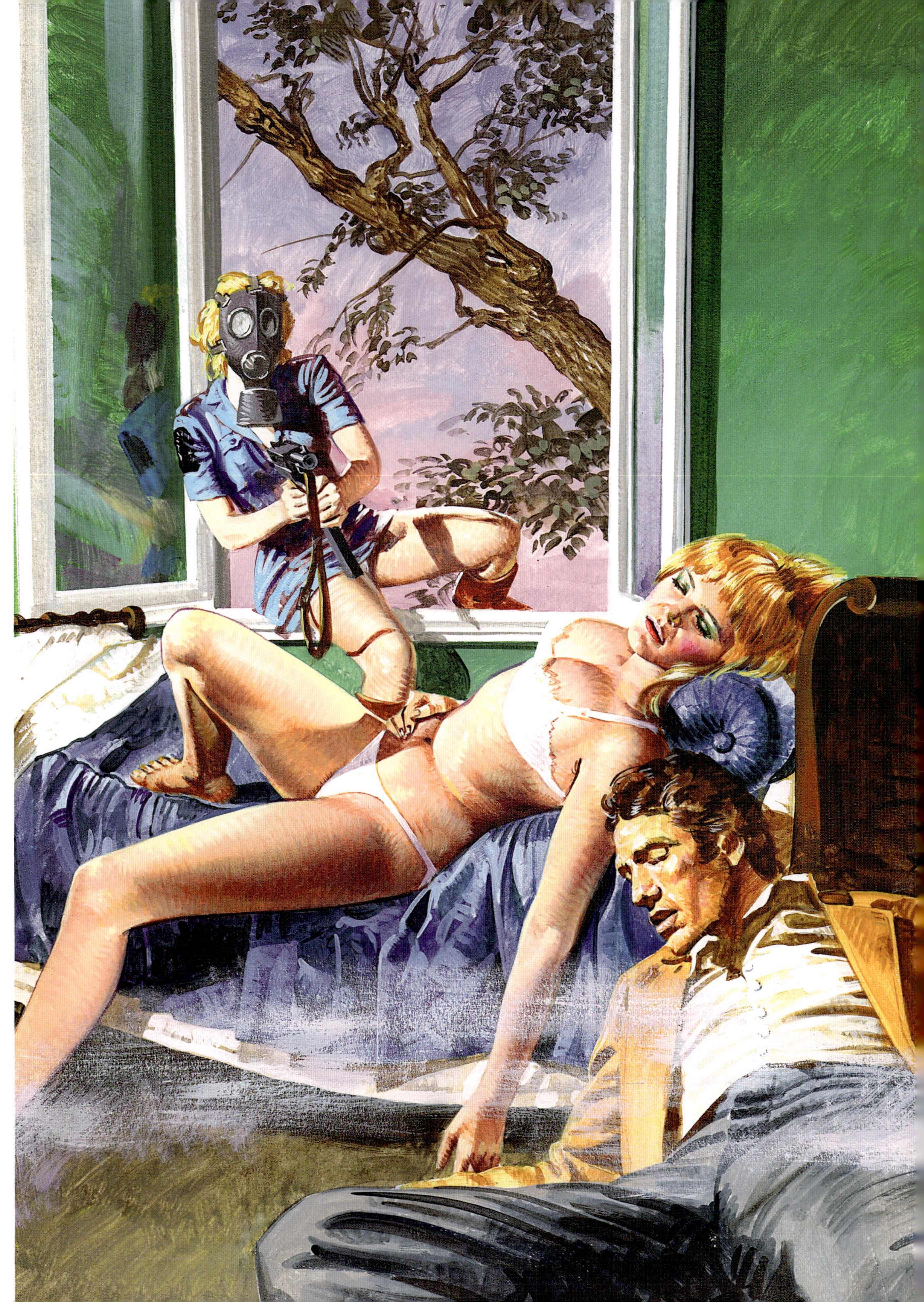

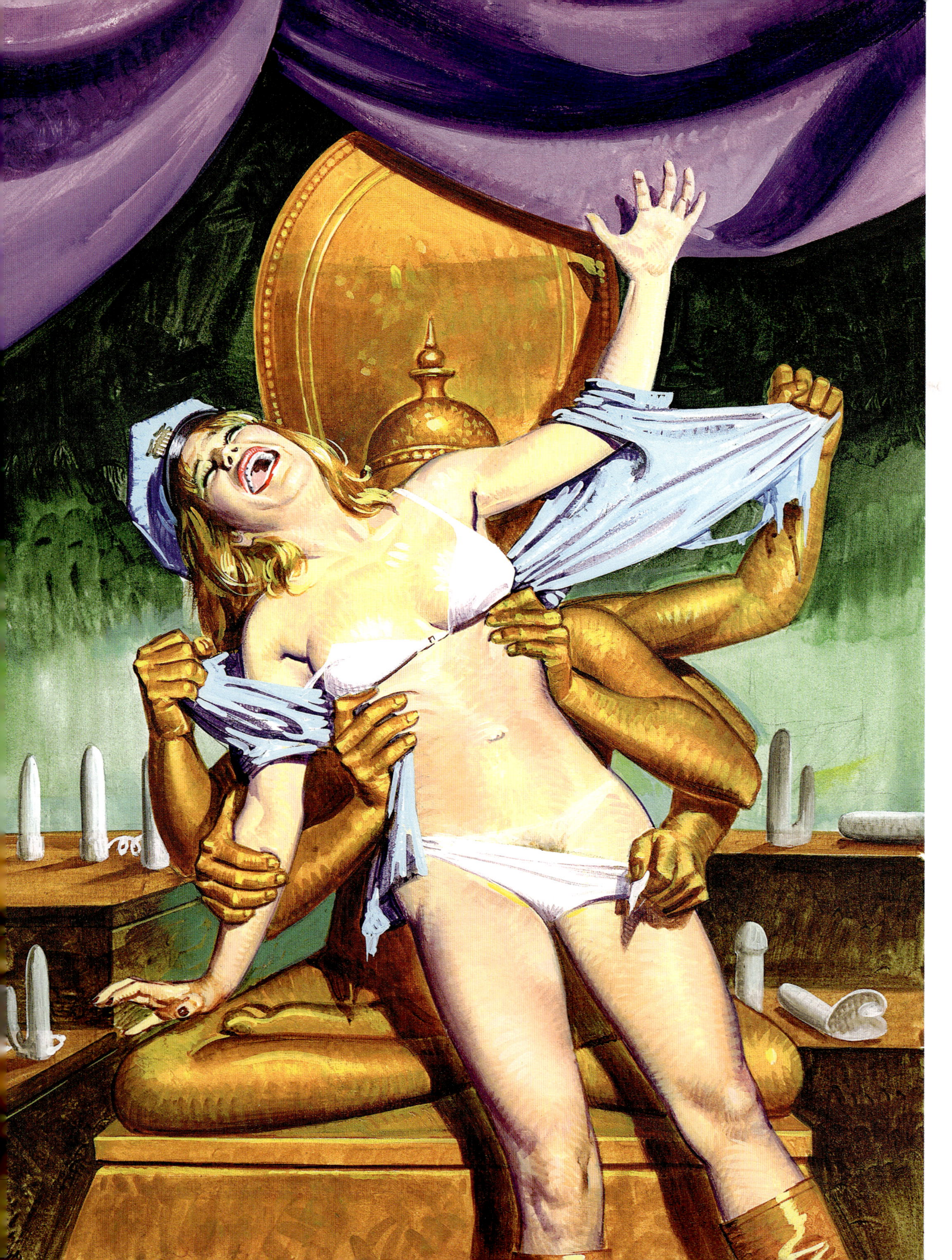

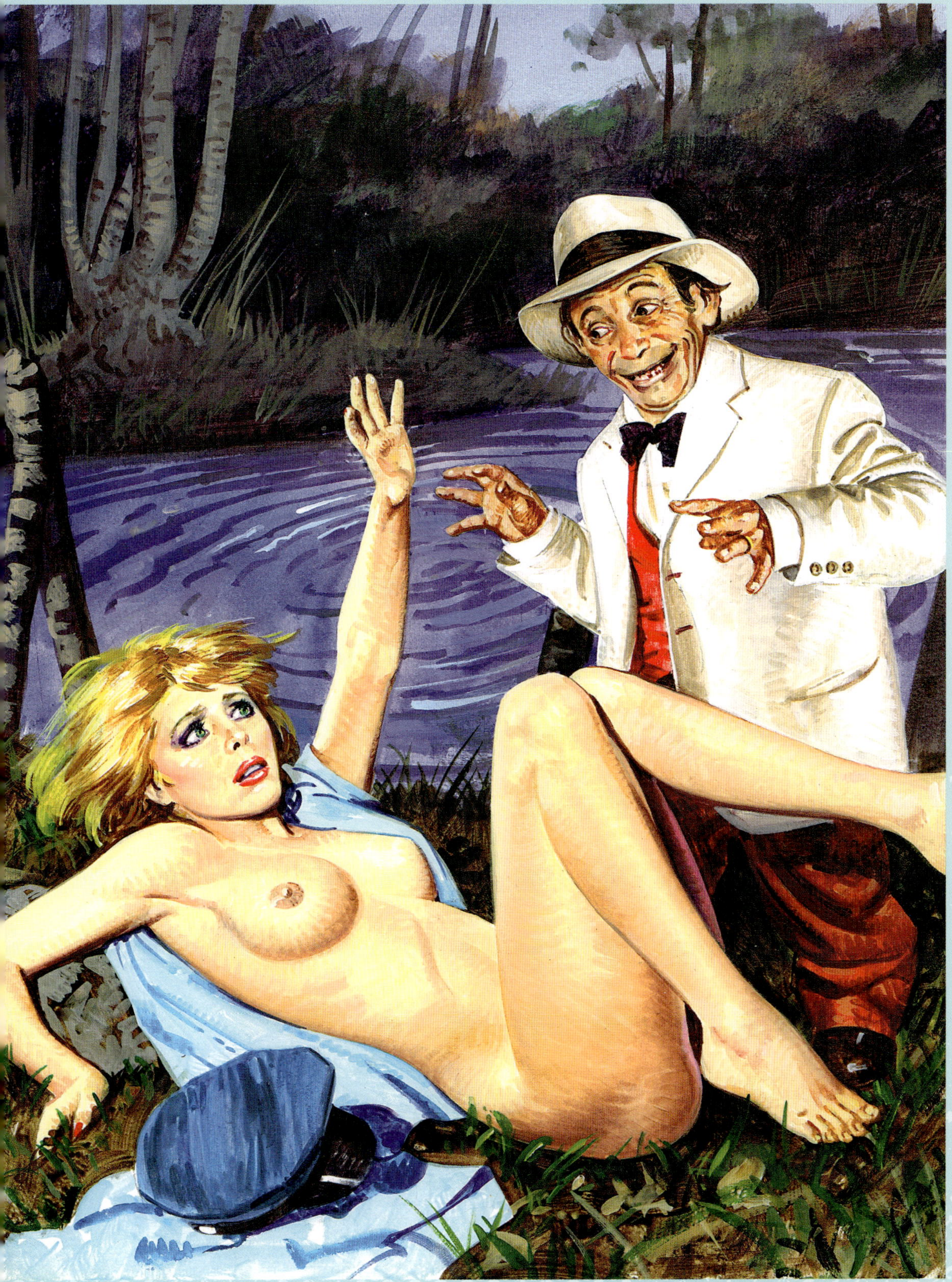

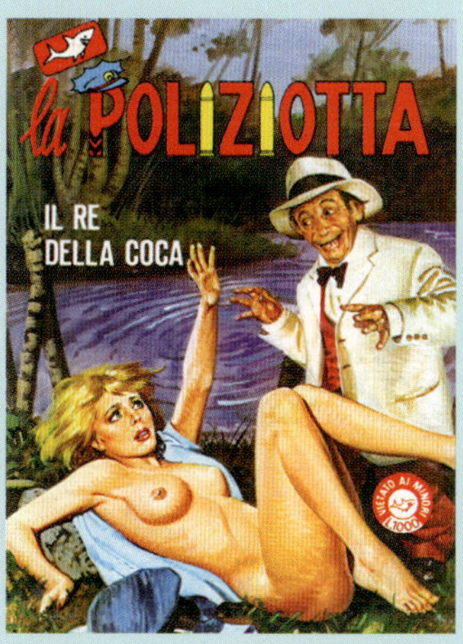

Left: La Poliziotta, n. 56, *Il Re della Coca*, The Coke King, January 1985.

Far left: La Poliziotta, n. 43, *Gli Attrezzi Erotici del Sexy Shop*, The Erotic Contraption of the Sex Shop, December 1983.

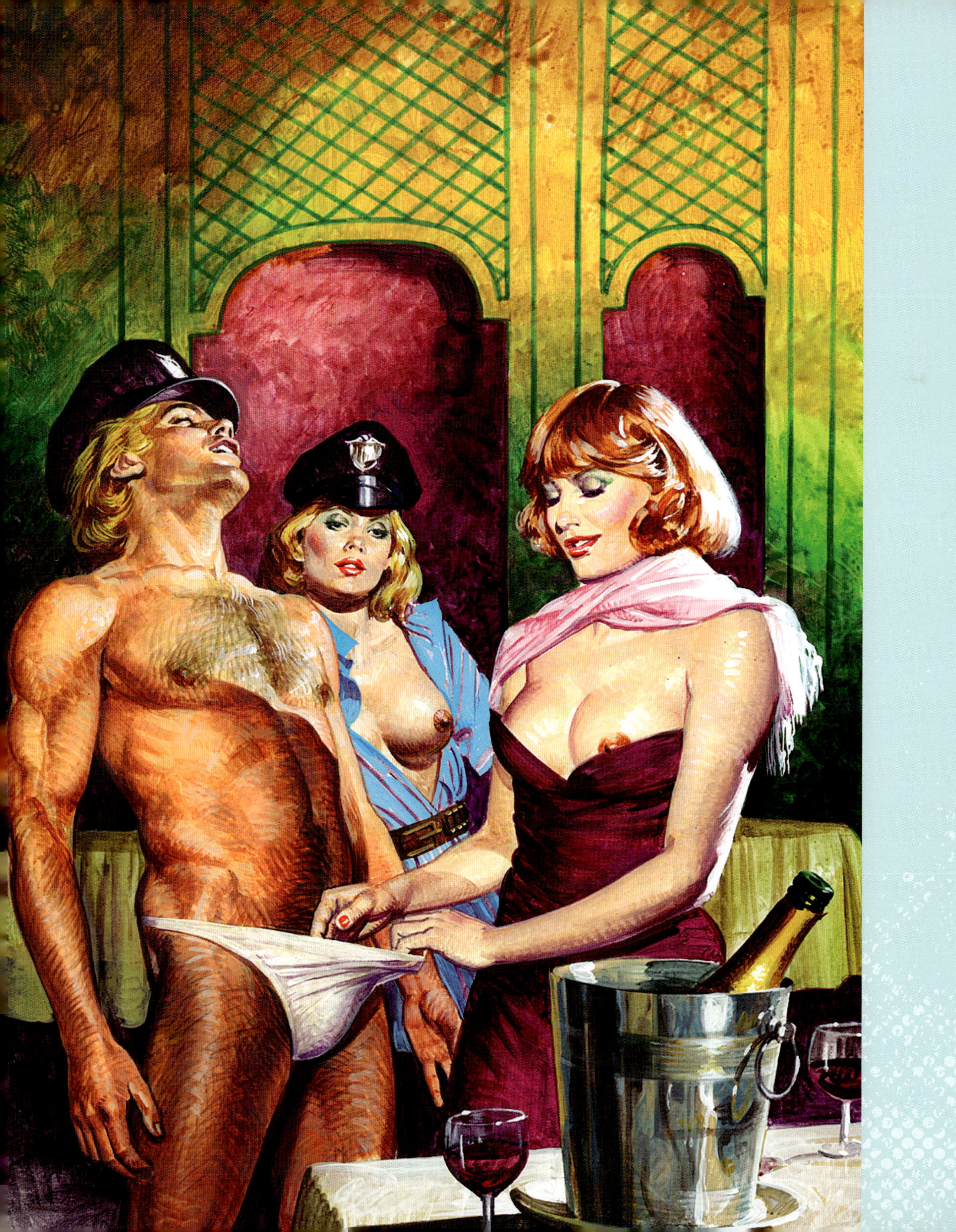

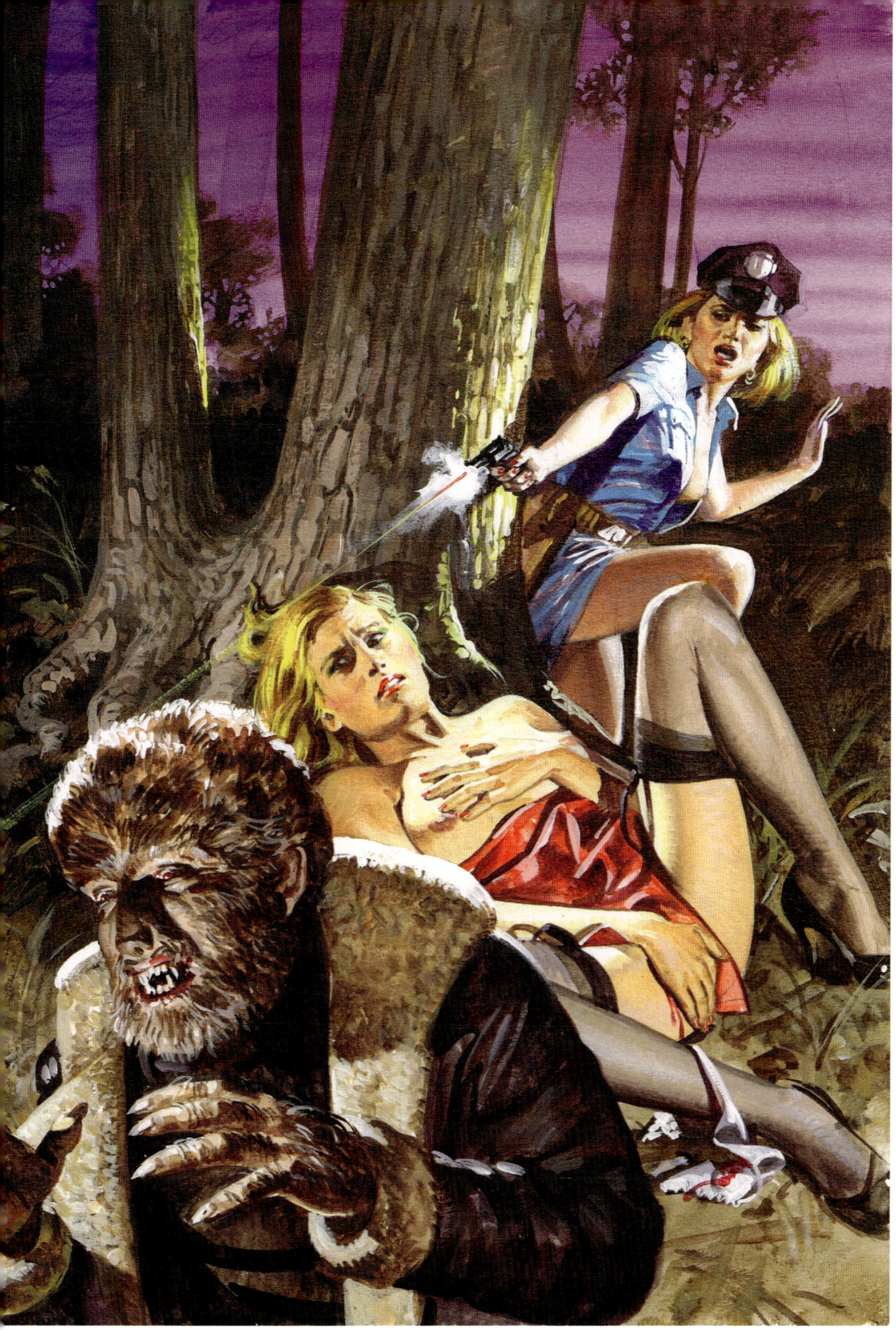

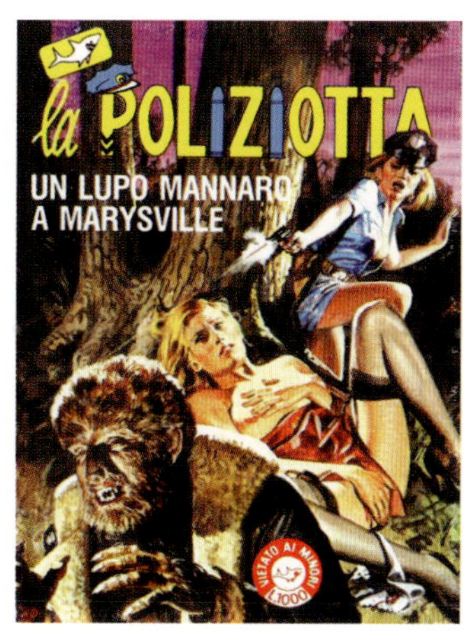

Far left: La Poliziotta, n. 60, *La Corsa agli Uccelli,* The Race for the Birds, May 1985.

Left: La Poliziotta, n. 68, *Un Lupo Mannaro a Marysville*, A Werewolf in Marysville, January 1986.

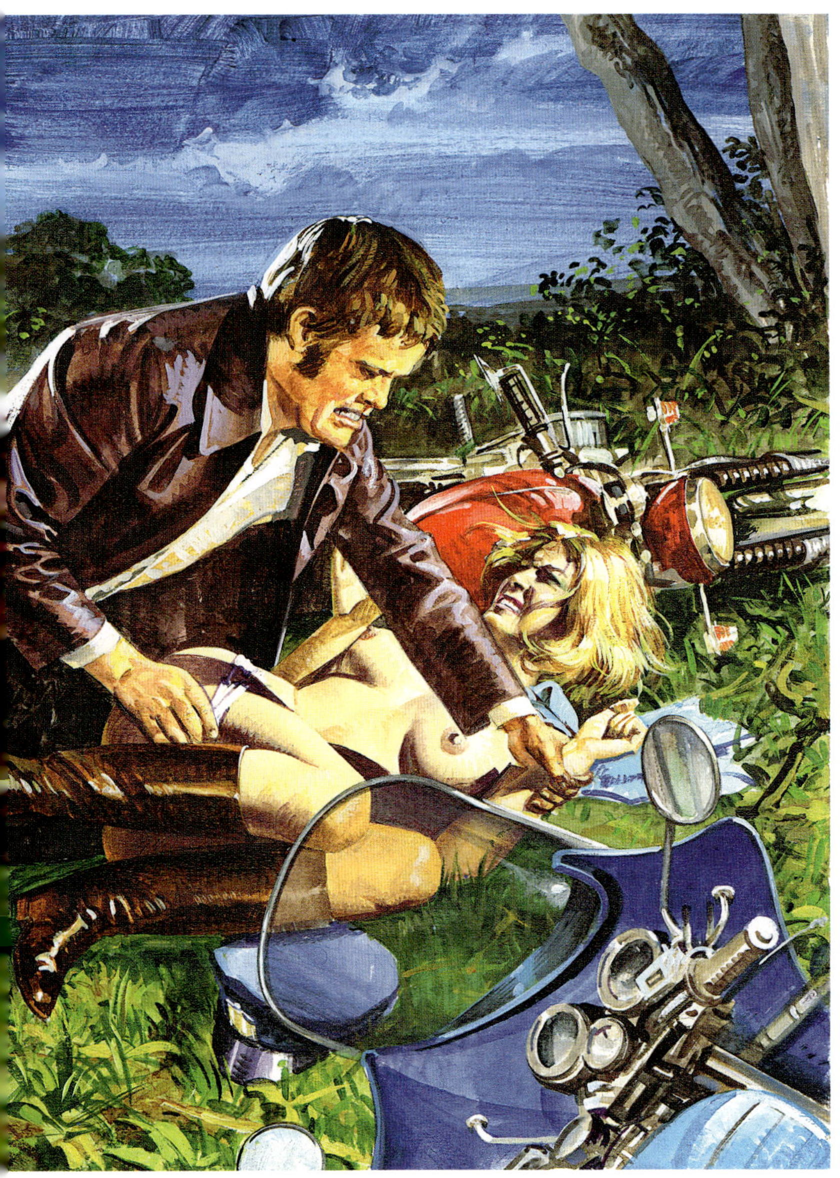

Above: La Poliziotta, n. 70, *Transex*, Shemale, March 1986.

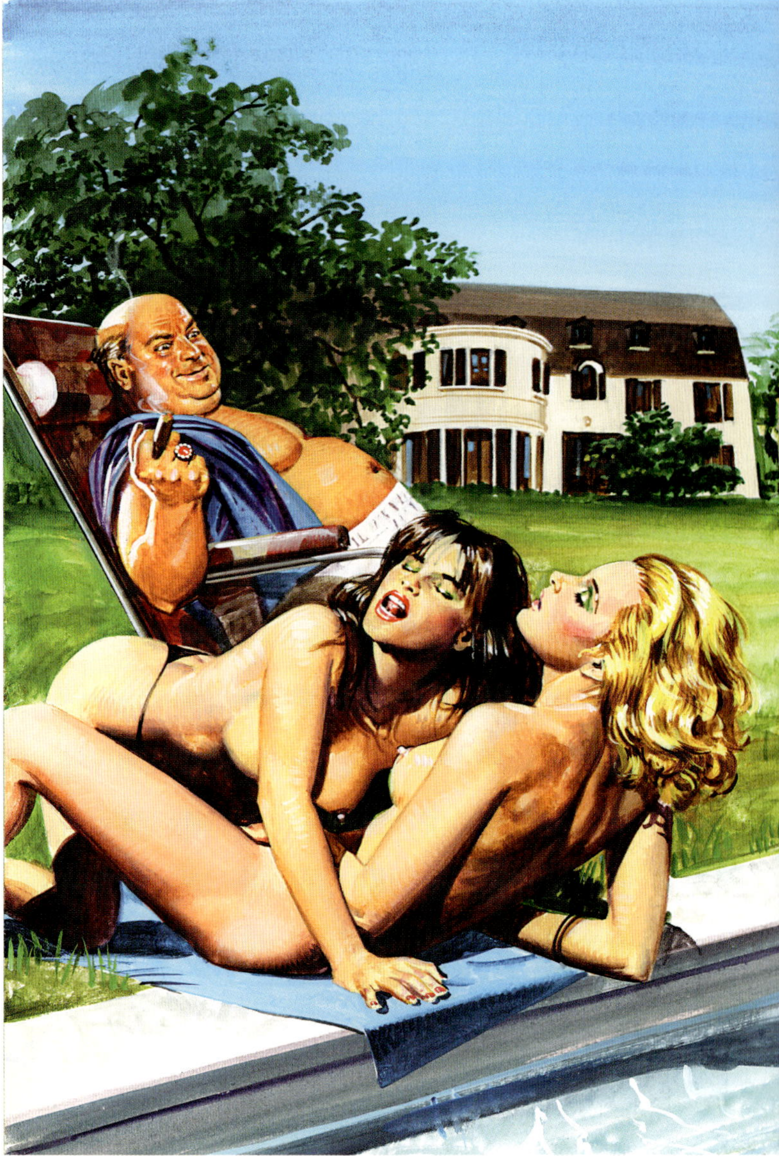

Above: La Poliziotta, n. 75, *Diabolico Piano*,
A Diabolical Plan, August 1986.

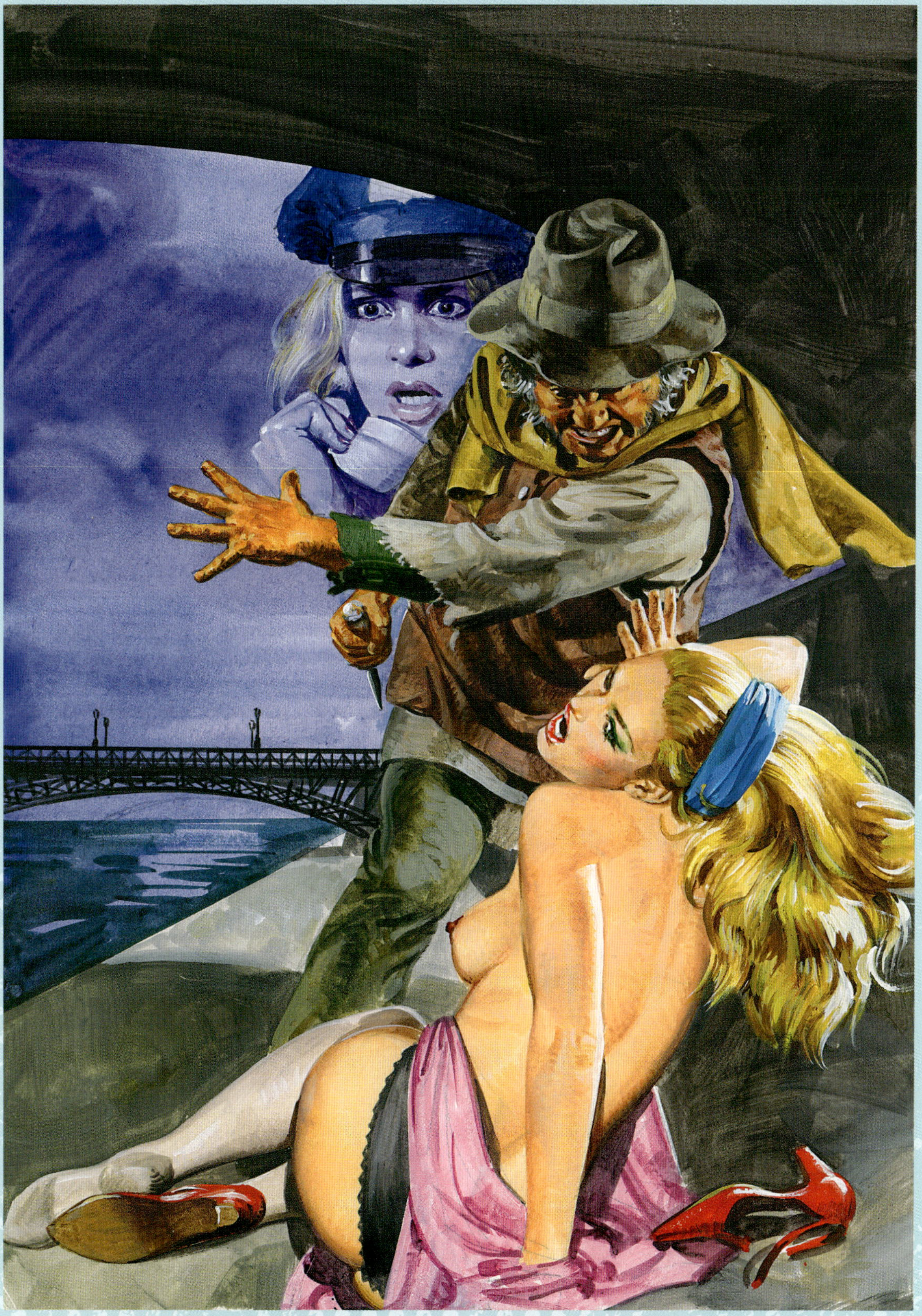

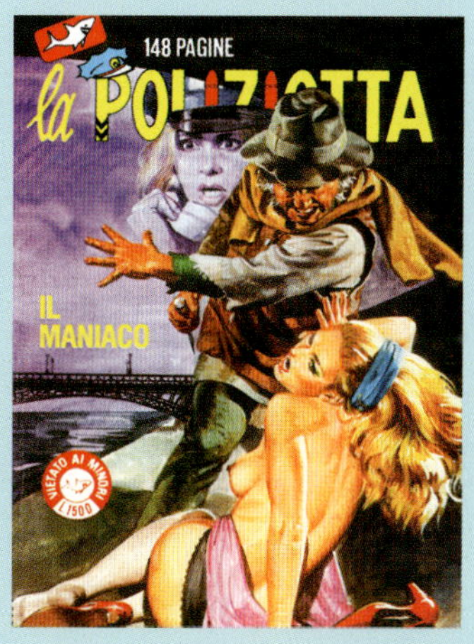

Left: La Poliziotta, n. 88, *Il Maniaco*, The Maniac, September 1988.

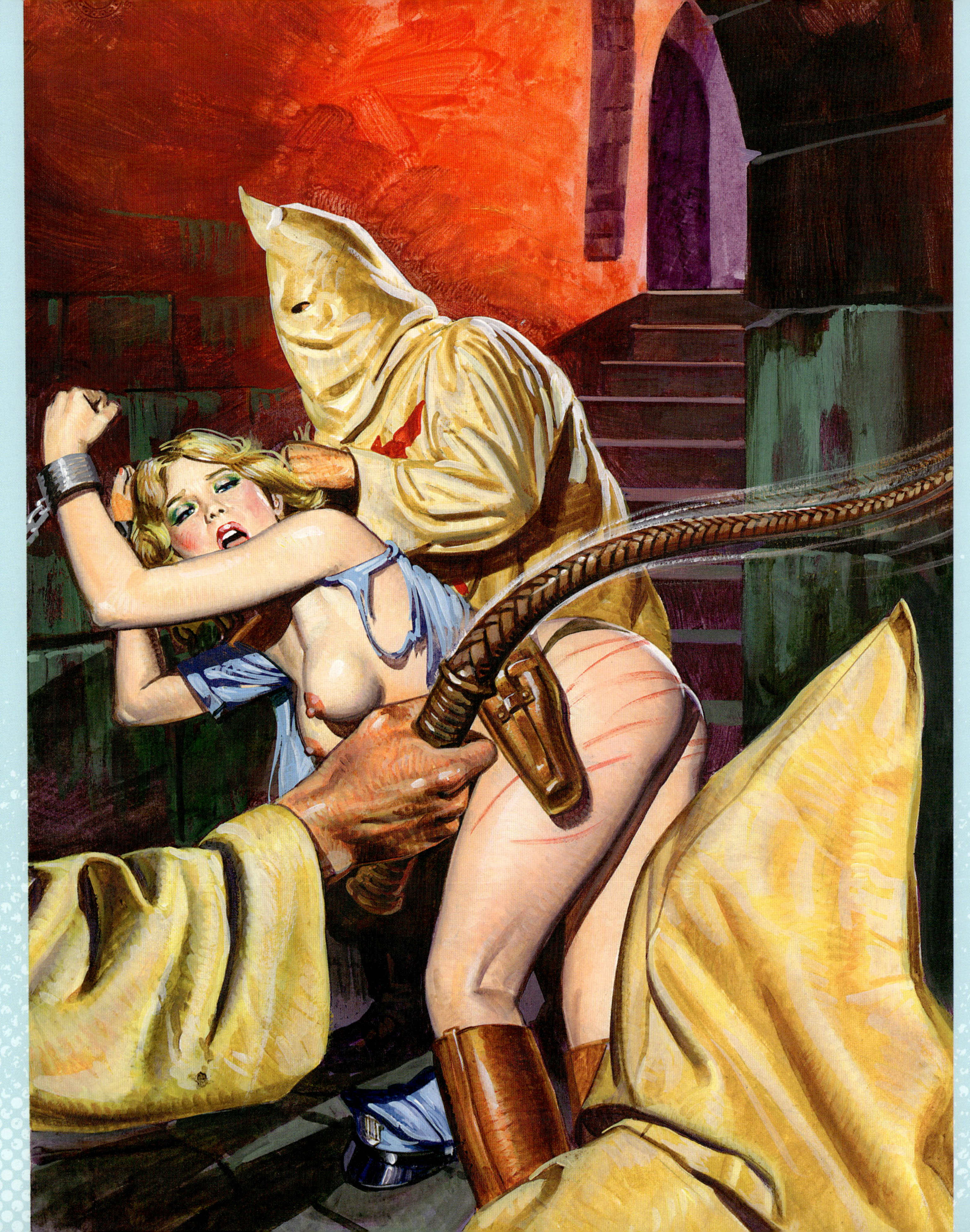

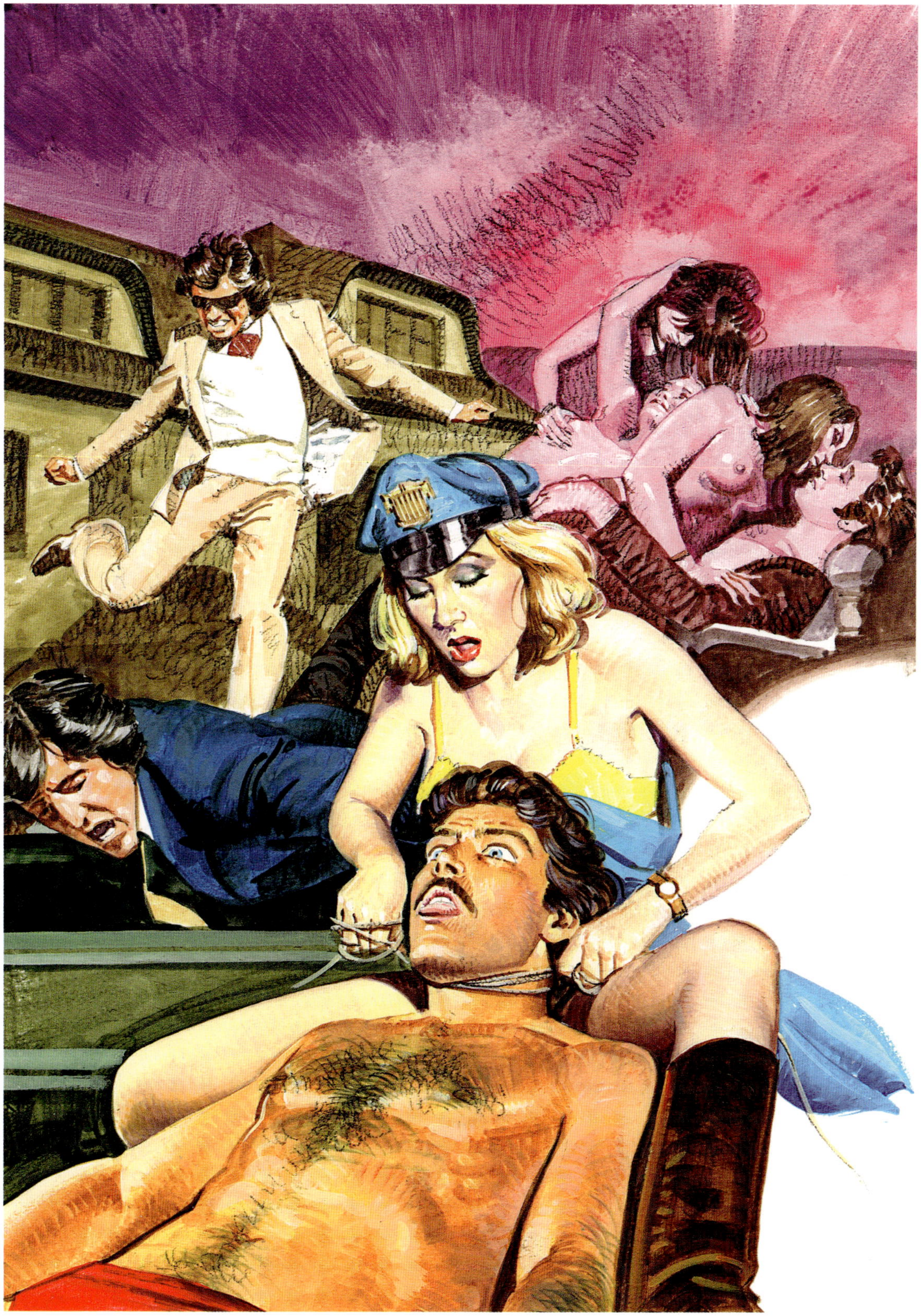

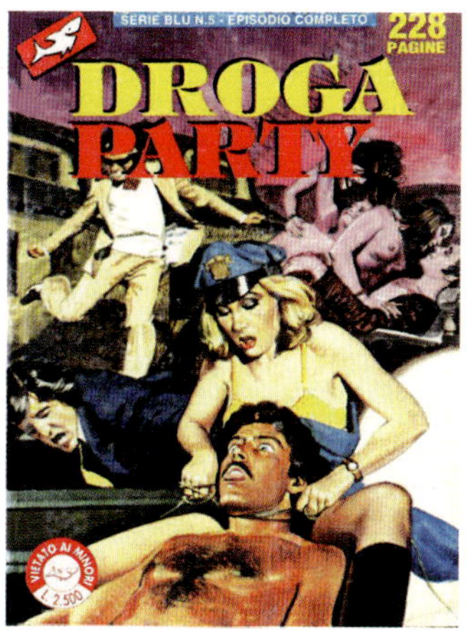

Left: La Poliziotta
Supplemento, n. 10,
Droga-Party a Marysville,
Marysville Drugs Party,
March 1981.

Far left: La Poliziotta
Supplemento, n. 5,
Il Clan dei Fustigatori,
The Clan of Whippers,
July 1983.

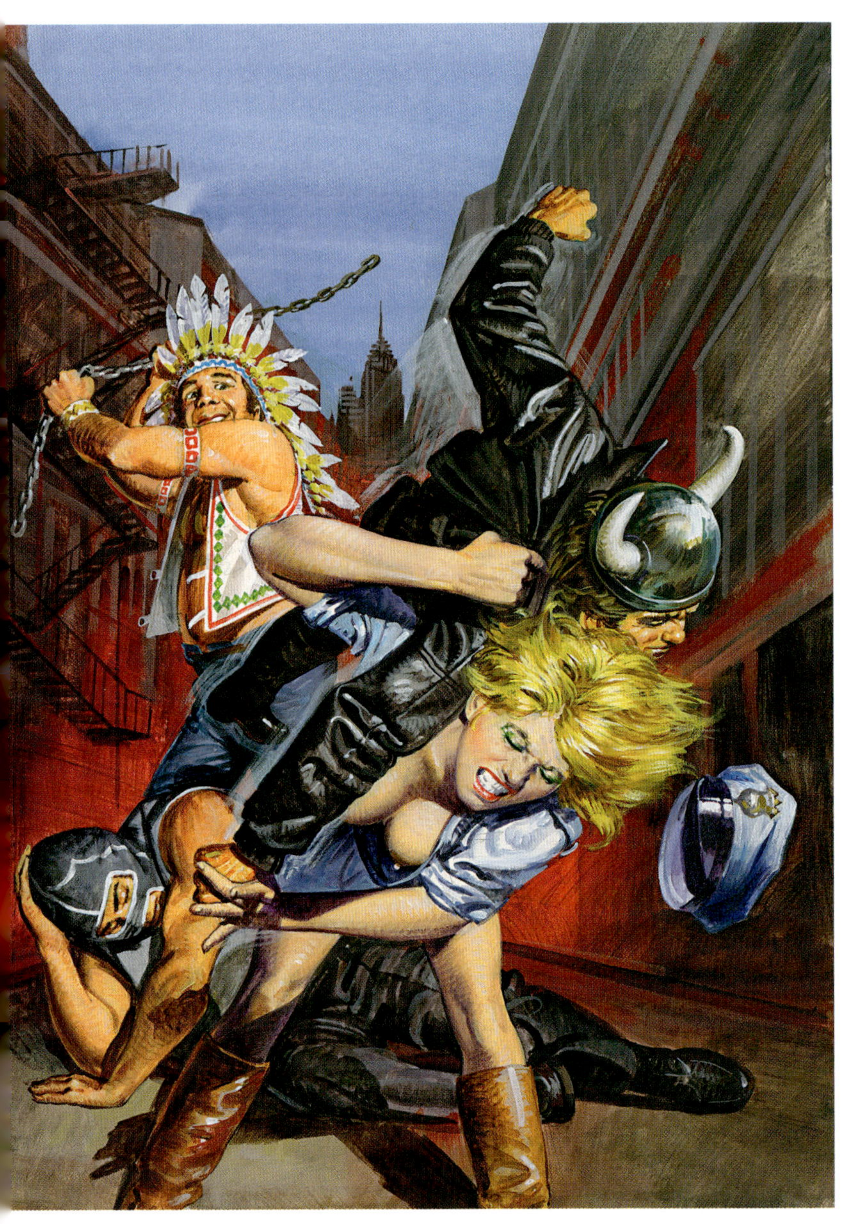

Above: Superpoliziotta, n. 1, *Contro una Sadica Banda di Finocchi Motociclisti*, Against a Sadistic Band of Gay Motorcyclists, June 1985.

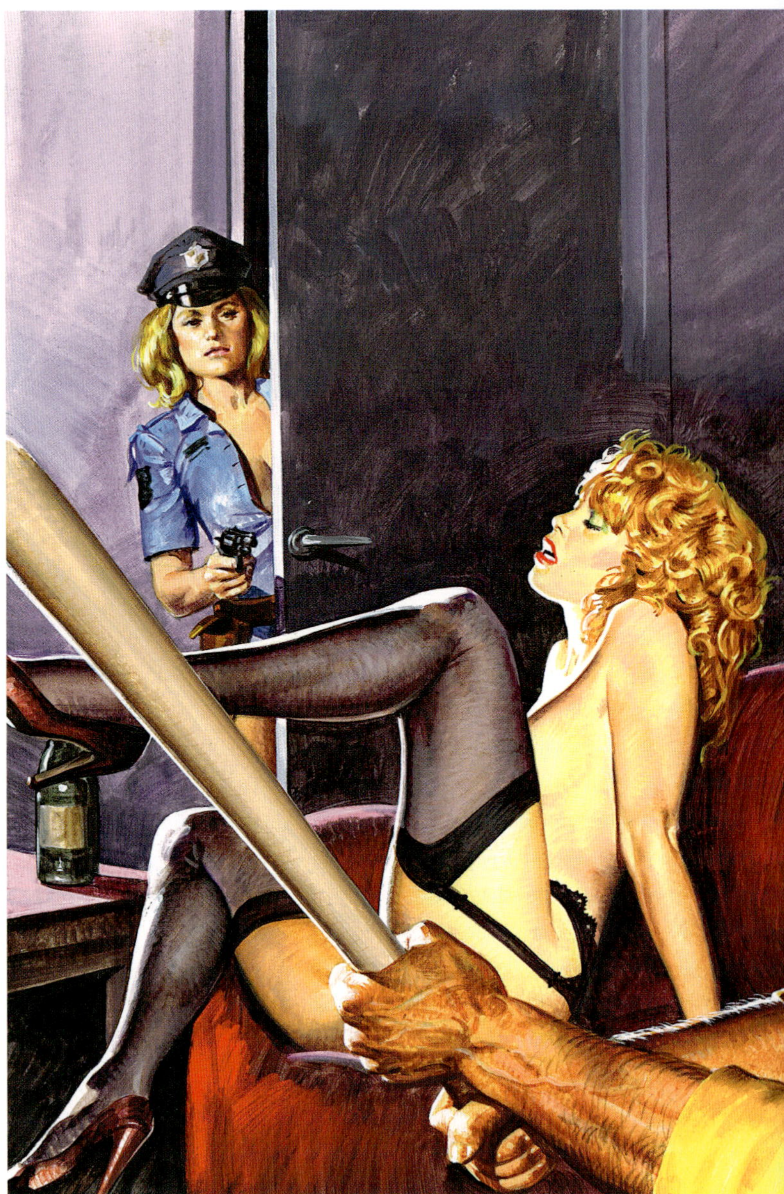

Above: Superpoliziotta, n. 2, *Due Palle e una Mazza*, Two Balls and a Bat, October 1987.

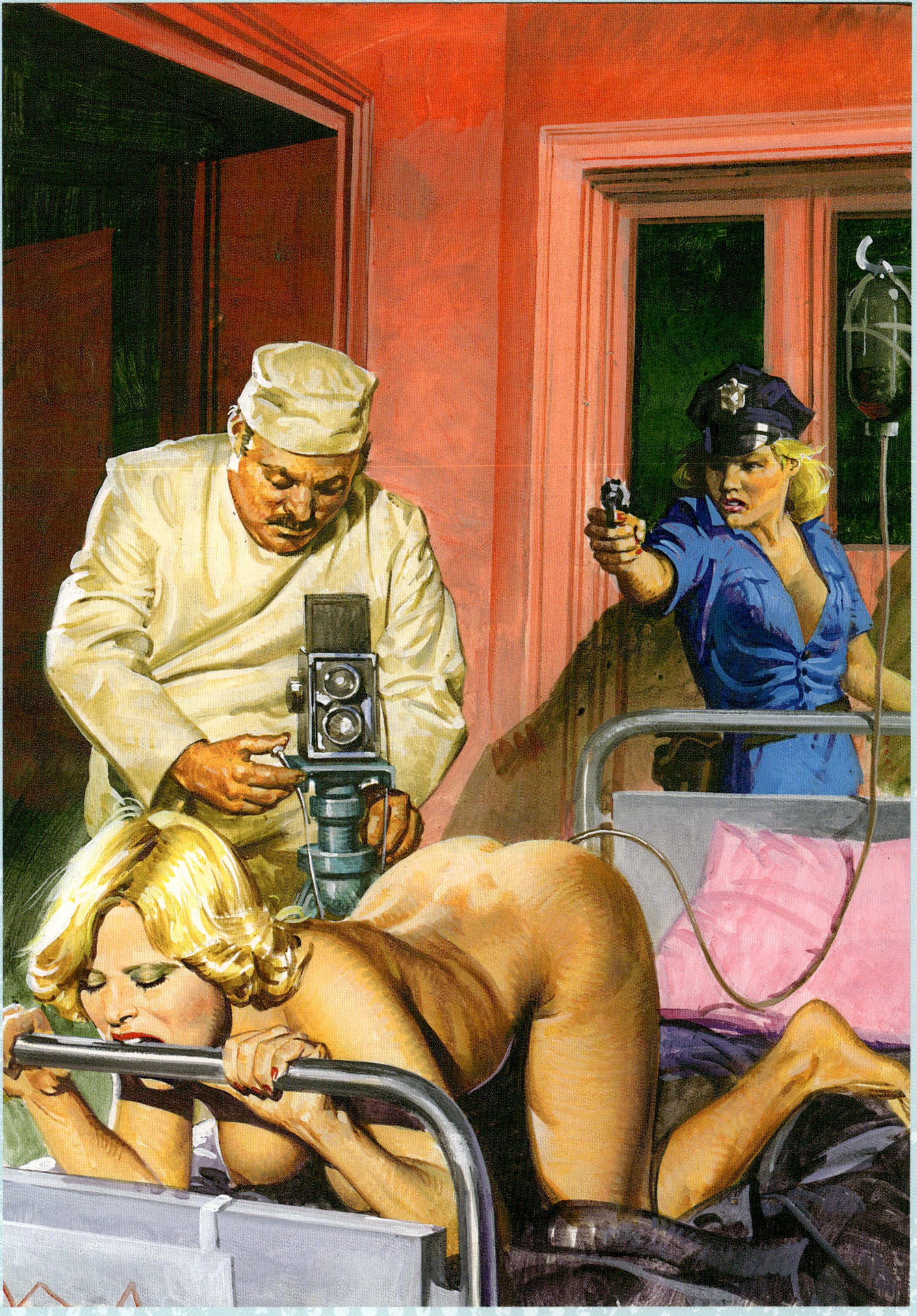

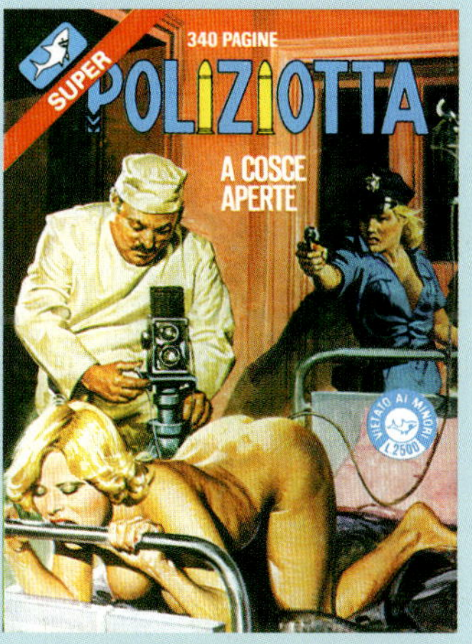

Left: Superpoliziotta, n. 3,
A Cosce Aperte, Open
Thighs, January 1986.

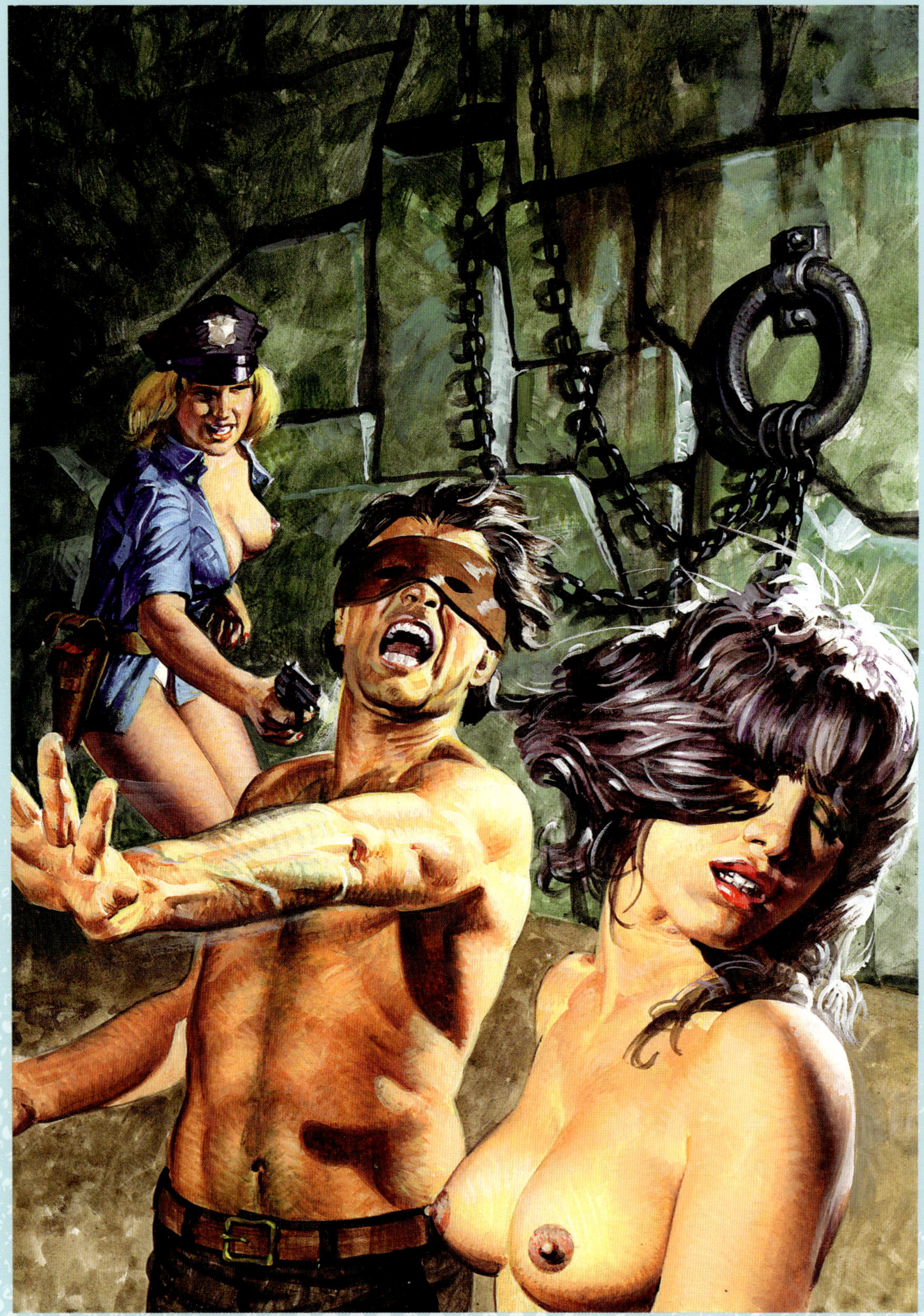

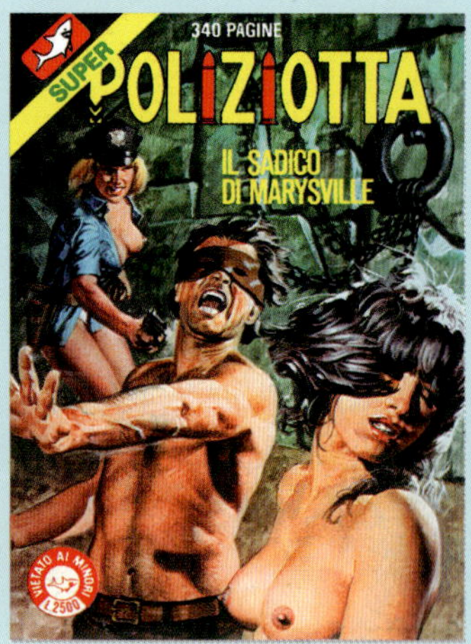

Left: Superpoliziotta, n. 1, *Il Sadico di Marysville,* The Sadist of Marysville, 1987.

OPPOSITE PAGE
Top left: Superpoliziotta, n. 12, *Prostitution,* Prostitution, May 1986.

Top right: Superpoliziotta, n. 14, *Ladri d'Auto,* The Car Thieves, July 1986.

Botton left: Superpoliziotta, n. 18, *Poker d'Assi,* Four Aces, January 1987.

Botton right: Superpoliziotta, n. 22, *Colta in Fallo,* Caught Out, May 1987.

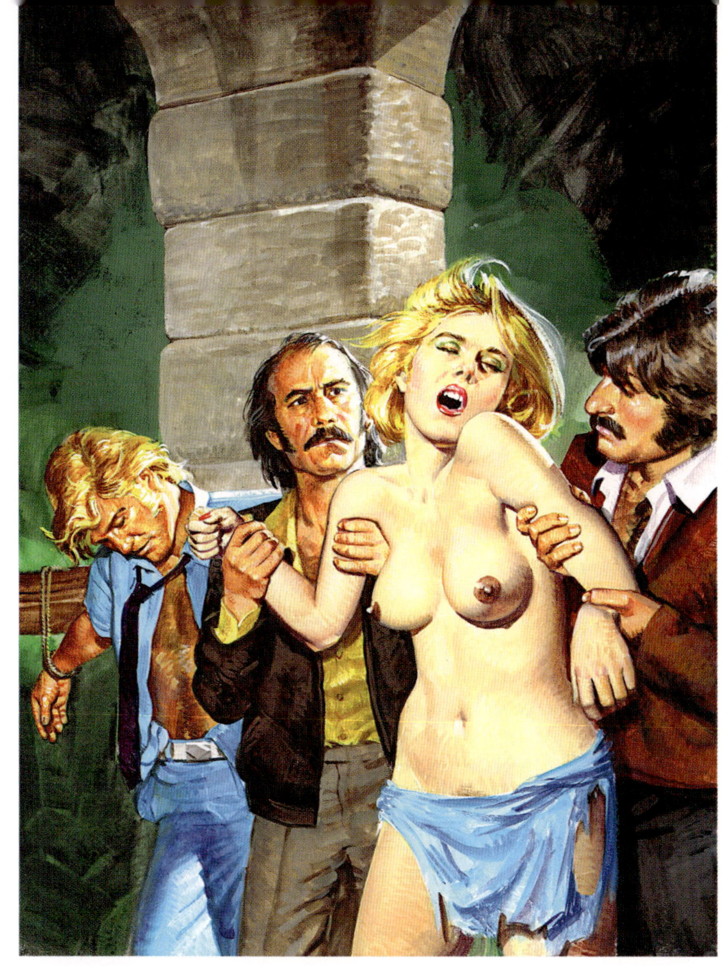
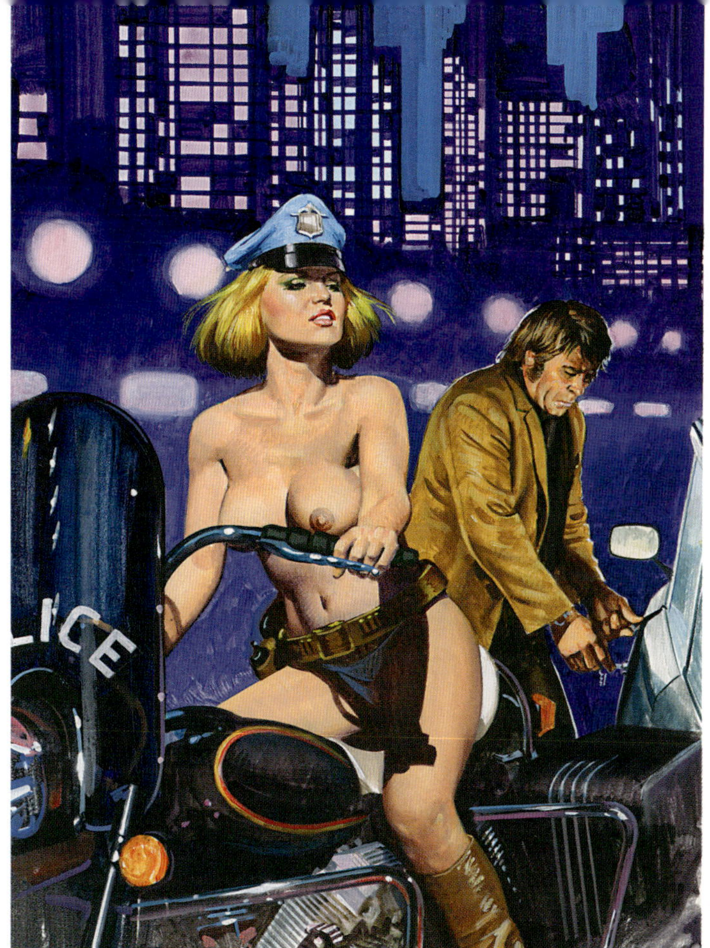
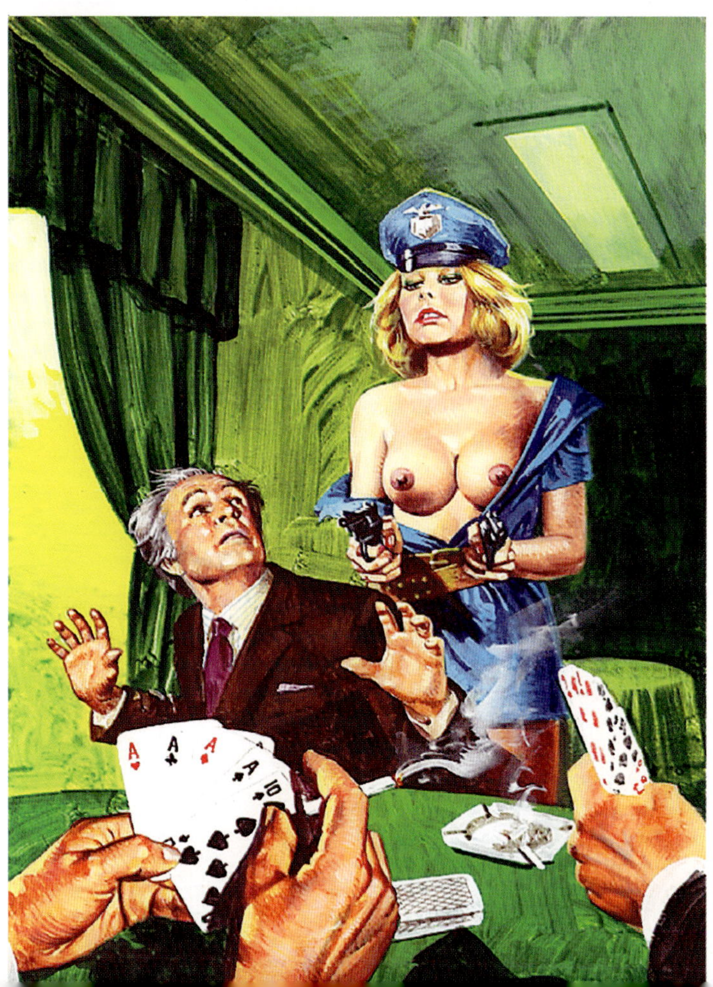
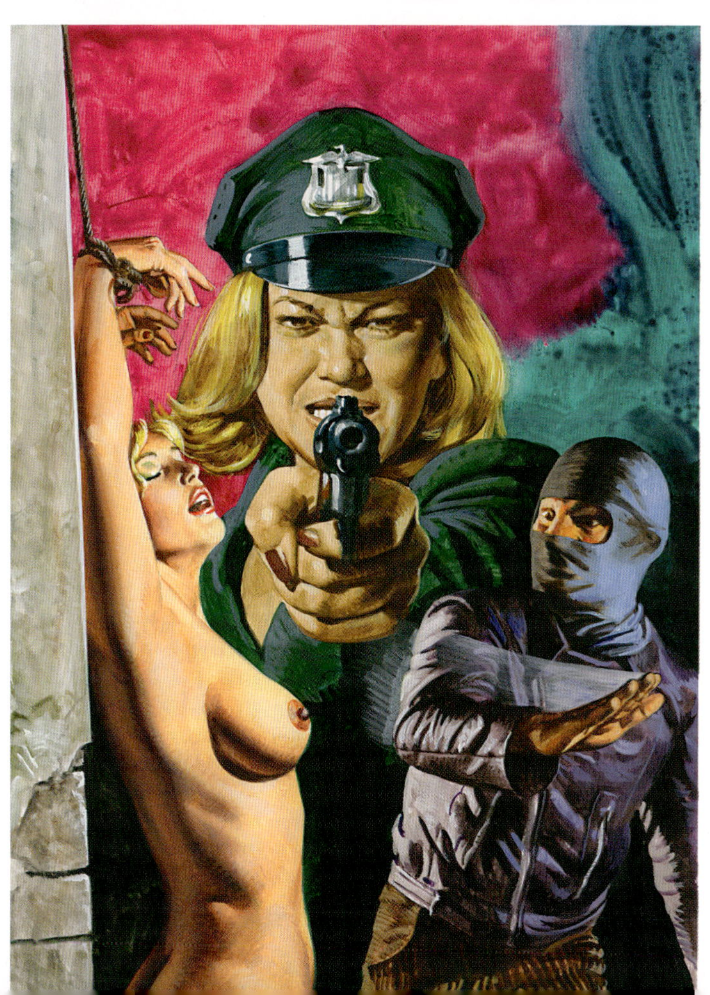

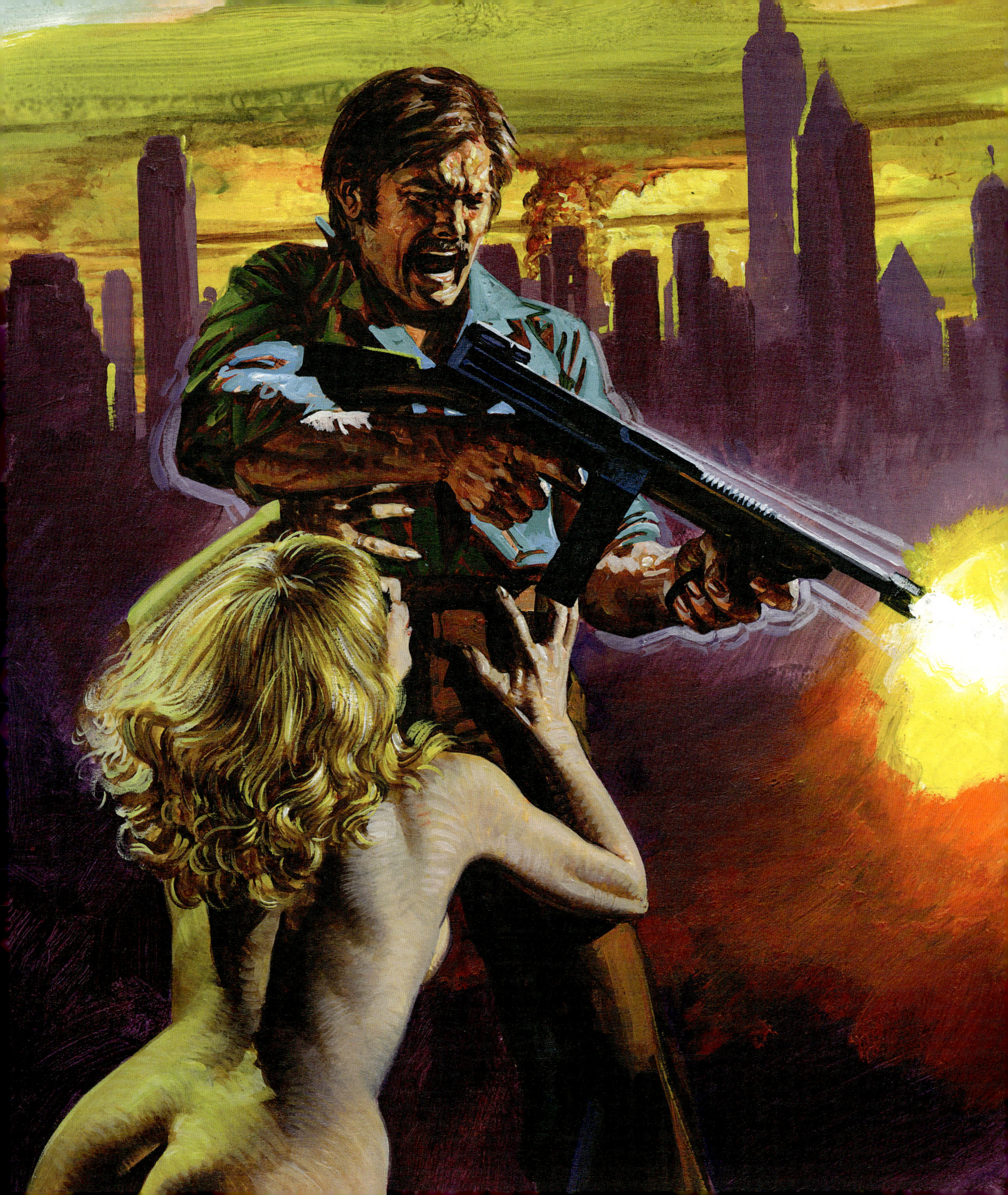

MAFIA

PUBLISHED 1979–1984; 77 ISSUES

The idea behind this series was to tell stories of sex and violence set in the world of international crime. It wasn't intended to portray the activities of the real Sicilian Mafia – the crime syndicate that primarily practises protection racketeering, drug-trafficking and fraud. The comic's protagonist, John "Baby" Lupano, is a young mobster who, due to a particular code of honour, stays away from such activities, preferring instead to indulge in diamond smuggling and the seduction of beautiful women, alongside running a seemingly legitimate business operation. The series had three supplements: *Shipwreck*, *Traitors Pay* and *The Tentacles of the Mafia*.

Left: Mafia, n. 22, *New York Apocalisse*, New York Apocalypse, March 1981.

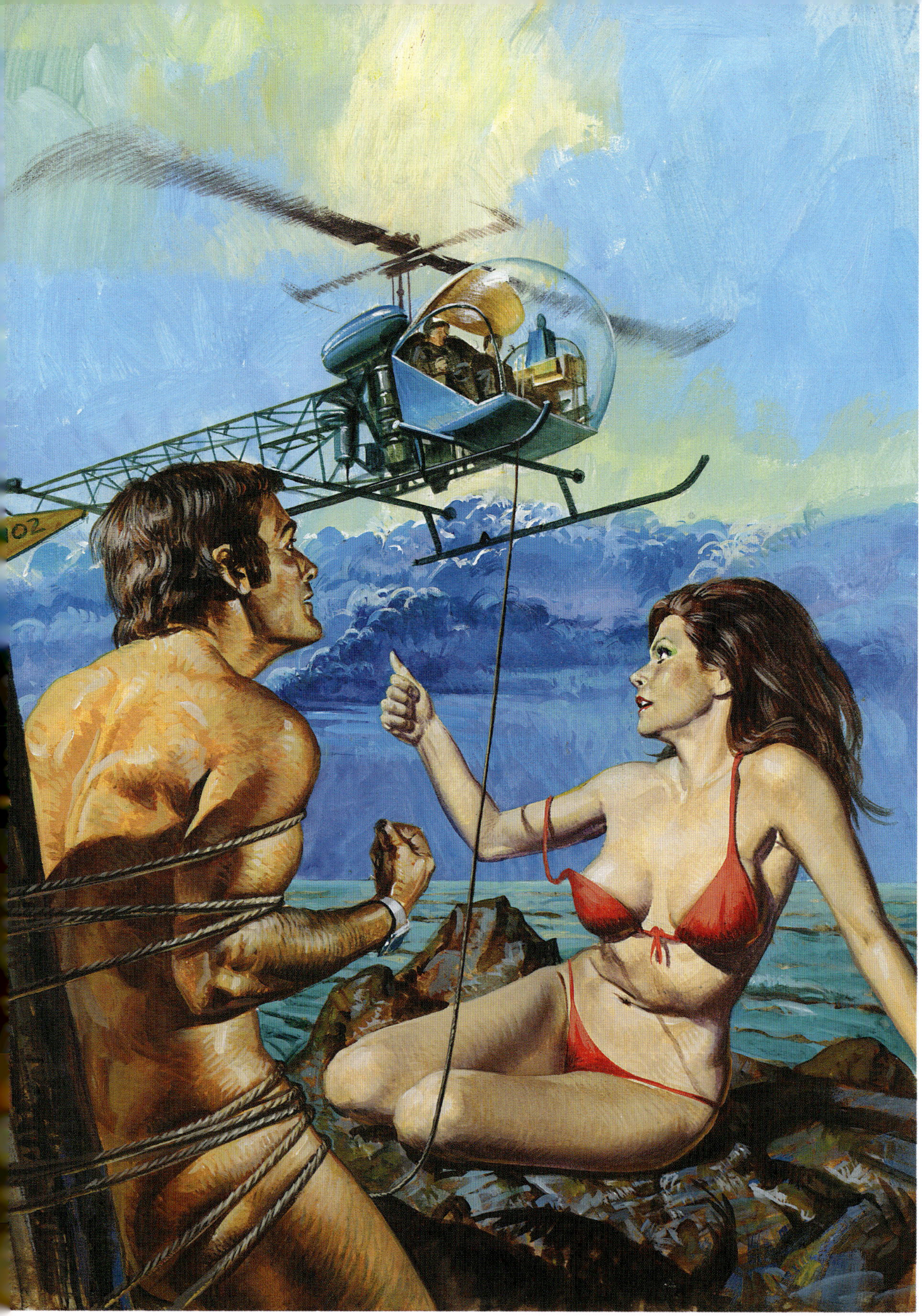

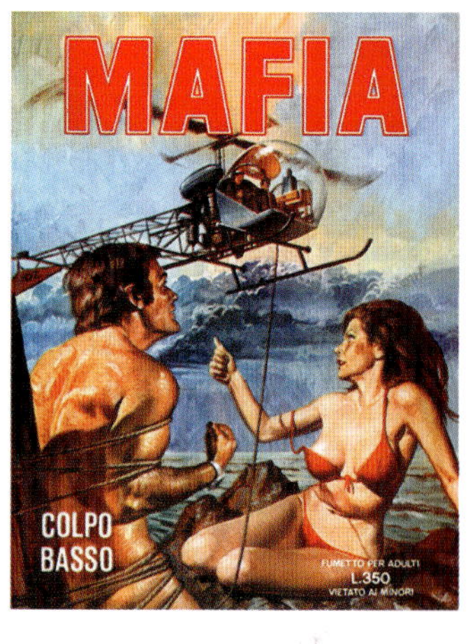

Left: Mafia, n. 7,
Colpo Basso,
A Blow Below the Belt,
December 1979.

Right: Mafia, n. 12,
L'Isola del Tesoro,
Treasure Island,
May 1980.

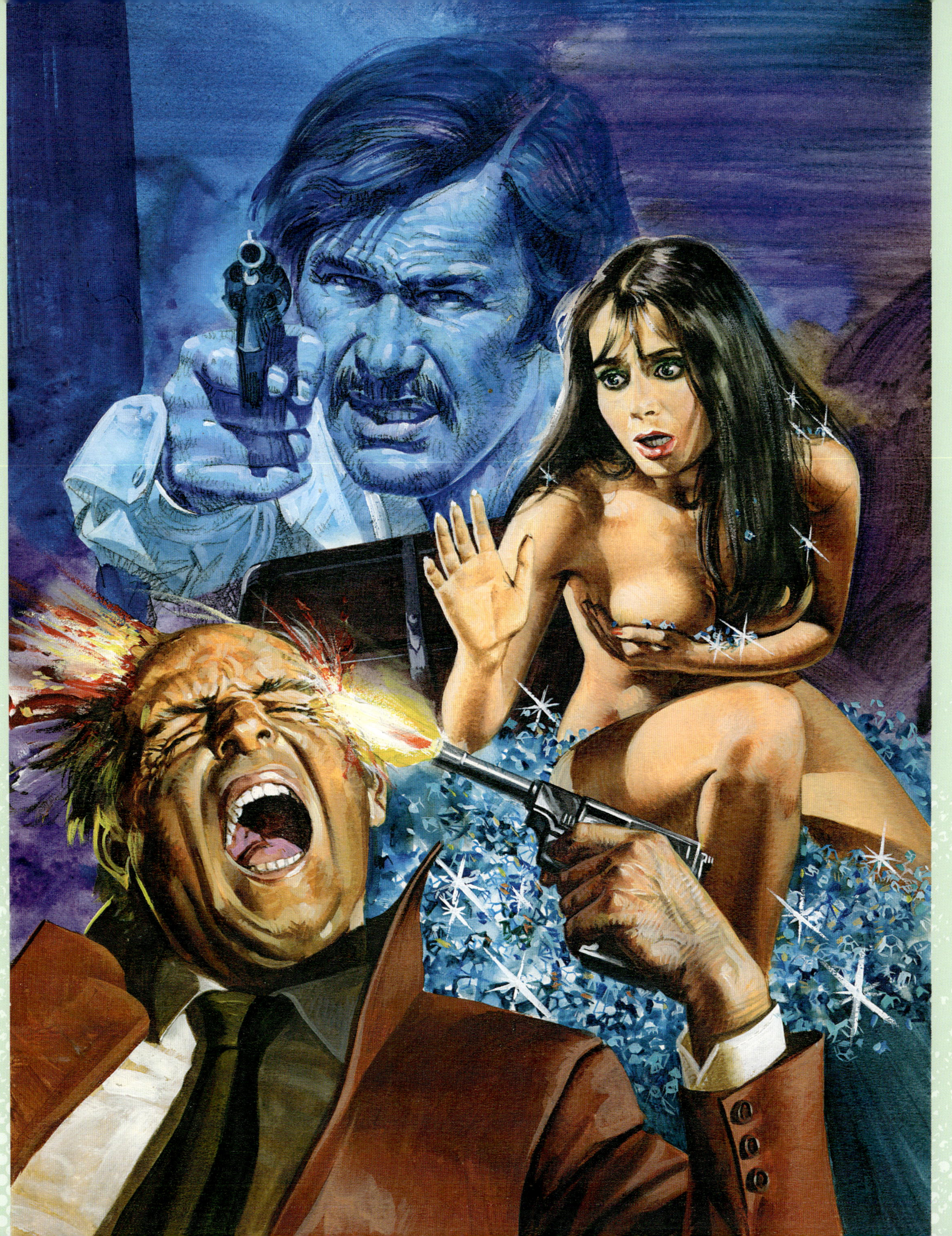

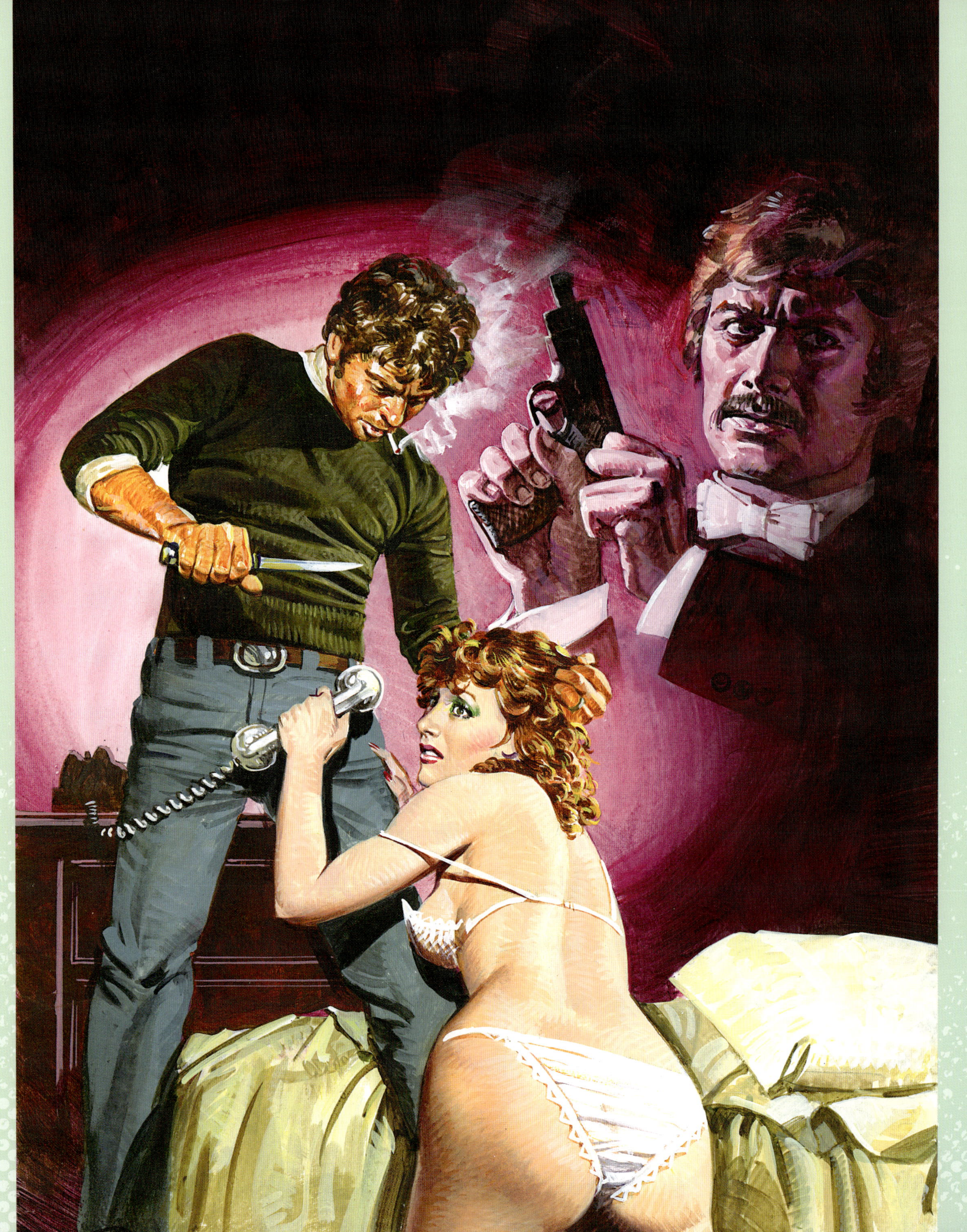

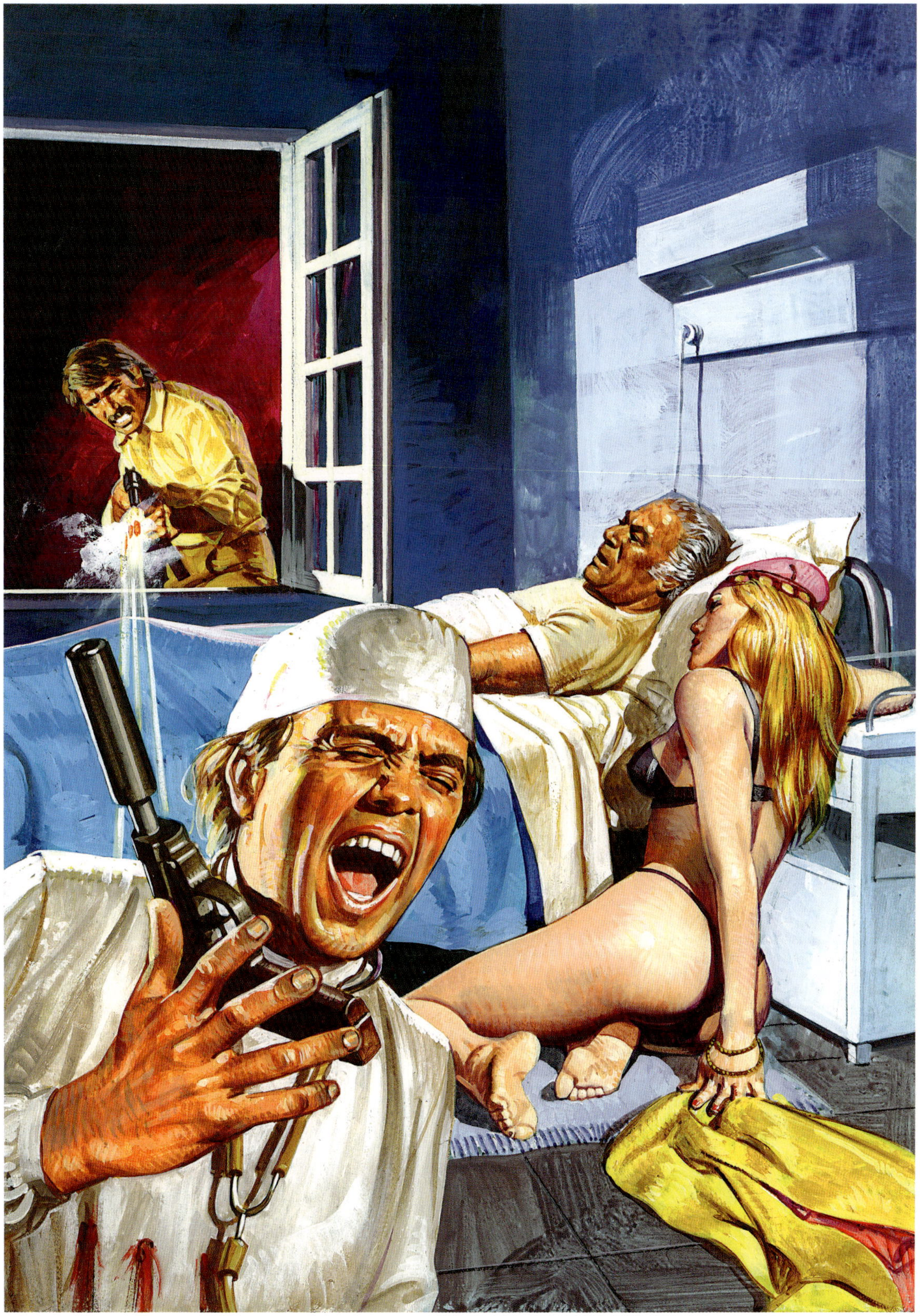

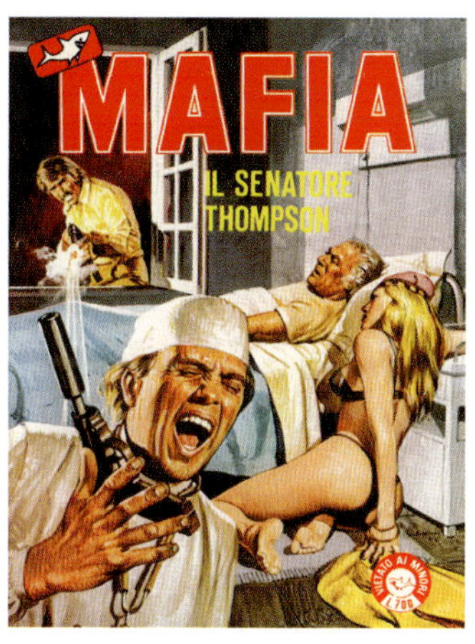

Left: Mafia, n. 47,
Il Senatore Thompson,
Senator Thompson,
April 1983.

Far left: Mafia, n. 45,
La Morte in Agguato,
Death Trap,
February 1983.

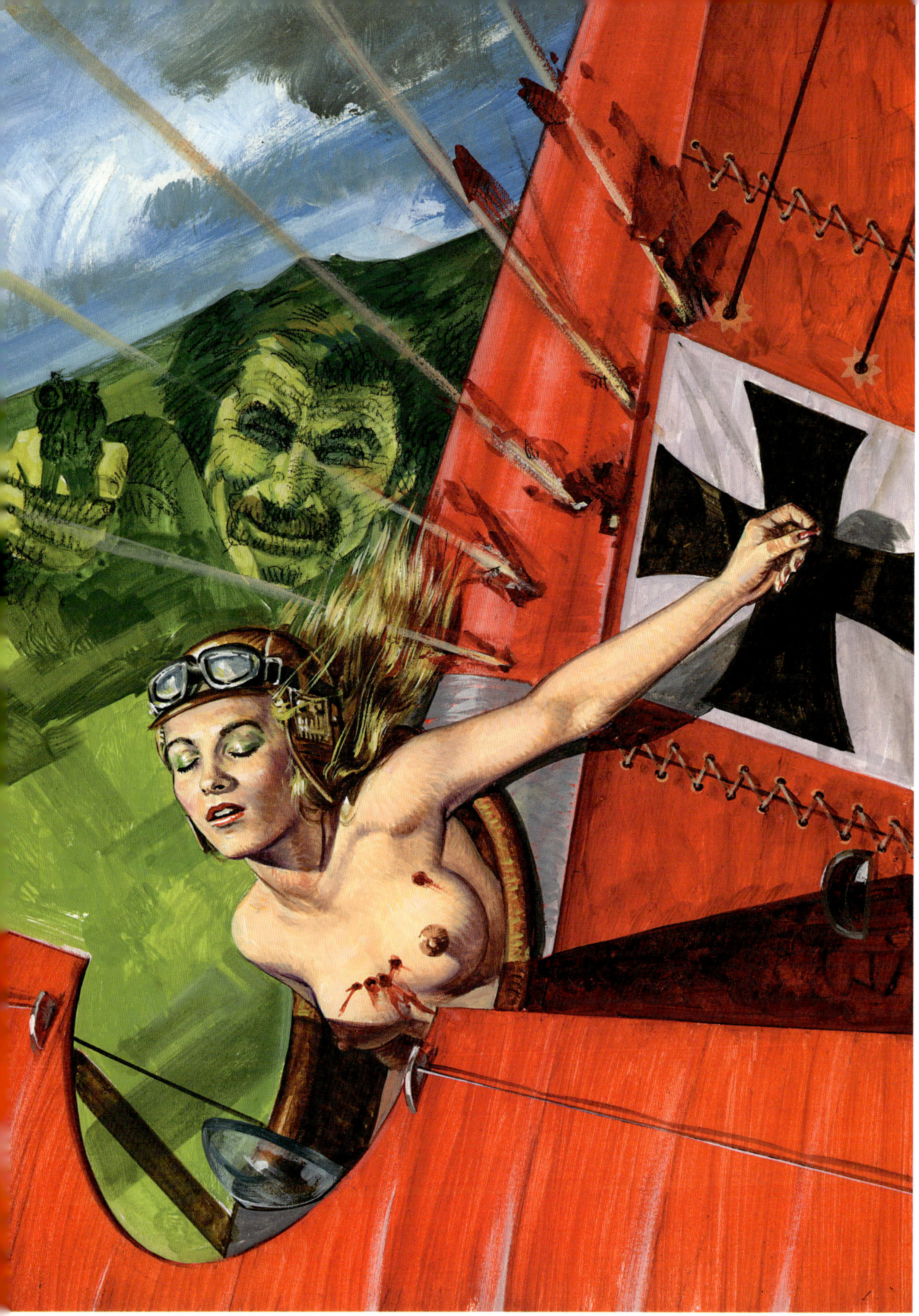

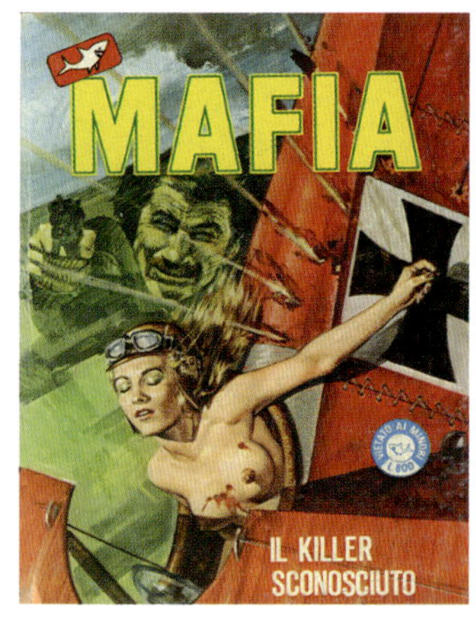

Left: Mafia, n. 50,
Il Killer Sconosciuto,
The Unknown Killer,
July 1983.

Right: Mafia Supplemento,
n. 9, *La Strage degli Innocenti,*
The Massacre of Innocents,
April 1986.

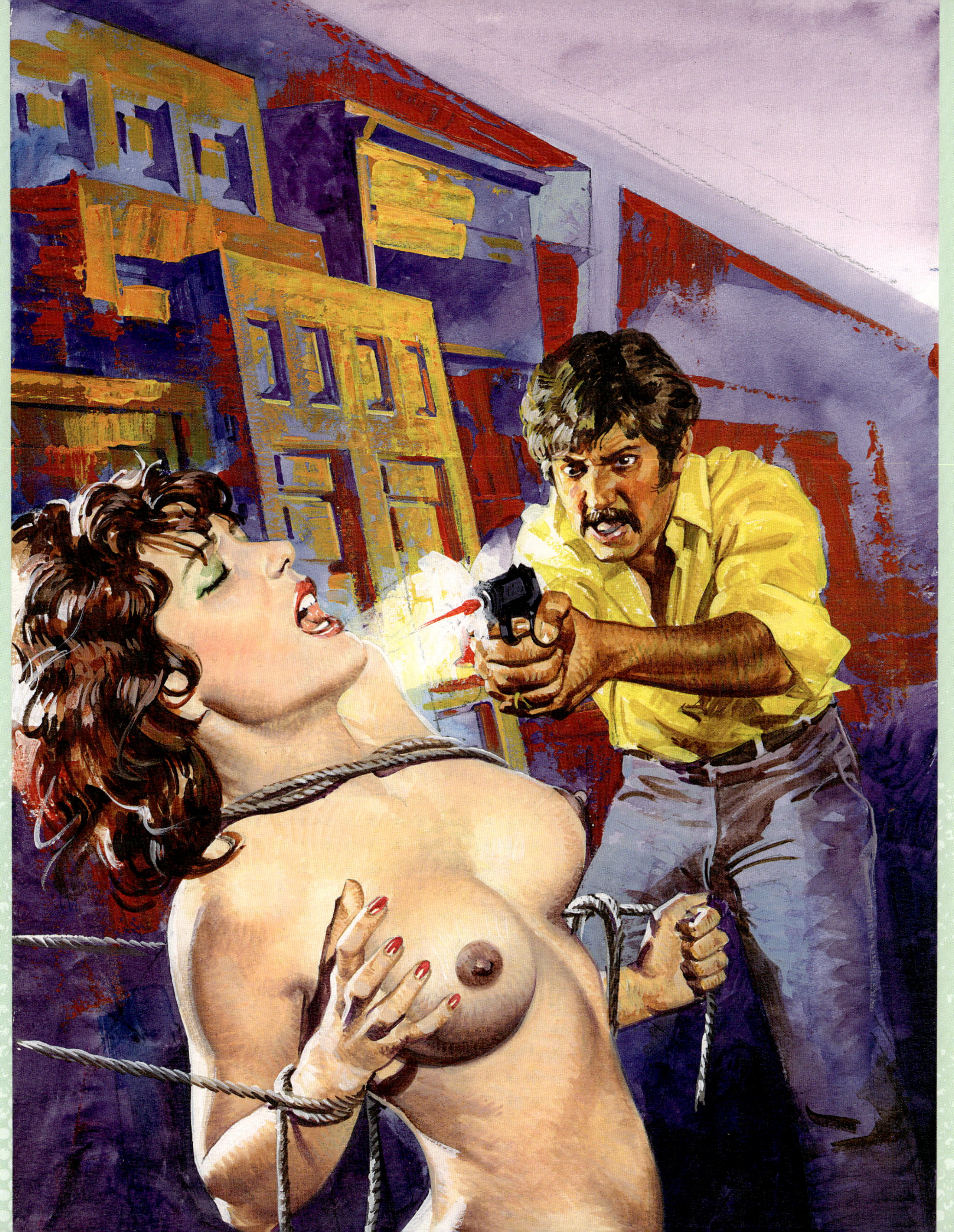

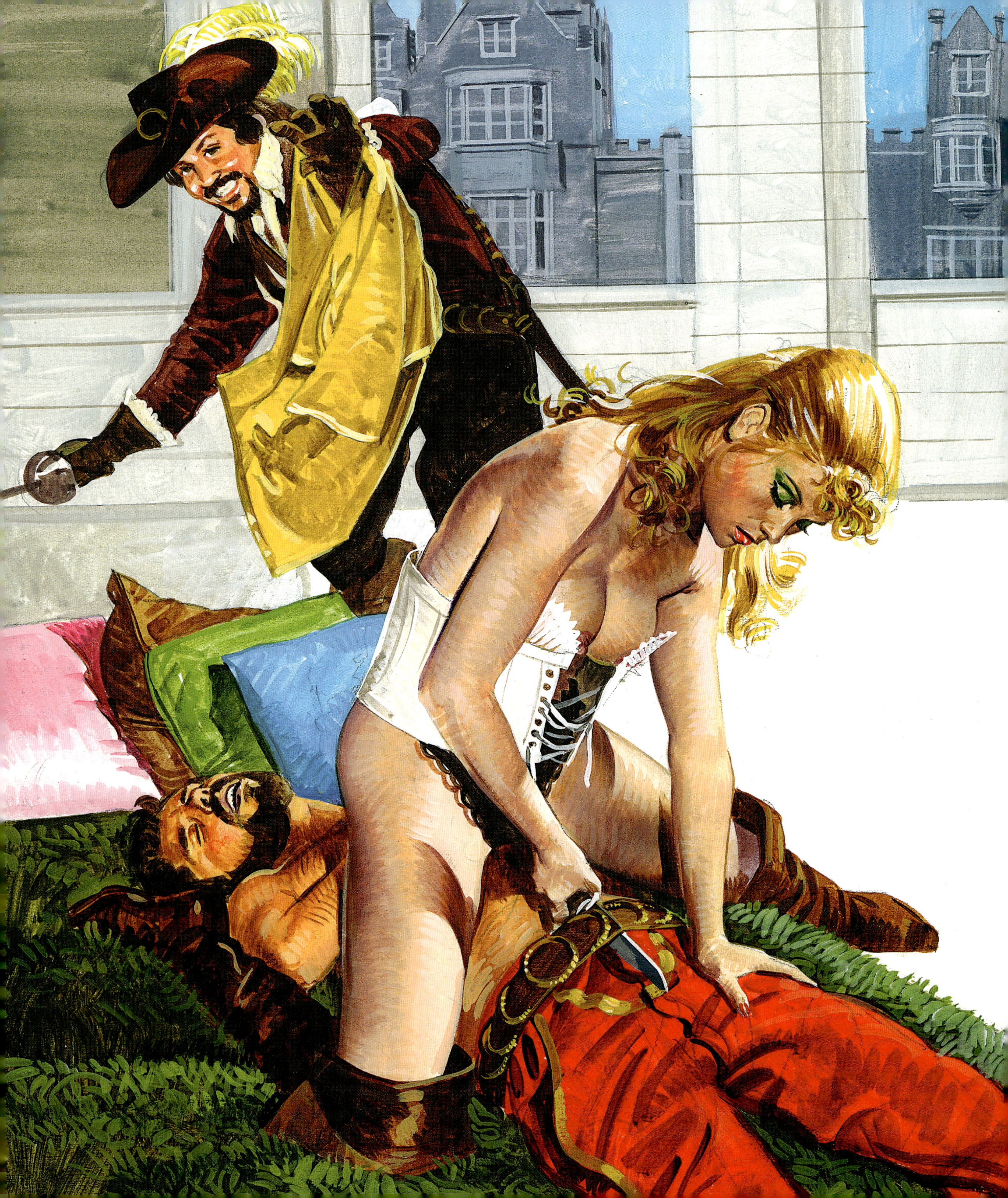

MOSCHETTIERA

PUBLISHED 1982–1982; 20 ISSUES.

Sweet, sensual and unstoppable Rosanna D'Armagnac is a skilled swordswoman who dices with danger, betrayal, conspiracies, corruption and political intrigue in the 16th-century court of France's King Louis XIII – with a touch of depravity and unrestrained lust along the way. On discovering that she is of noble birth, Rosanna heads to the royal court in Paris to try to regain her family's property, which has been confiscated. She gets in the good books of the king's wife, Anne of Austria, but unfortunately her plans are then thwarted by Anne's evil mother, Marie de Medici, who is effectively ruling the kingdom from behind the throne, aided by her sinister Italian lover Concino Concini. Our Musketeer decides to unravel Marie's web of intrigue, and enlists the help of the Gypsies of the Court of Miracles. Finally, the Countess Rosanna manages to regain possession of her land and property and wreaks her revenge on Marie de Medici, who was responsible for her family's downfall.

Left: Moschettiera, n. 7, *Trame d'Amore e di Vendetta*, Plotting Love and Revenge, August 1982.

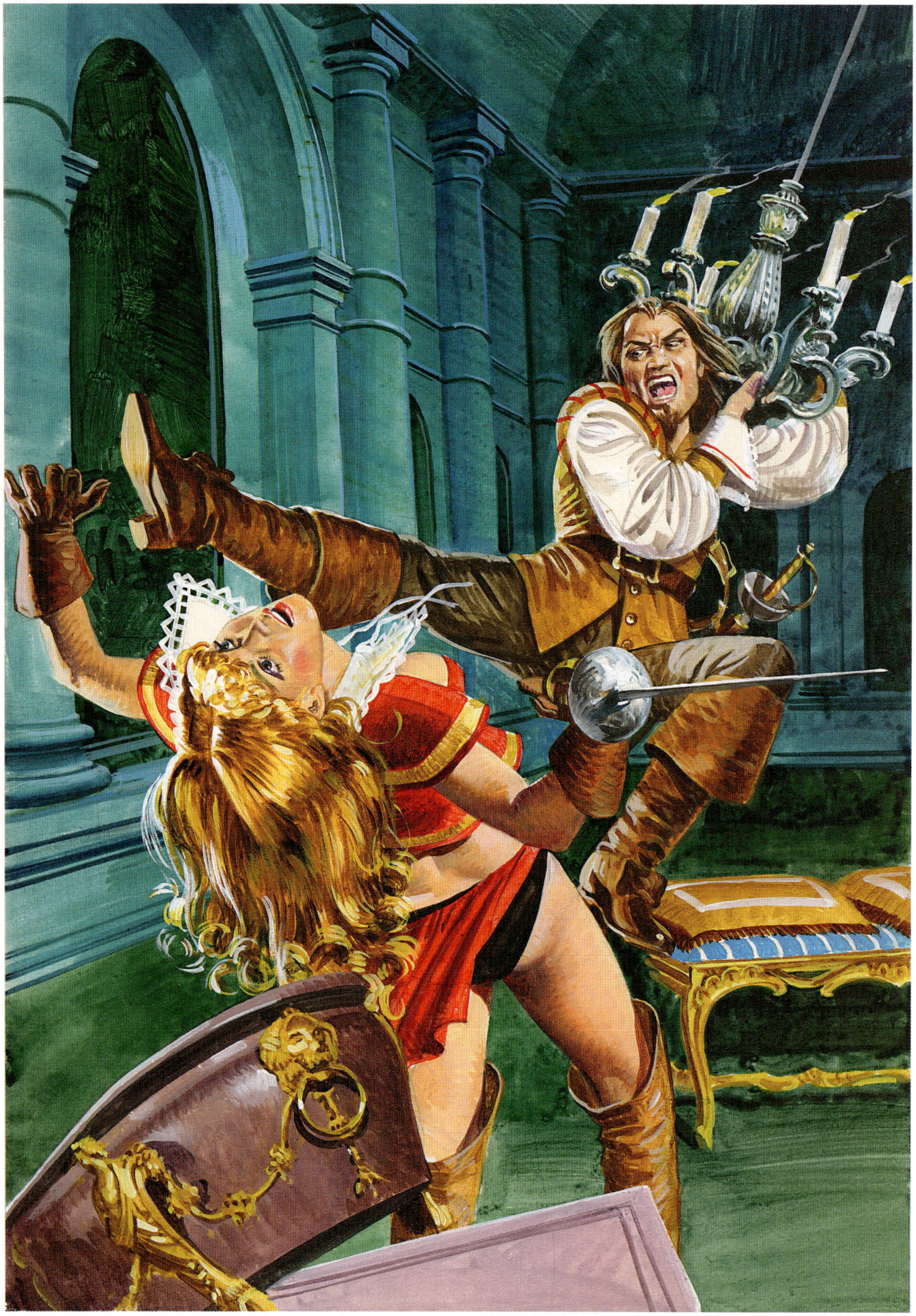

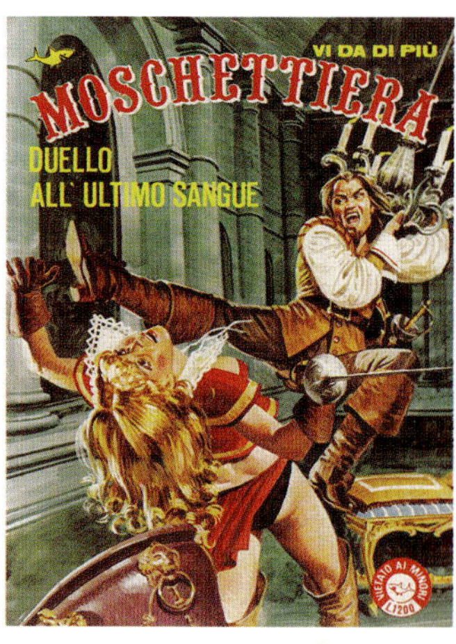

Left: Moschettiera, n. 12,
Duello all'Ultimo Sangue,
Duel to the Death,
January 1983.

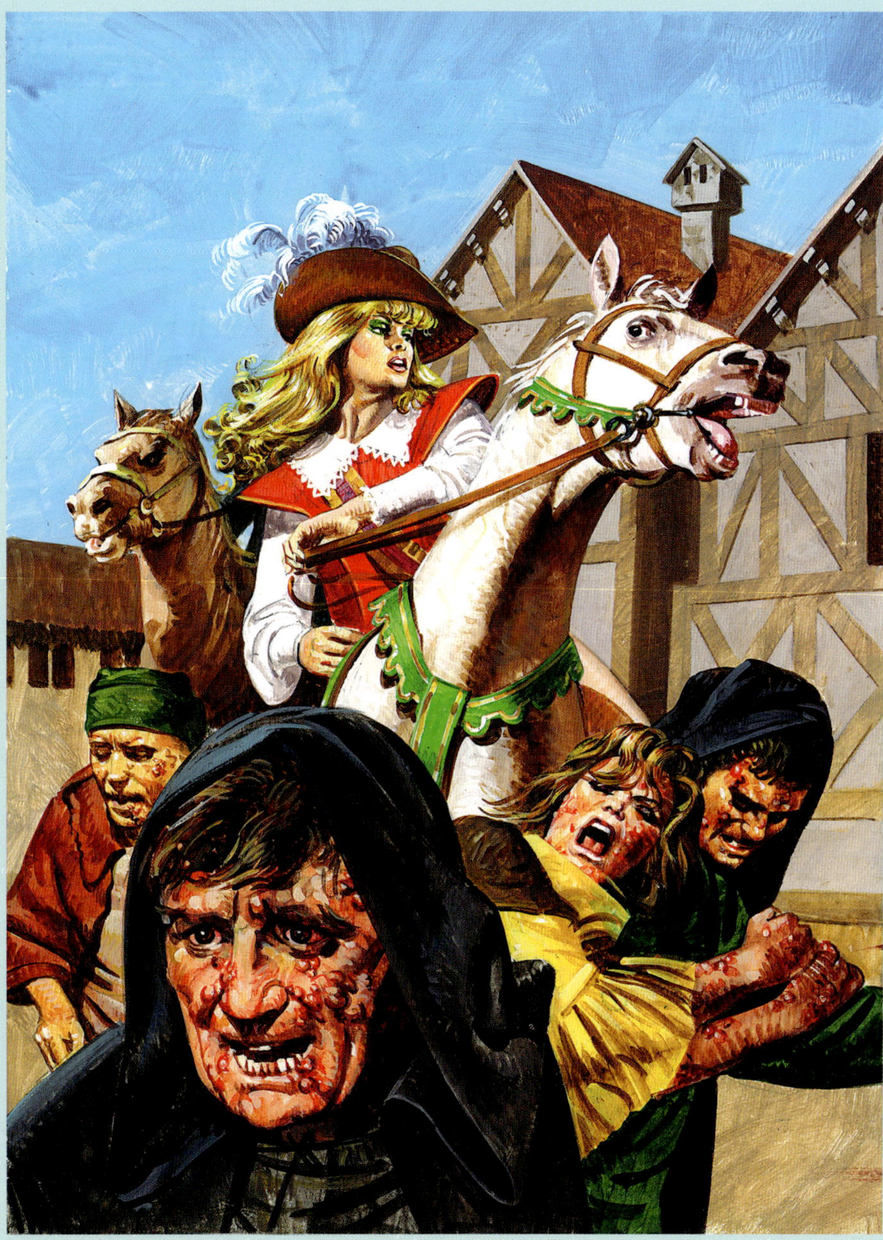

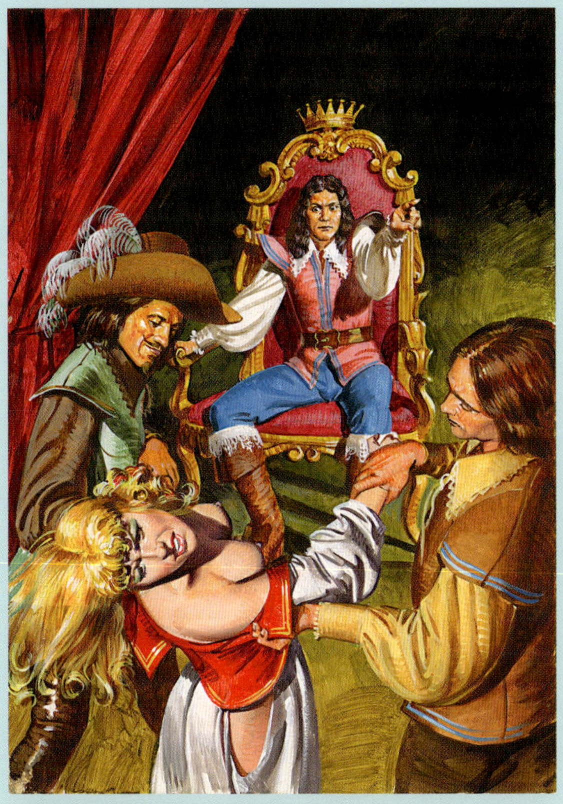

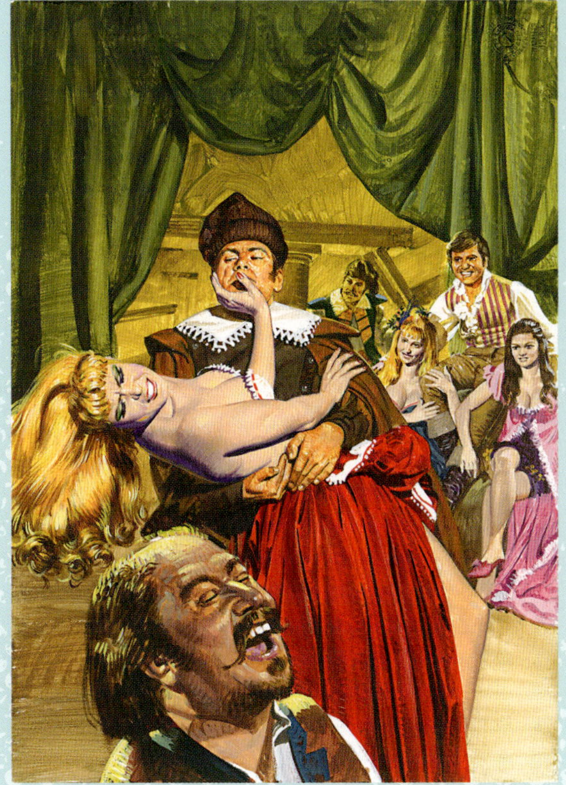

Above: Moschettiera, n. 17, *La Peste di Parigi,*
The Plague of Paris, June 1983.

Top left: Moschettiera, n. 13, *Scacciata da Corte,*
Banished from Court, February 1983.

Left: Moschettiera, n. 14, *Nel Bordello di Nantes,*
In the Bordello of Nantes, March 1, 1983.

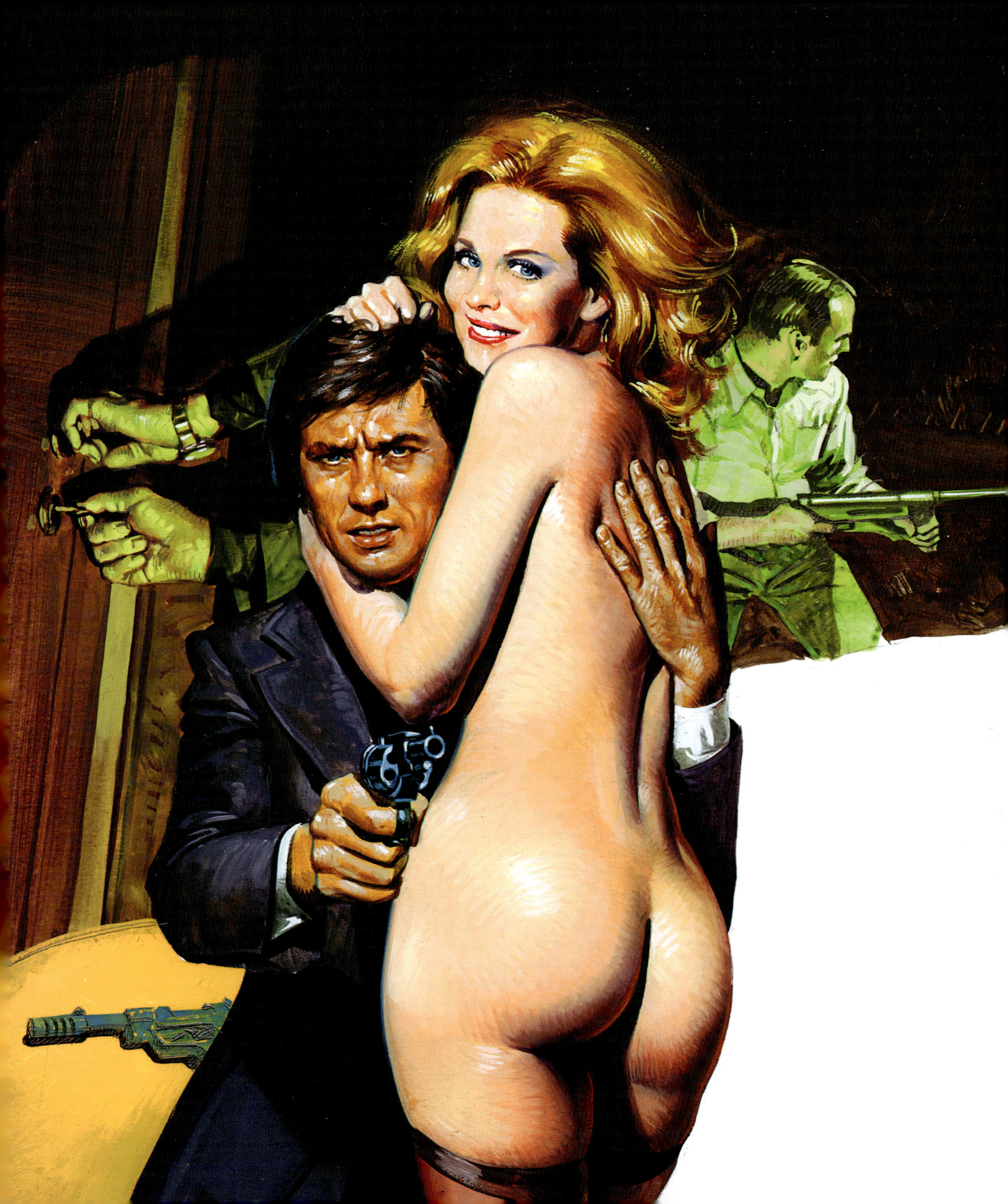

PUBLISHED 1972–1979; 128 ISSUES

The hero of Playcolt is 34-year-old Alan Velon, a super-rich American playboy with interests in a publishing empire; his appearance and name are based on those of the handsome French actor Alain Delon. Velon's a broadminded, daring and adventurous character who lives for most of the year on Barracuda, his private, shark-shaped island, and while he is romantically linked to sex bomb actress Scarlett Lizzy, he continues to flirt with beautiful women wherever he goes. Velon has a strong sense of justice, and often switches to his secret identity: the cynical and ruthless Playcolt, an avenger and crime-fighting hero who goes to the aid of the weak and the oppressed. Playcolt's storylines cover everything from espionage and action to science fiction and horror, and throughout the series there are cameos from international jetsetters of the '70s, from Frank Sinatra to Aristotle Onassis. The content here is pretty subtle compared with what was to follow in '80s comics.

Left: Playcolt, n. 66, *Il Grande Slam*, The Grand Slam, April 1978.

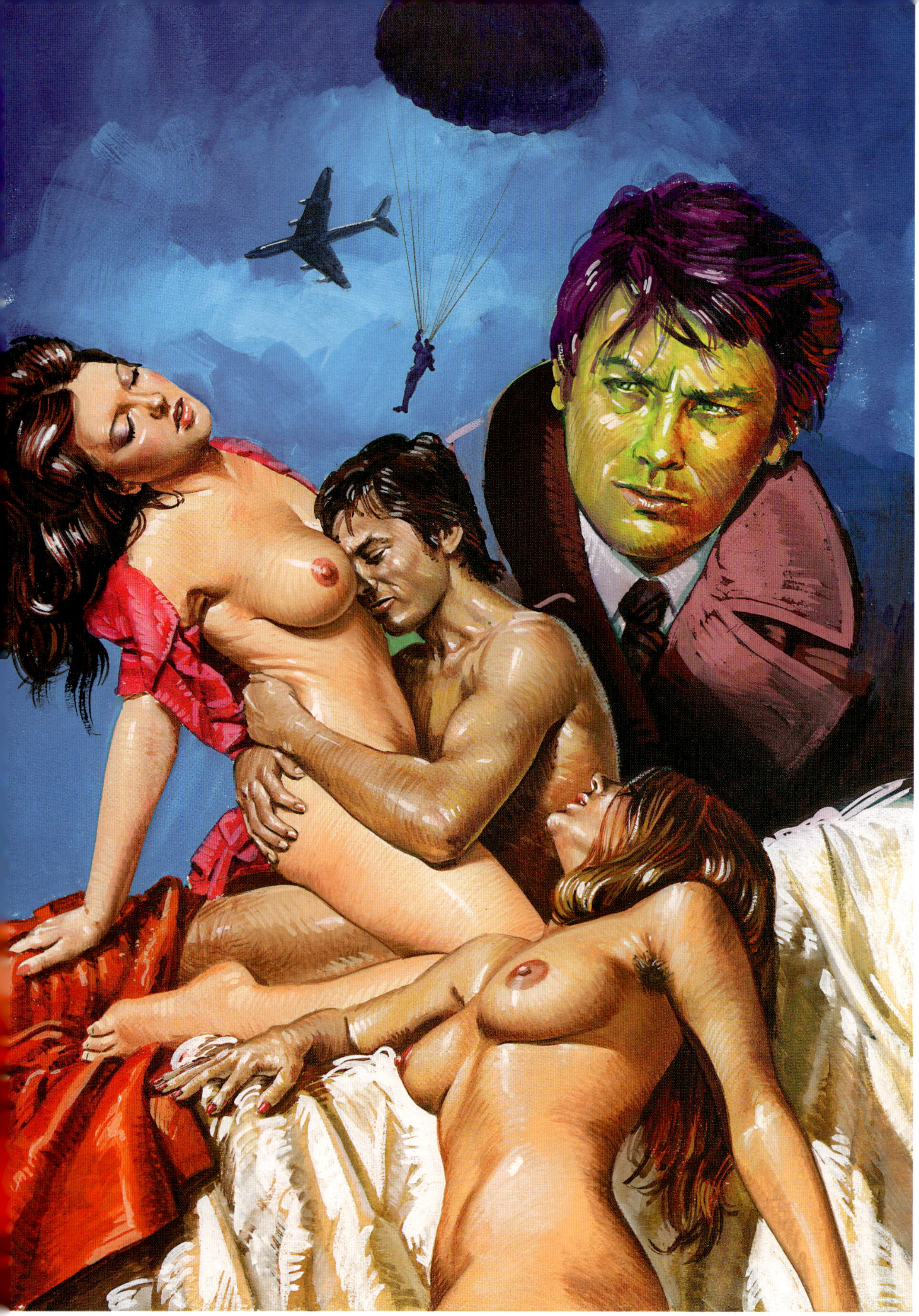

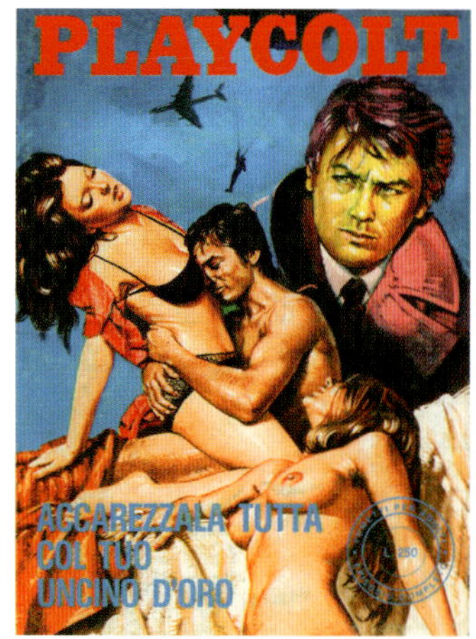

Left: Playcolt, n. 3,
*Accarezzami tutta col tuo
Uncino d'Oro,* Caress me all
over with your Golden Hook,
February 1975.

OPPOSITE PAGE
Top left: Playcolt, n. 12,
Col Ghiaccio me la Faccio,
I Screw her with Ice,
June 1974.

Top right: Playcolt, n. 21,
Operazione Rompiballe,
Operation Ballbreaker,
November 1975.

Bottom left: Playcolt, n. 26,
Stringi le Chiappe e Vai,
Get off your Backside and Go,
January 1976.

Bottom right: Playcolt, n. 58,
Giorni Violenti, Violent Days,
August 1, 1977.

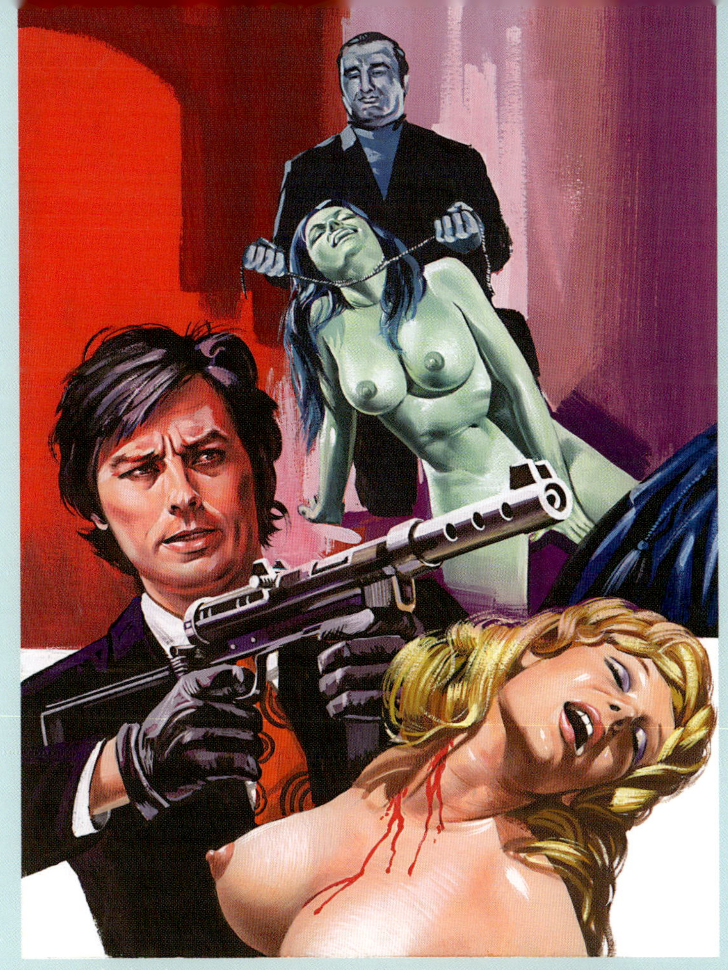
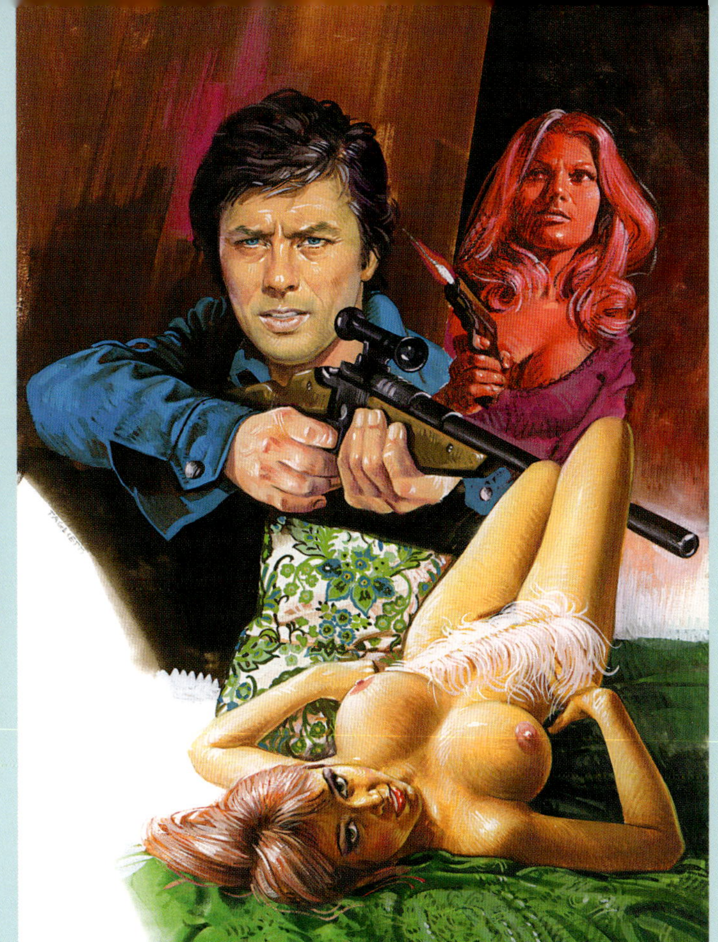
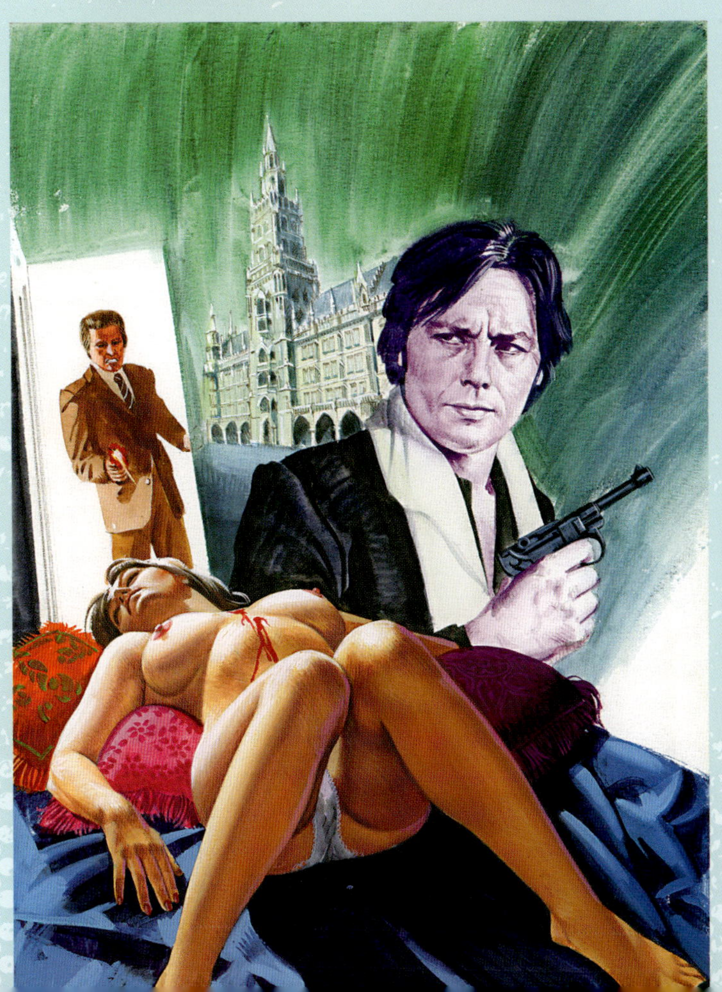
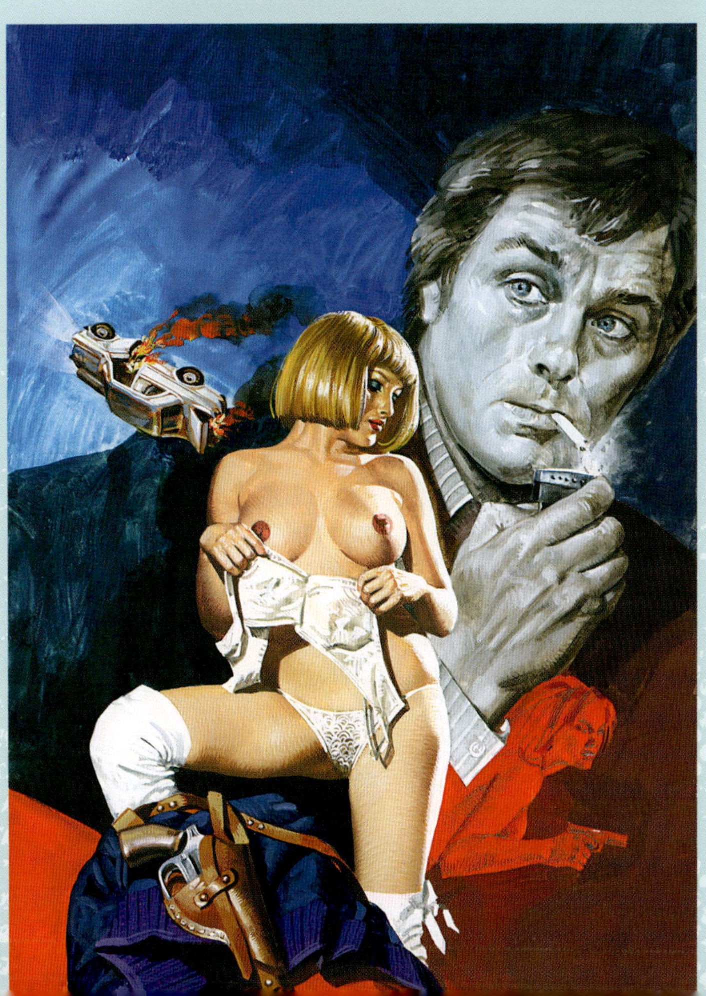

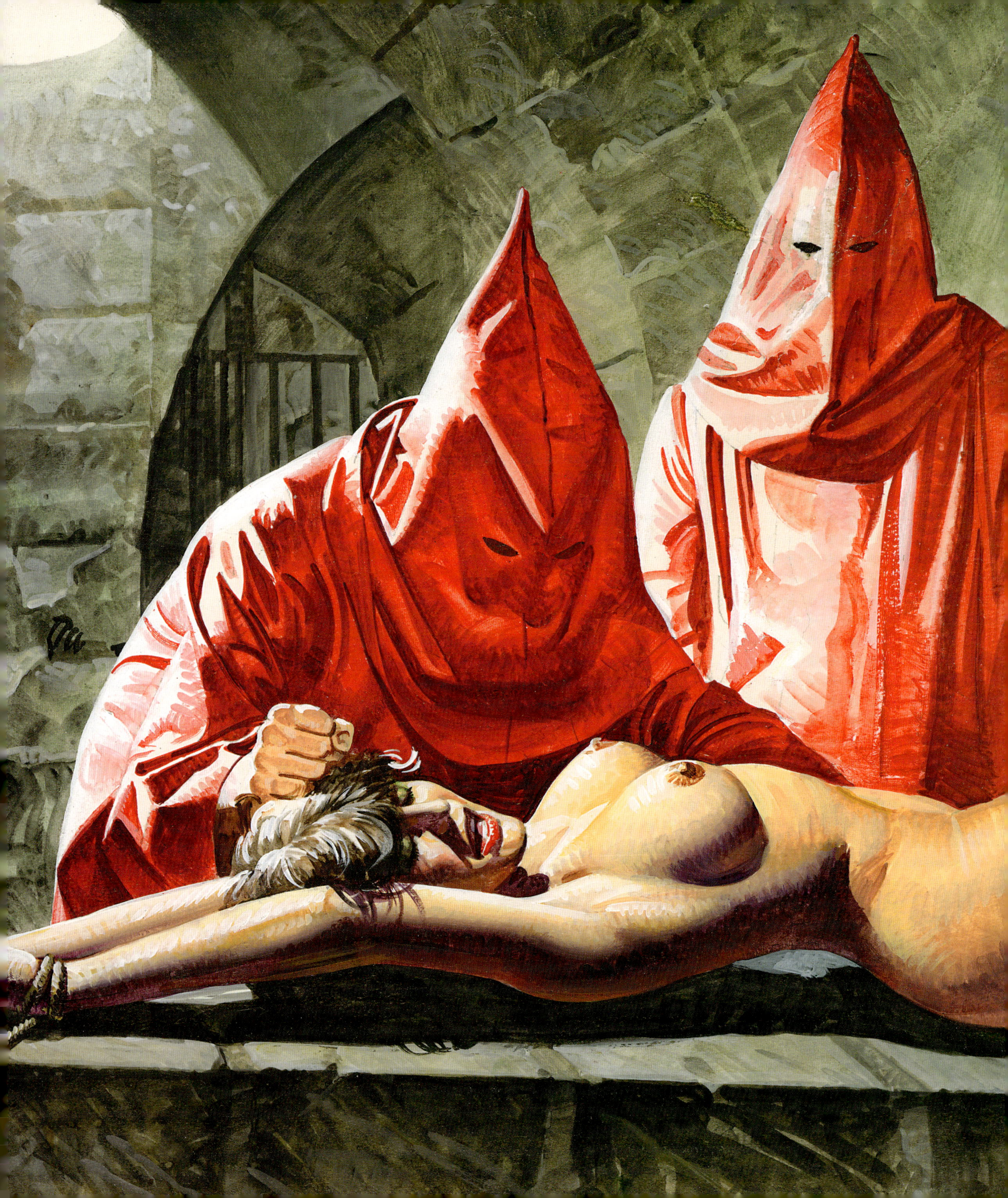

STREGONERIA

PUBLISHED 1984–1986; 10 ISSUES

"Sorcery" was an erotic horror series featuring tales of witchcraft across the centuries. It's populated by all manner of bizarre and depraved characters – including serial killers and people possessed by demons – and the intriguing plots are shot through with cruelty and terror. All the covers bar the final one were painted by Emanuele.

Left: Stregoneria, n. 3, *Il Sabba delle Beffe,* The Witches Sabbath of Mischief, January 1985.

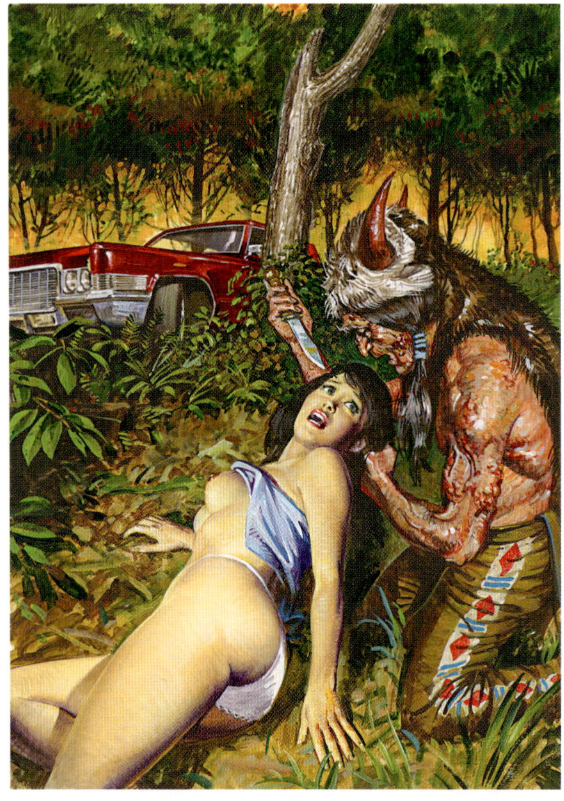

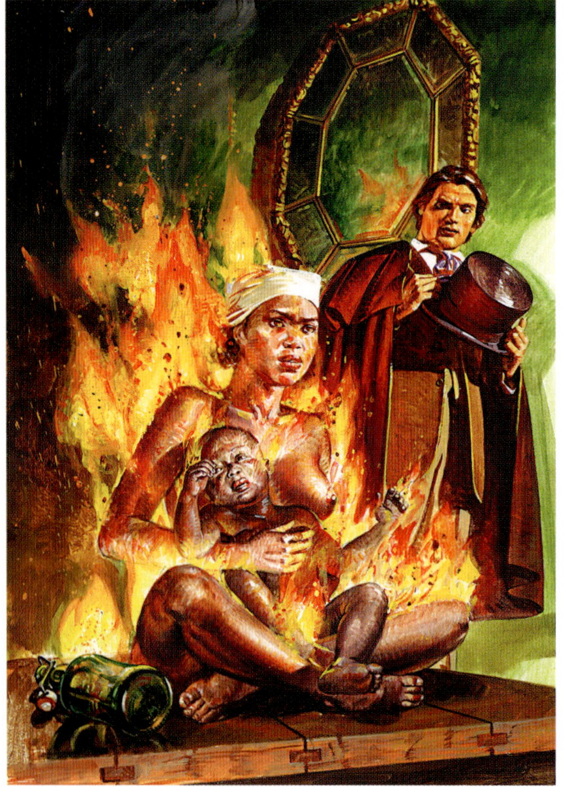

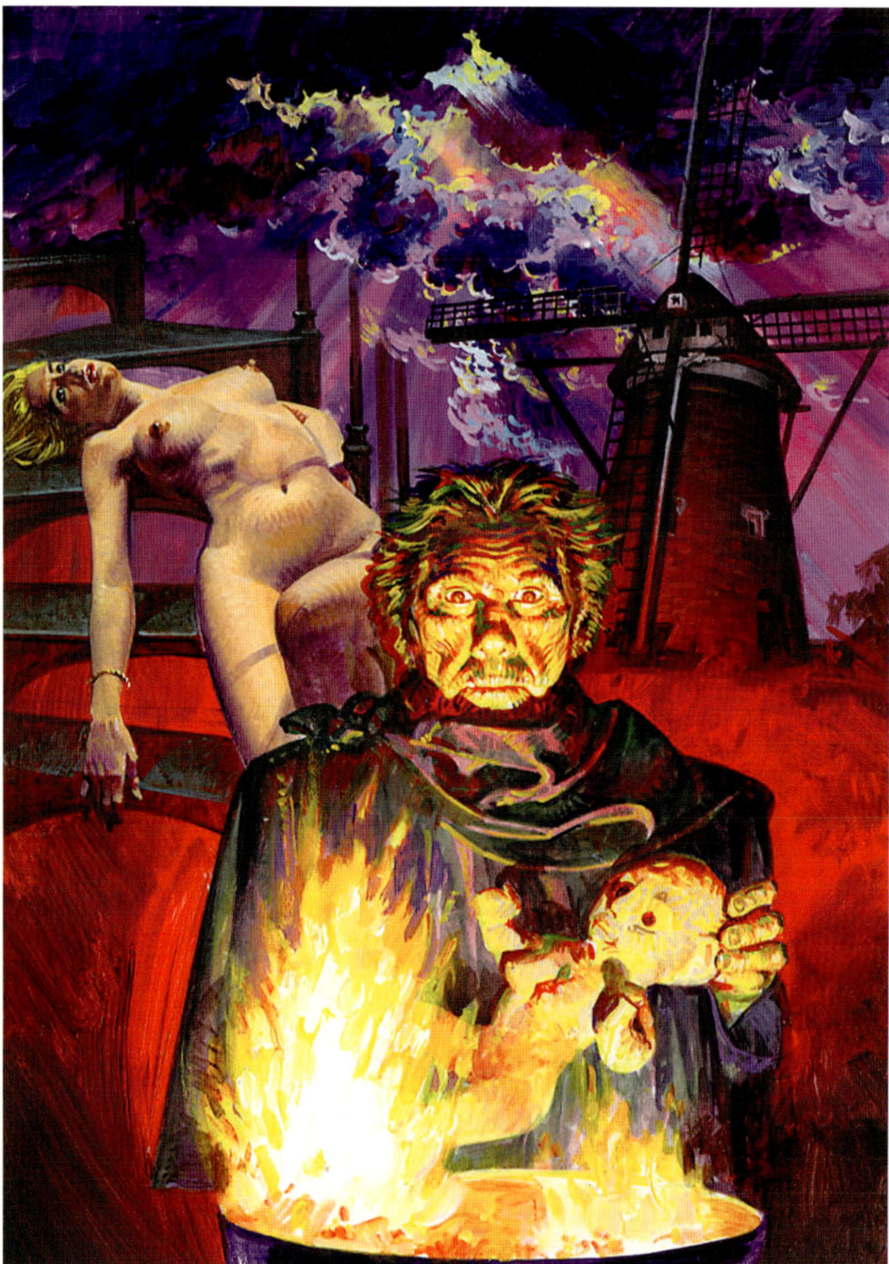

Above: Stregoneria, n. 7, *Il Mulino delle Bambole Maledette*,
The Cursed Doll of the Windmill, May 1985.

Top left: Stregoneria, n. 4, *Weekend di Sangue*,
Weekend of Blood, February 1985.

Left: Stregoneria, n. 5, *Rituale Macabro*, Macabre Ritual, March 1985.

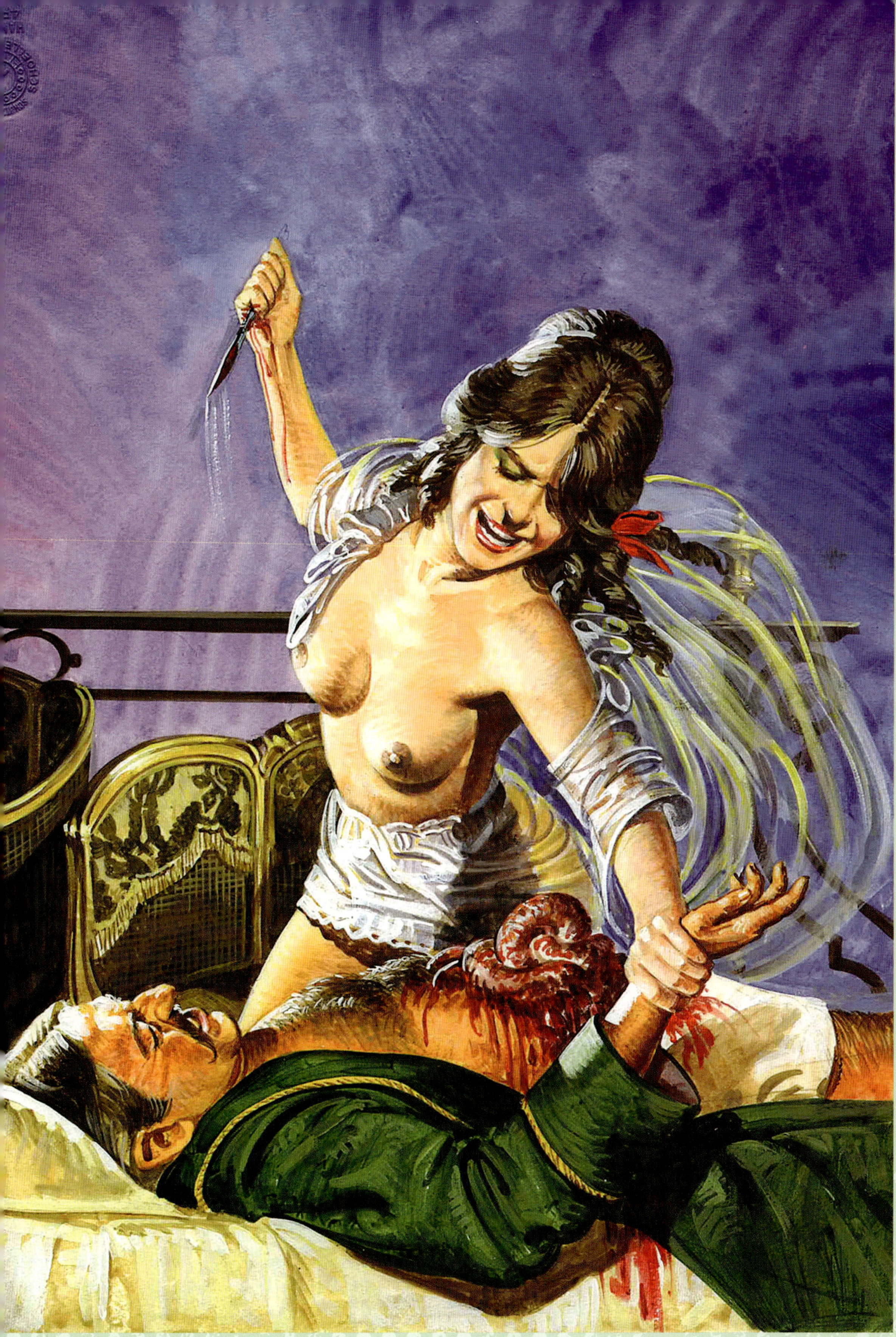

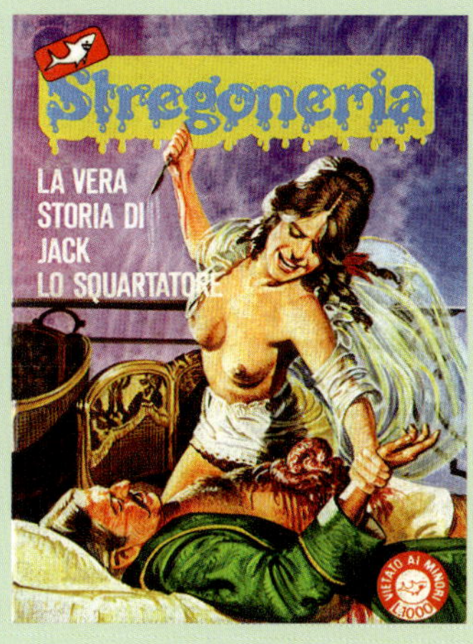

Left: Stregoneria, n. 9,
*La Vera Storia di Jack lo
Squartatore,* The True Story
of Jack The Ripper,
July 1985.

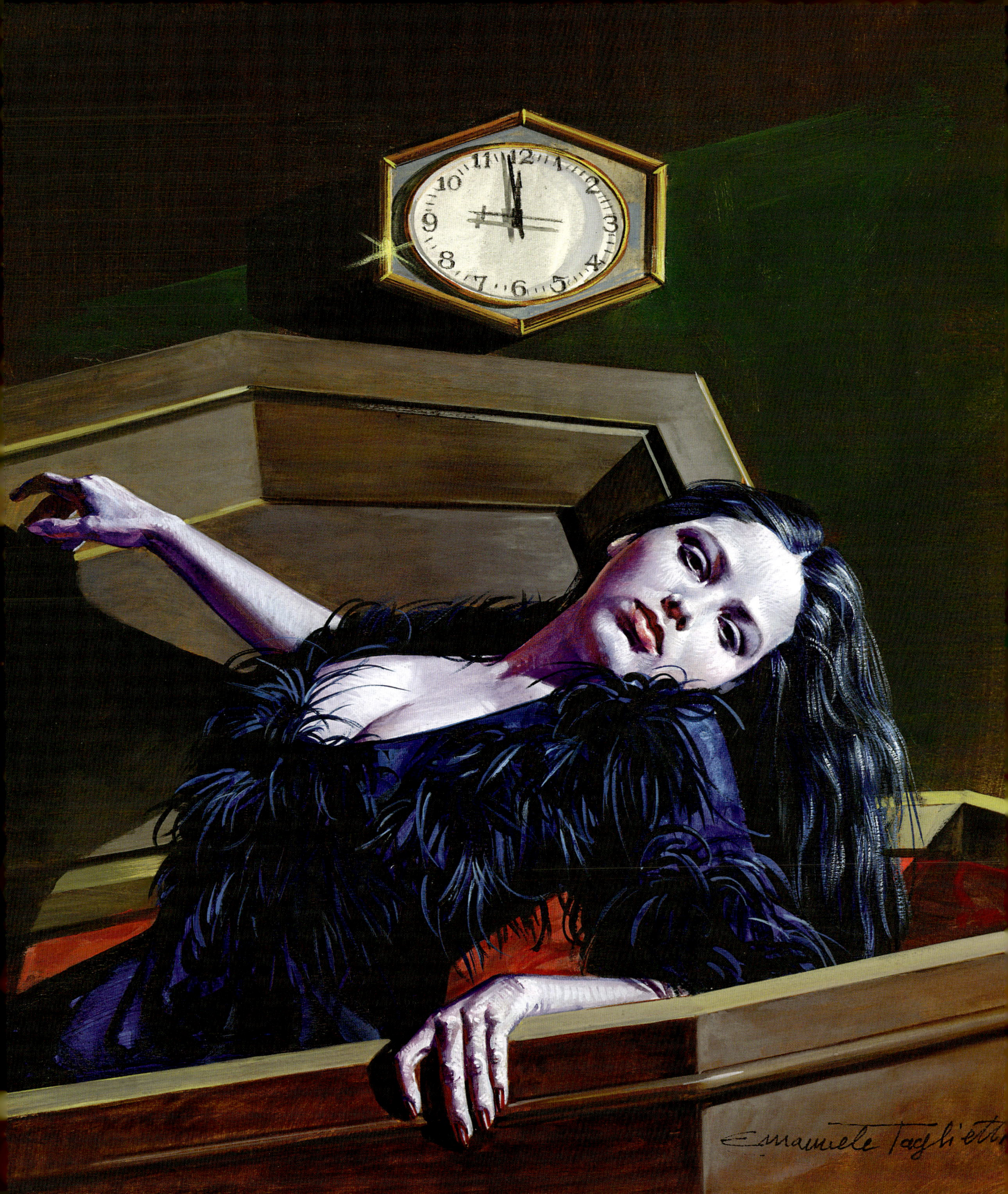

Emanuele Taglietti

SUKIA

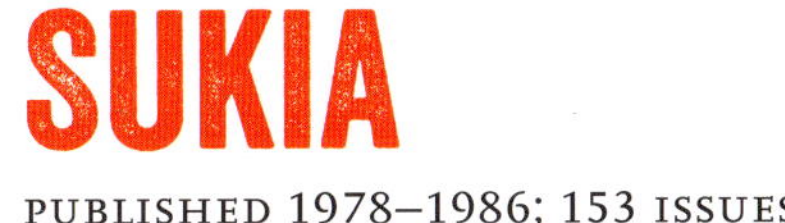

PUBLISHED 1978–1986; 153 ISSUES

Sukia Dragomic is one of the sexiest, and most popular, vampire characters ever created: her physical appearance is closely modelled on that of the beautiful Italian actress Ornella Muti. Sukia is a descendant of the Counts Dragomic, who originate from Transylvania. She is cursed by vampirism, which was passed to her by her father, Drakul Dragomic, who tried to rape and kill her, but although she drinks blood, she seems to have few other classic vampiric powers. Sukia dies in the 13th century and is accidentally revived in 1724; she then moves to the US where she dies again in 1801. In the first issues we find her alive again and living it up in New York, having killed her husband in order to inherit his name and fortune. Sukia's often disturbing and horrific adventures play out against a backdrop of night-lit city skylines. She's accompanied throughout by her ever-faithful companion, a gay man called Gary, who indulges his insatiable sexual appetite at every opportunity. Sukia's main adversary is a journalist who is determined to expose her true nature, and carry out the scoop of the century: the first interview with a real vampire! Emanuele painted all the covers except one.

Left: Sukia, n. 9, *Come Risorge una Vampira,* How to Resurrect a Vampire, September 1978.

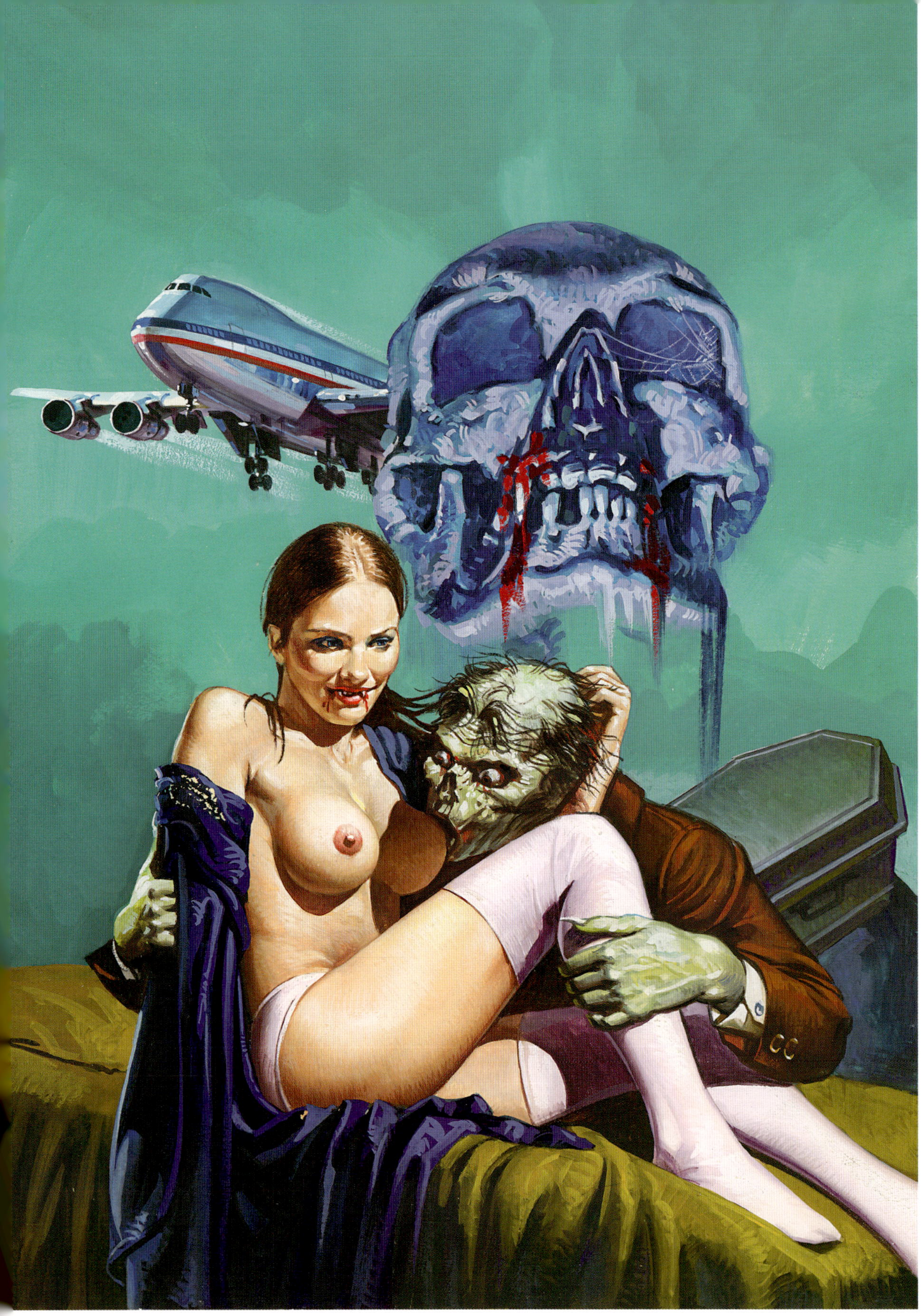

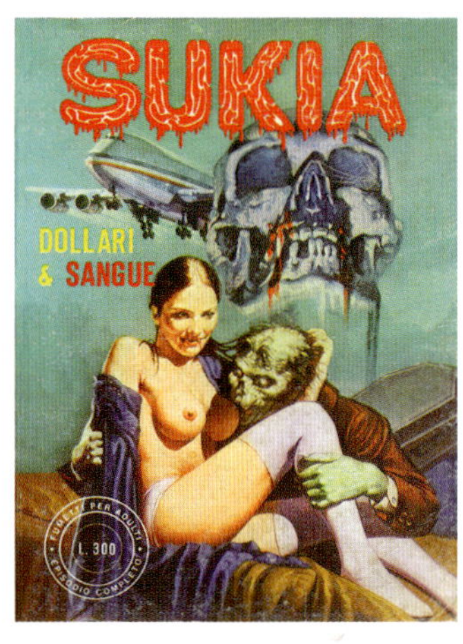

Left: Sukia, n. 2, *Dollari & Sangue*, Dollars & Blood, June 1978.

Right: Sukia, n. 8, *Sangue e Orina*, Blood and Urine, August 1978.

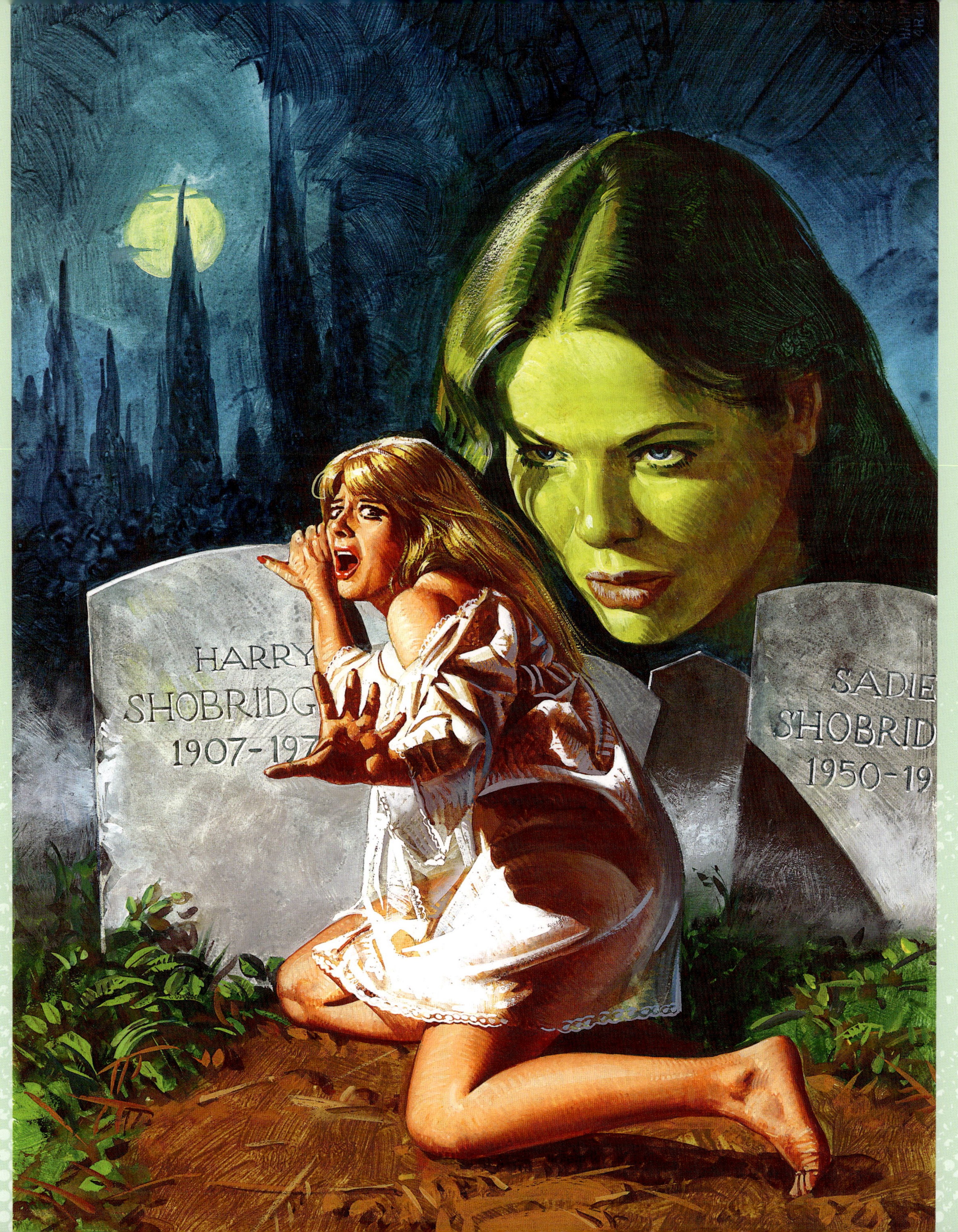

HARRY
SHOBRIDG
1907-197
SADIE
SHOBRID
1950-19

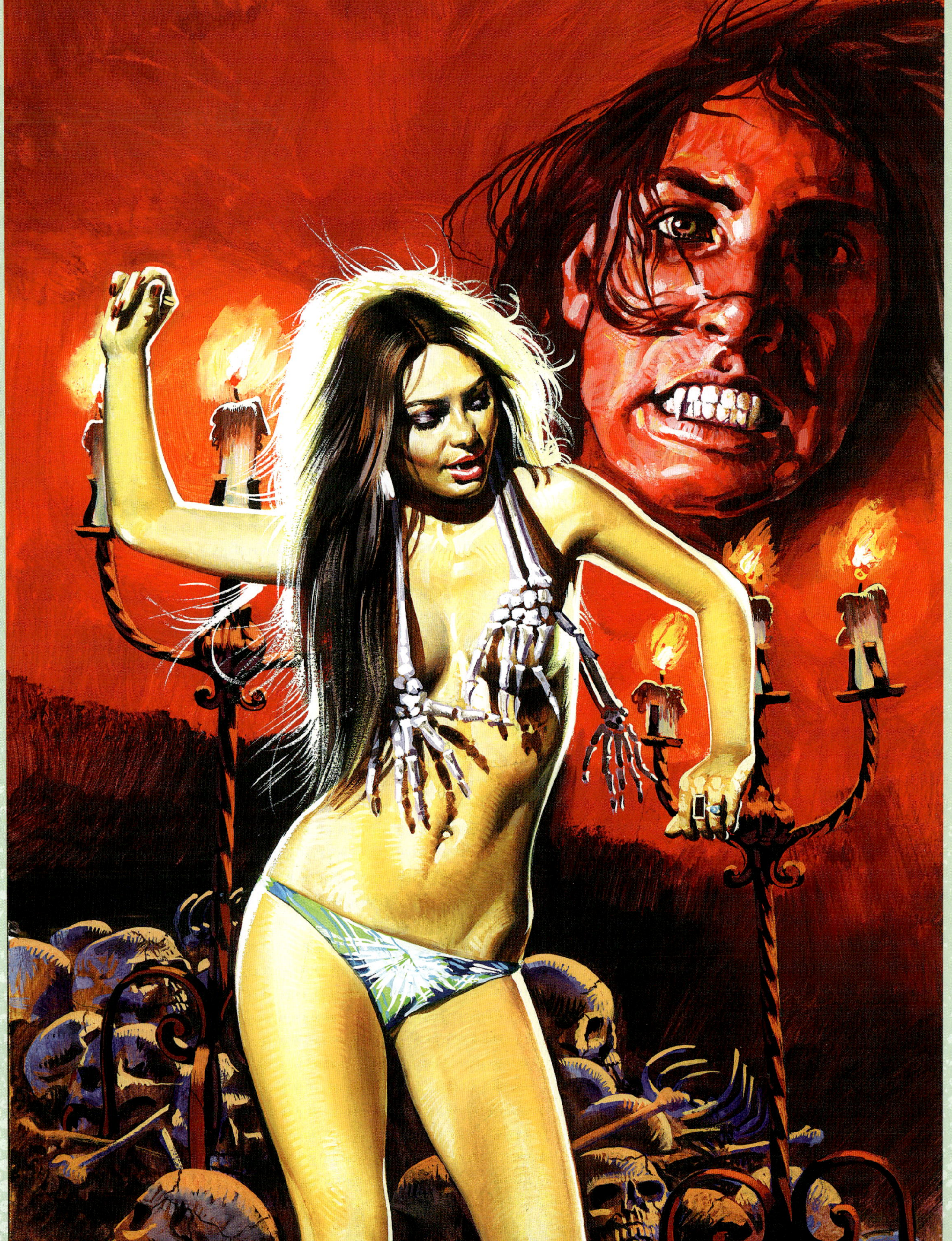

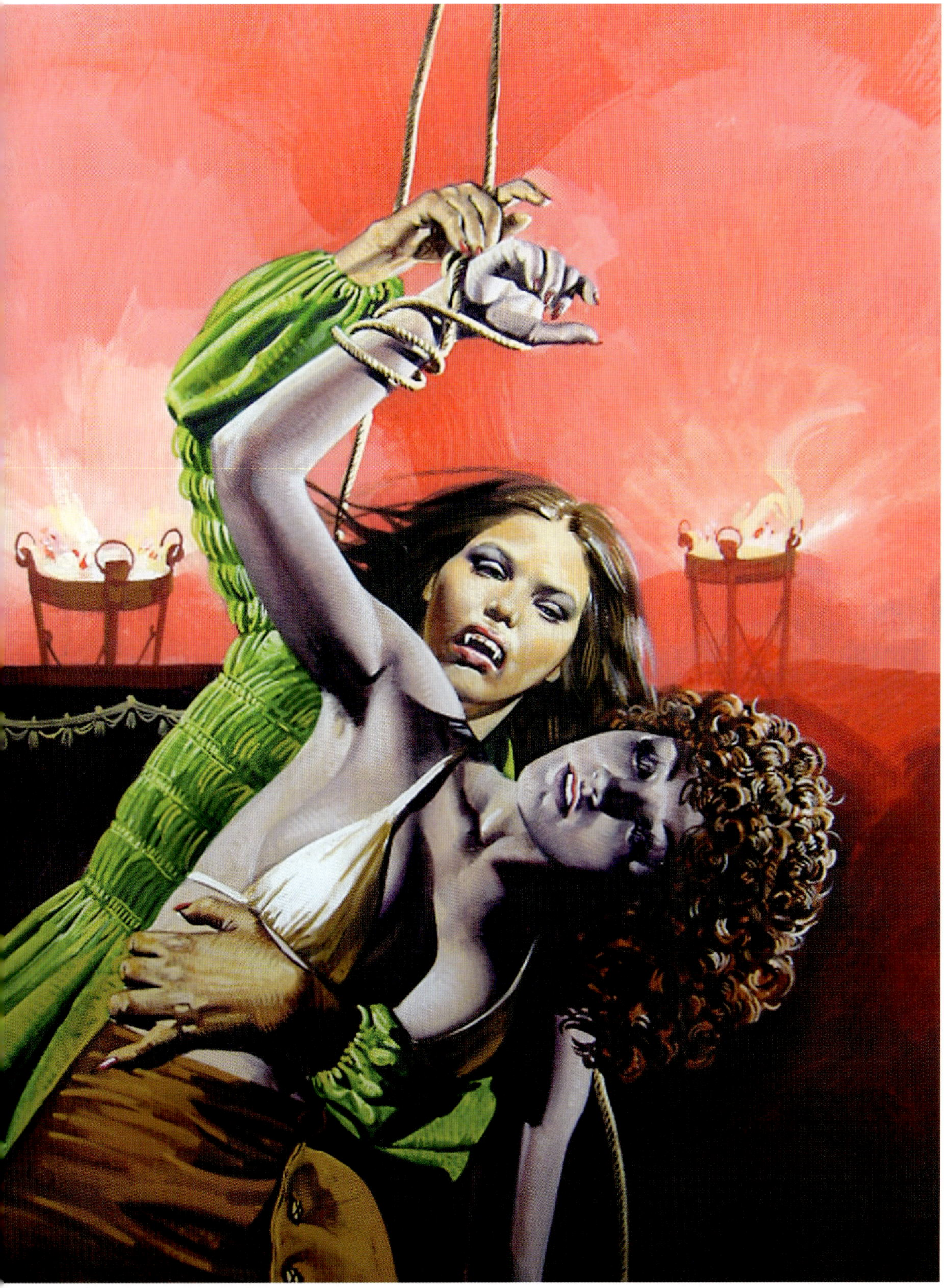

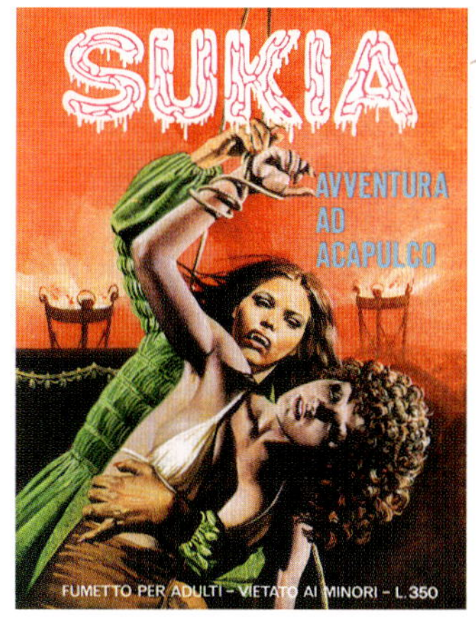

Left: Sukia, n. 20,
Avventura ad Acapulco,
Adventure in Acapulco,
February 1979.

Far left: Sukia, n. 19,
Tra Le Fauci dello Squalo,
In the Jaws of a Shark,
February 1979.

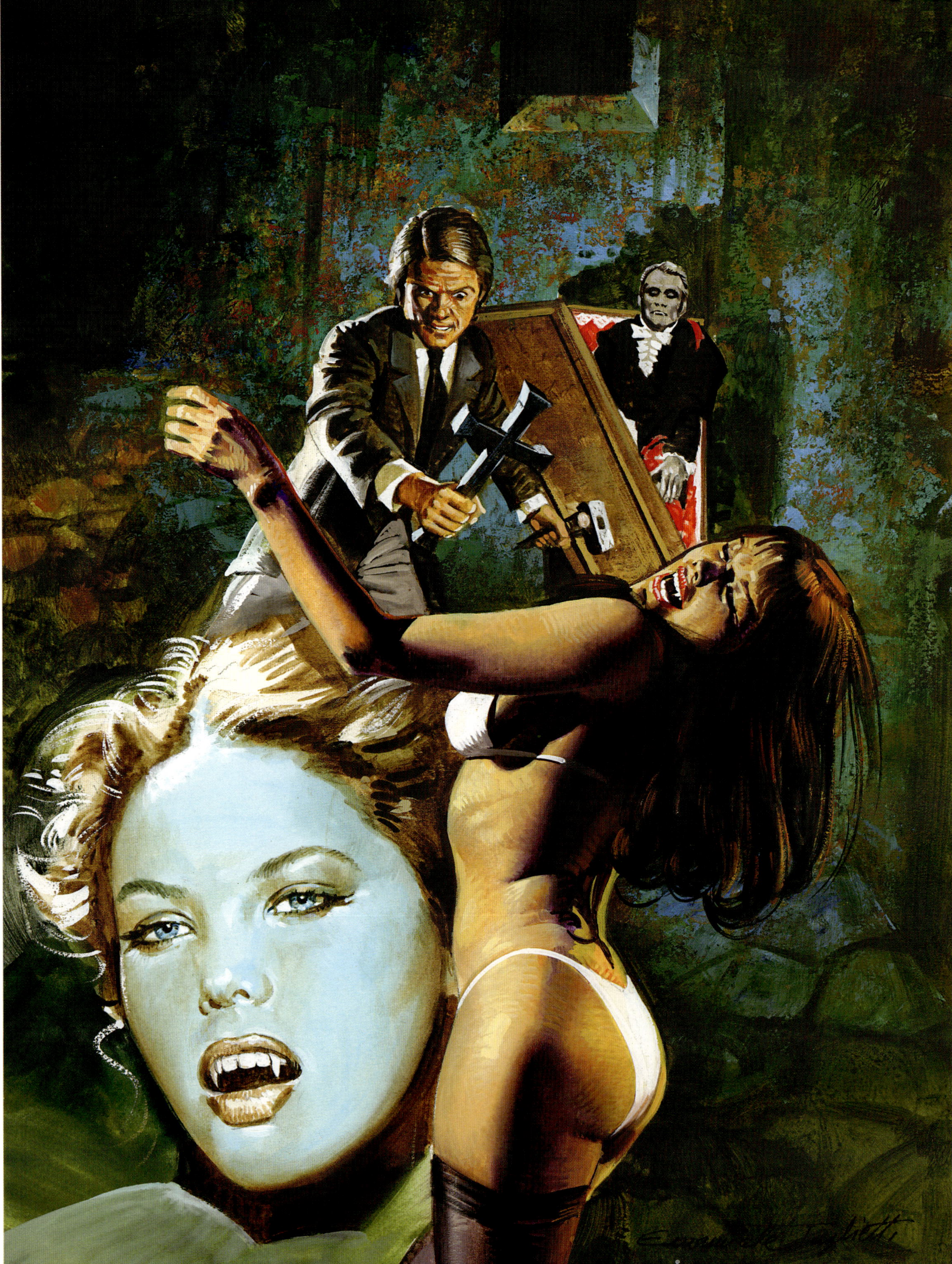

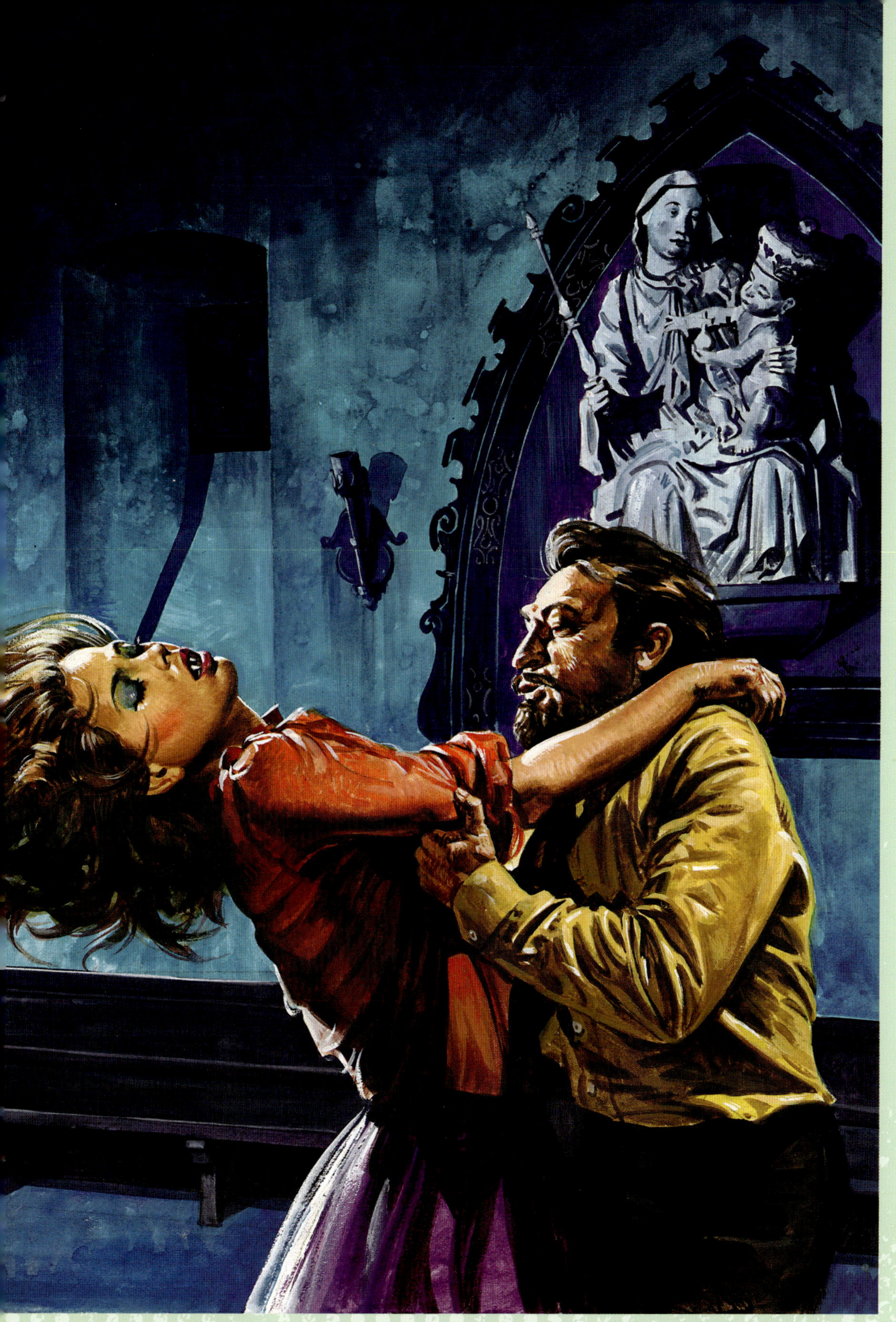

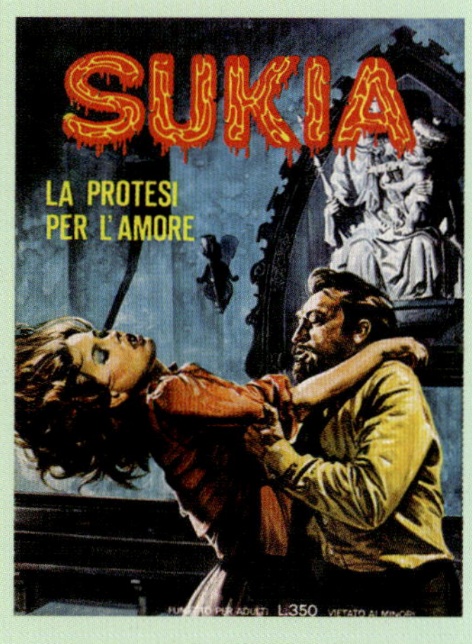

Left: Sukia, n. 31,
La Protesi per l'Amore,
The Prostheses for Love,
July 1979.

Far left: Sukia, n. 27,
Chi ha Paura del Culo Mannaro,
Who's Afraid of the Ass Werewolf,
June 1979.

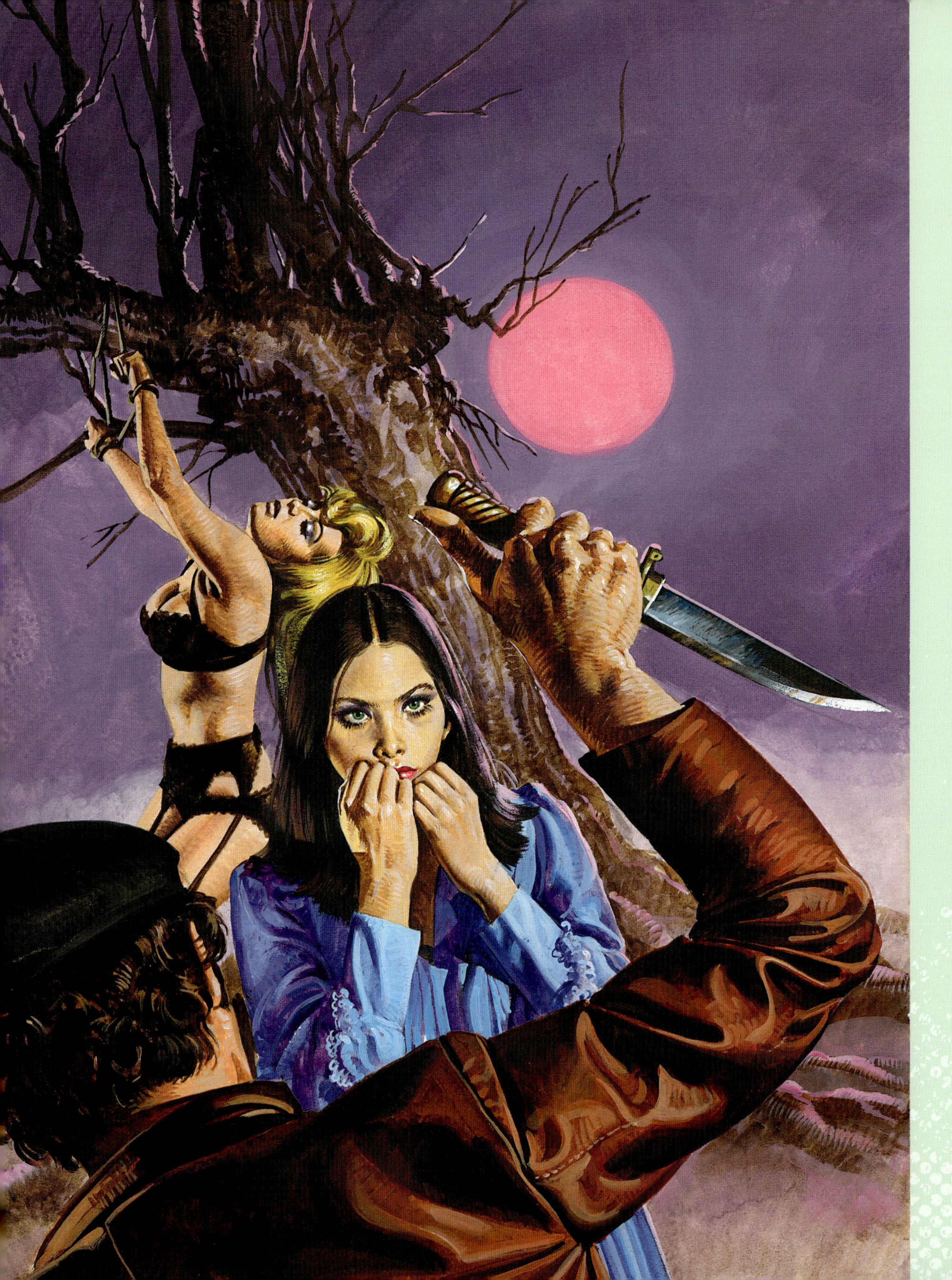

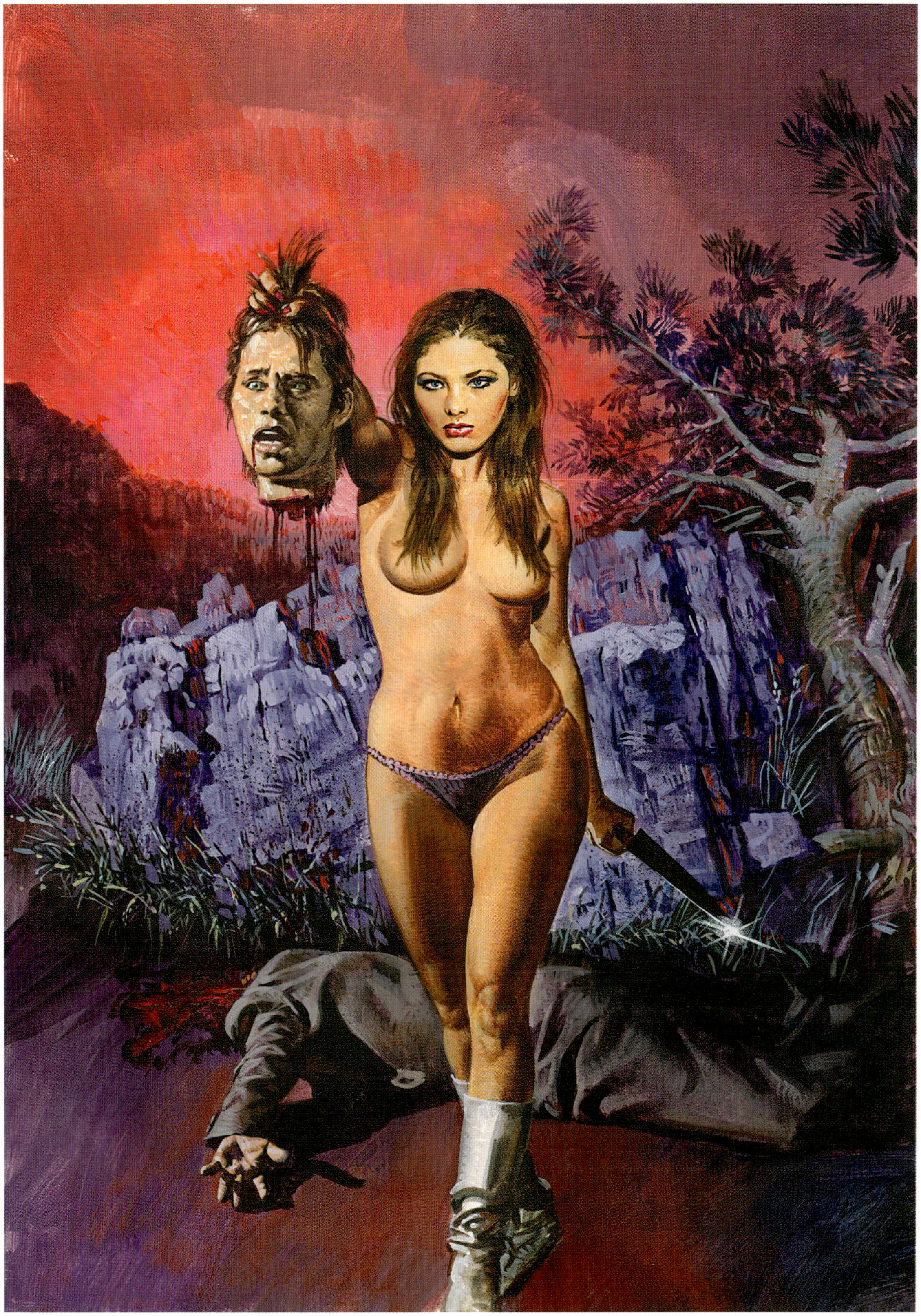

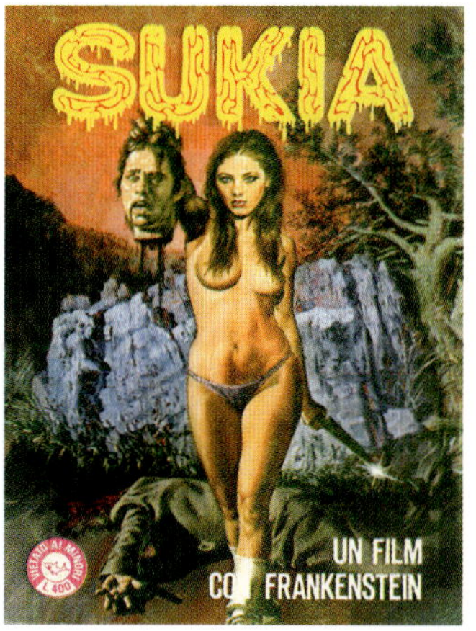

Left: Sukia, n. 46,
Un Film con Frankenstein,
A Film with Frankenstein,
March 1980.

Far left: Sukia, n. 38,
Tortura, Torture,
October 1979.

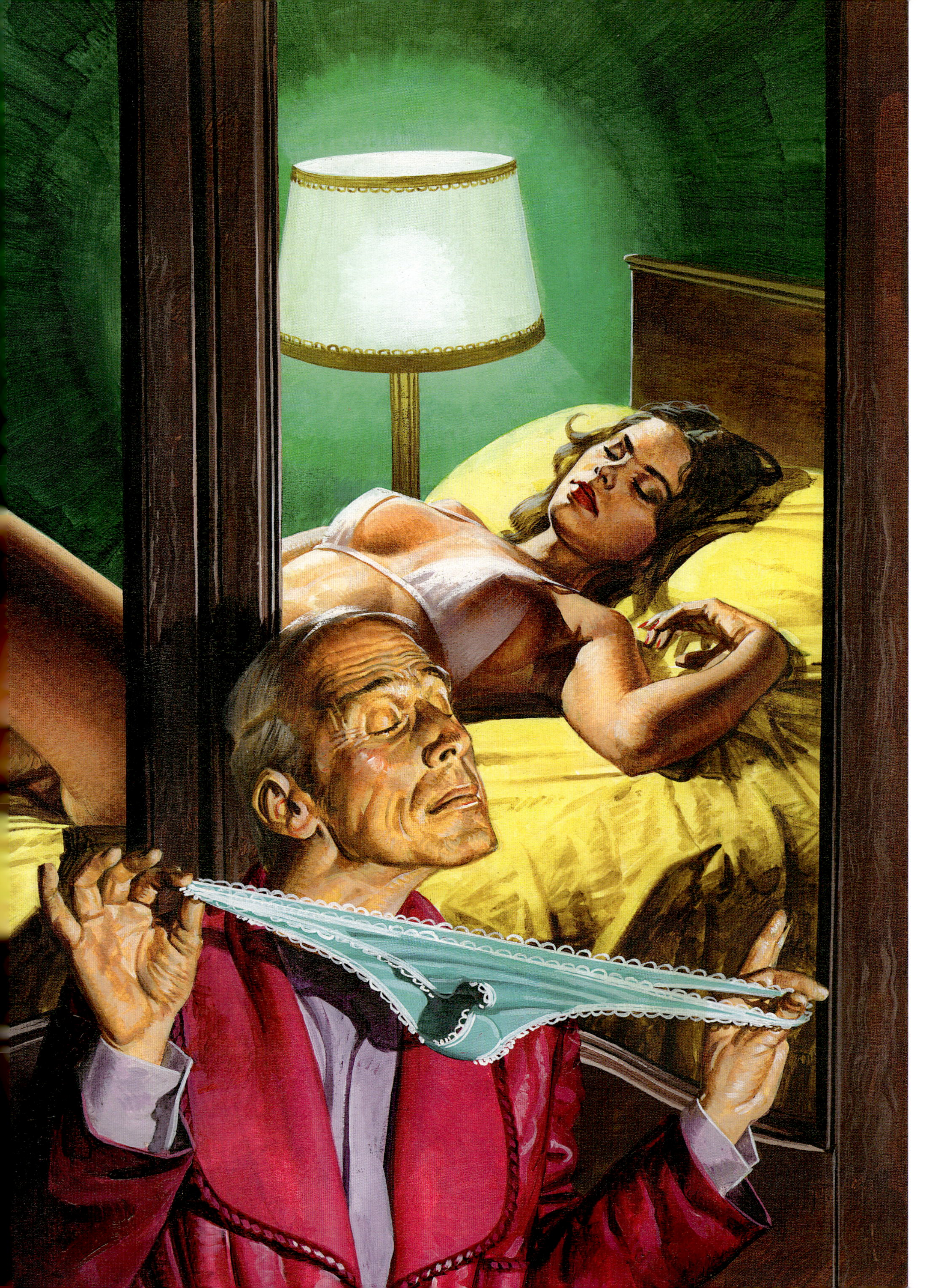

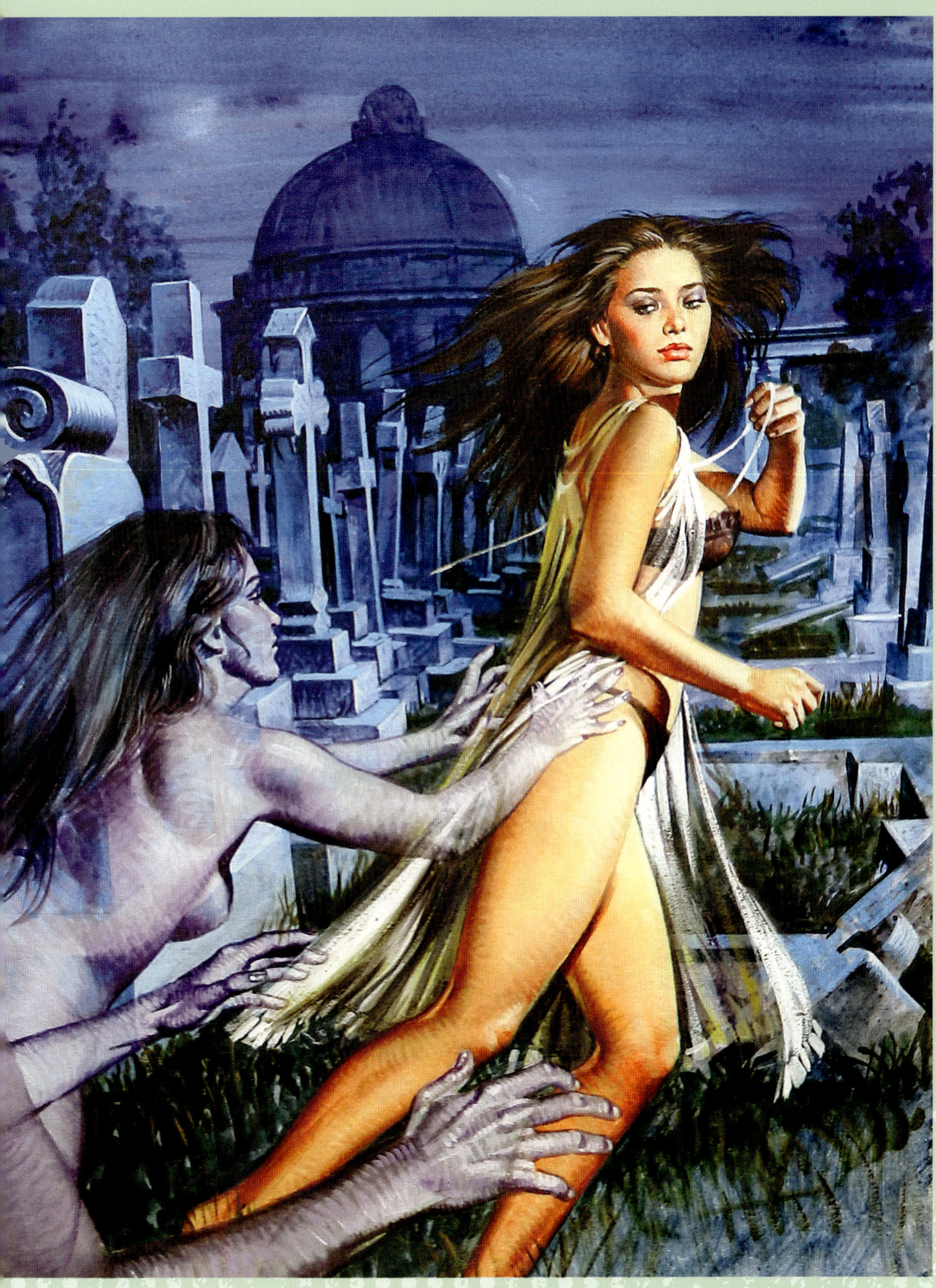

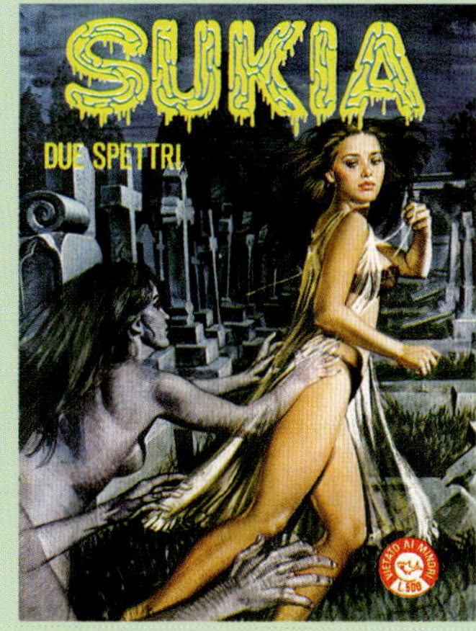

Left: Sukia, n. 65,
Due Spettri, Two Ghosts,
November 1980.

Far left: Sukia, n. 48,
Il Collezionista di Puzze,
The Puzzle Collector,
April 1980.

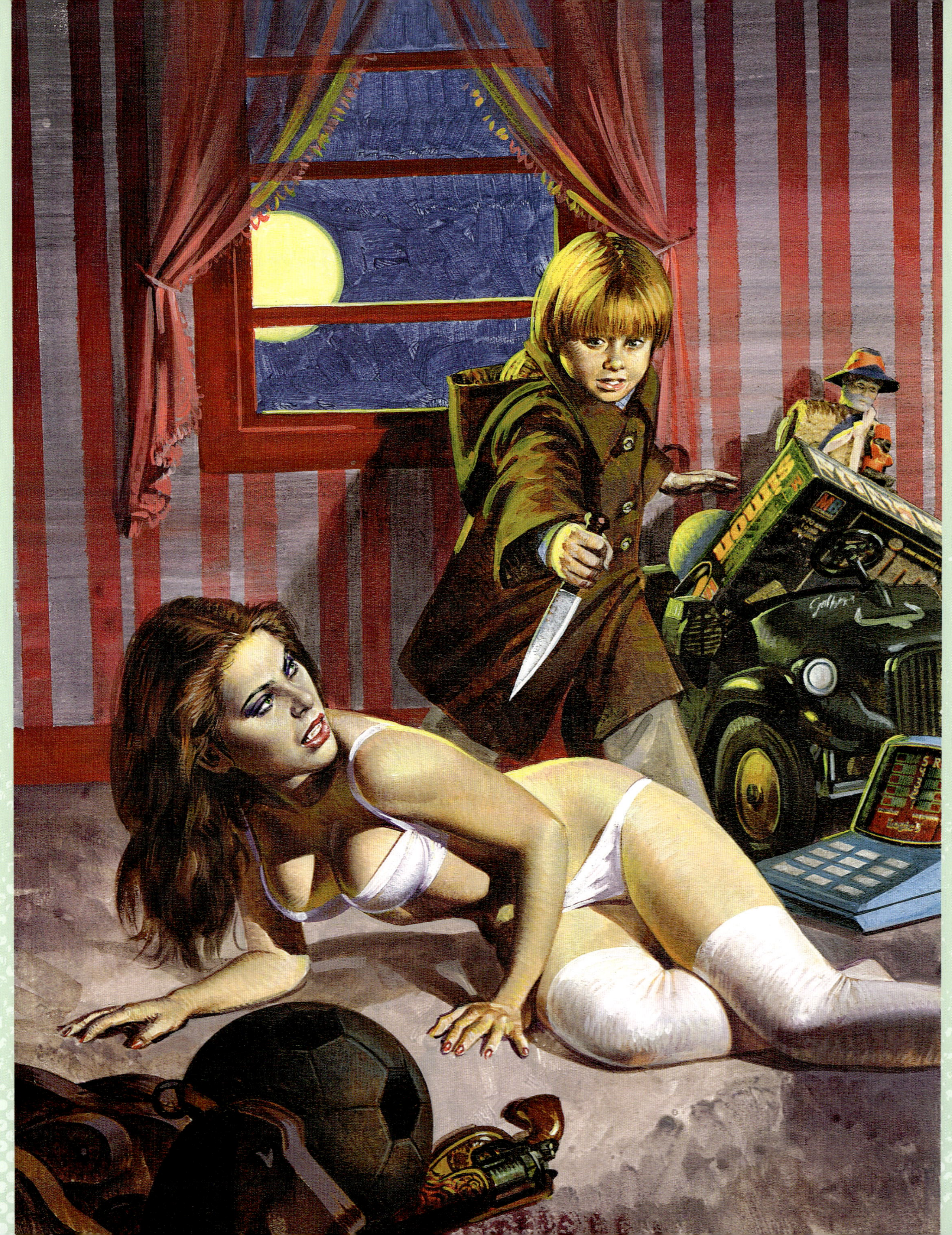

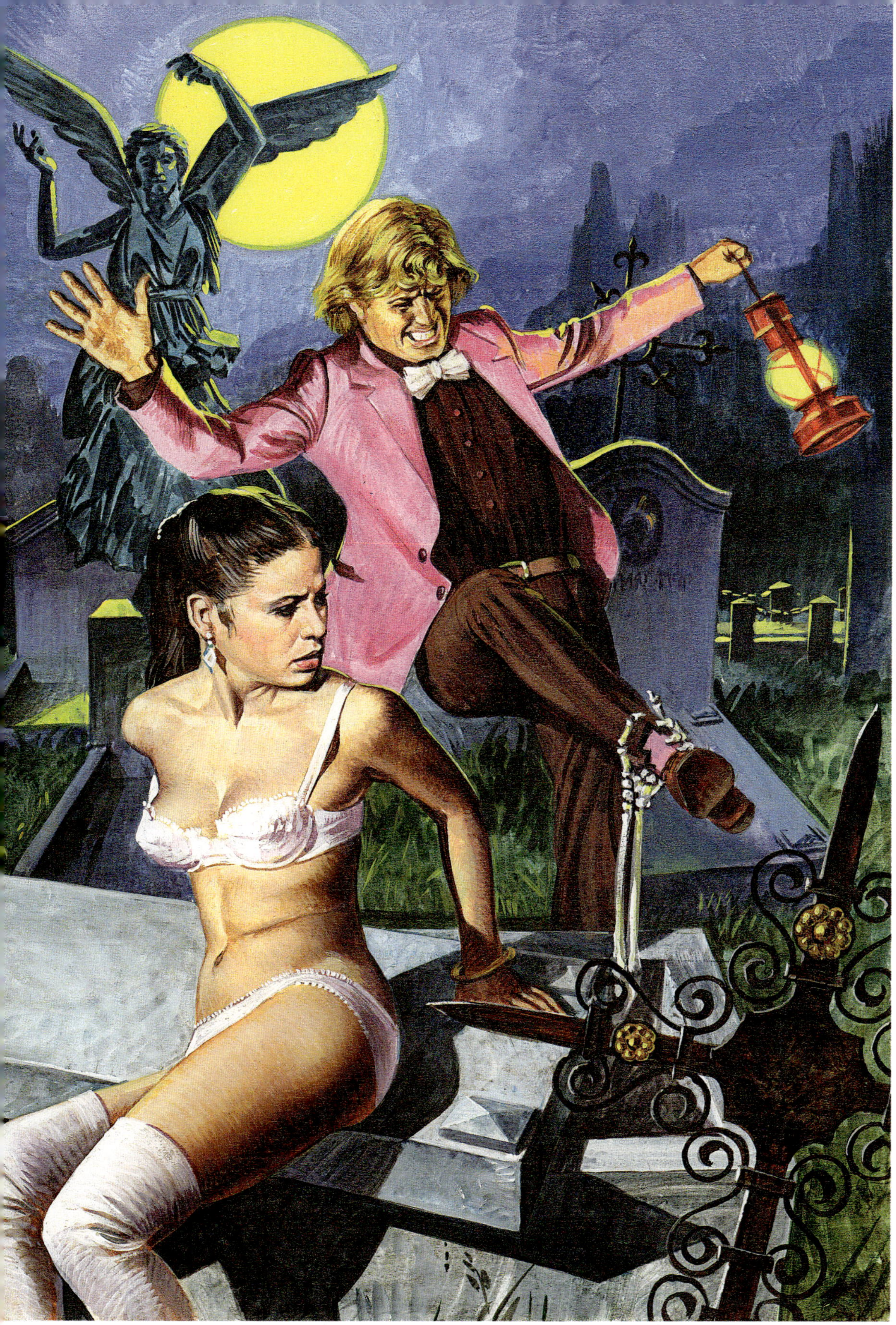

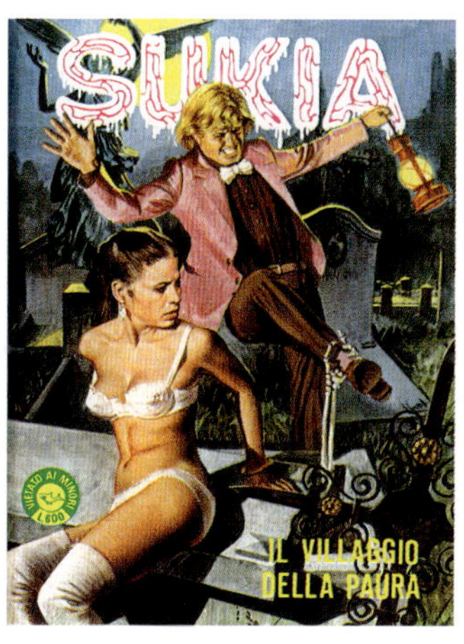

Left: Sukia, n. 68,
Il Villaggio della Paura,
The Village Of Fear,
February 1981.

Far left: Sukia,
n. 66, *Reincarnazione*,
Reincarnation,
December 1980.

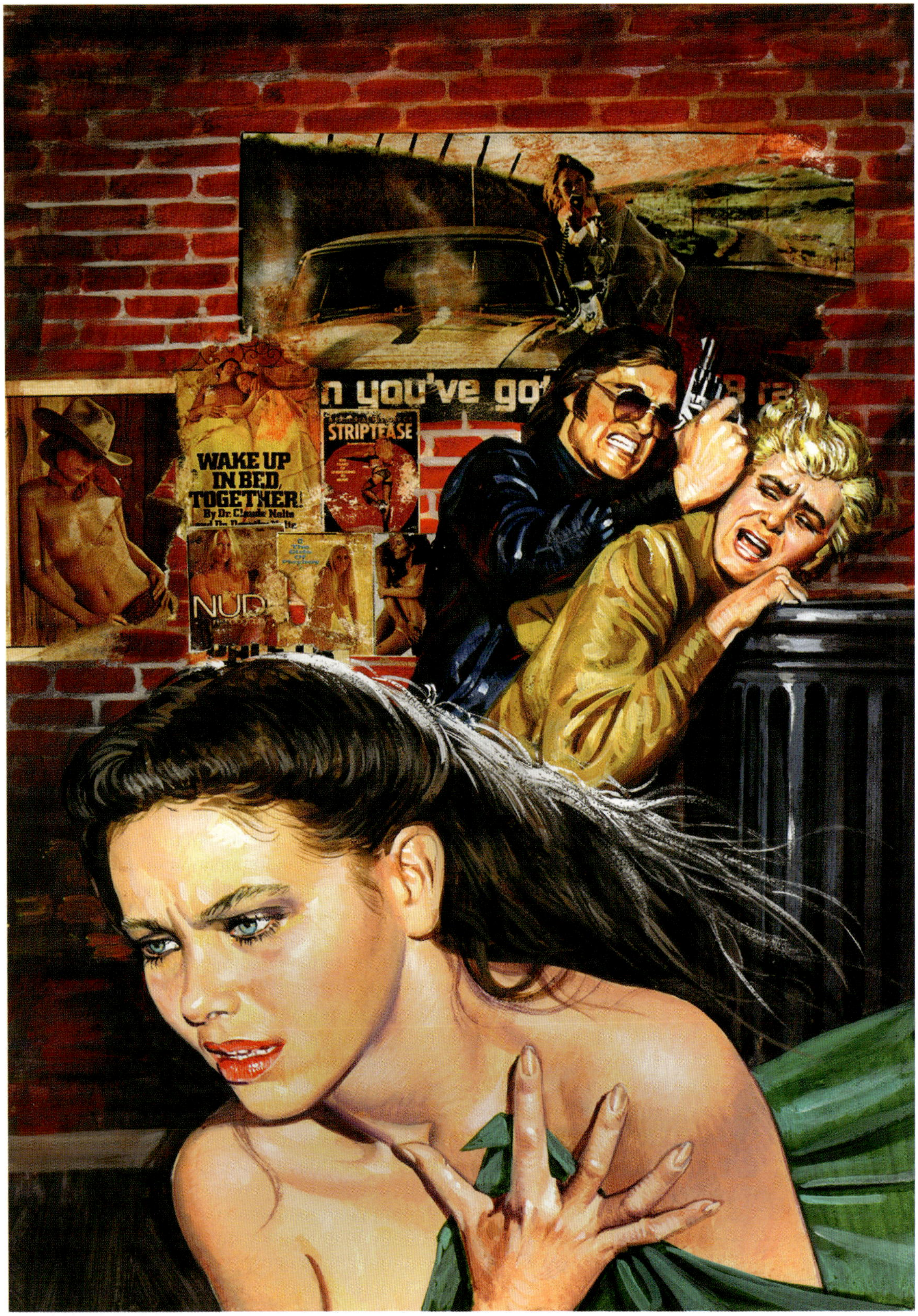

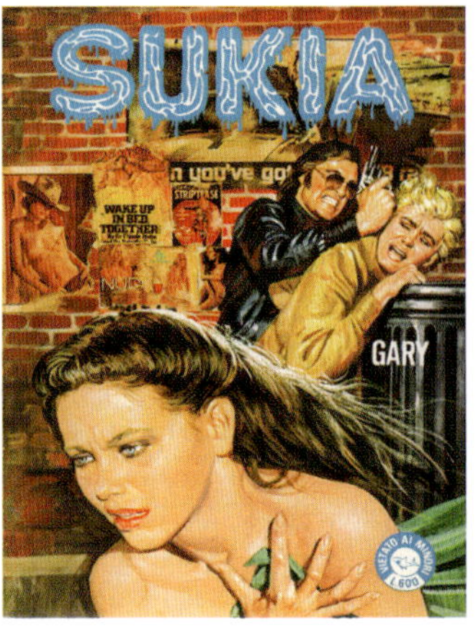

Left: Sukia, n. 74,
Gary, Gary,
April 1981.

Right: Sukia, n. 83,
Dracula, Dracula,
September 1981.

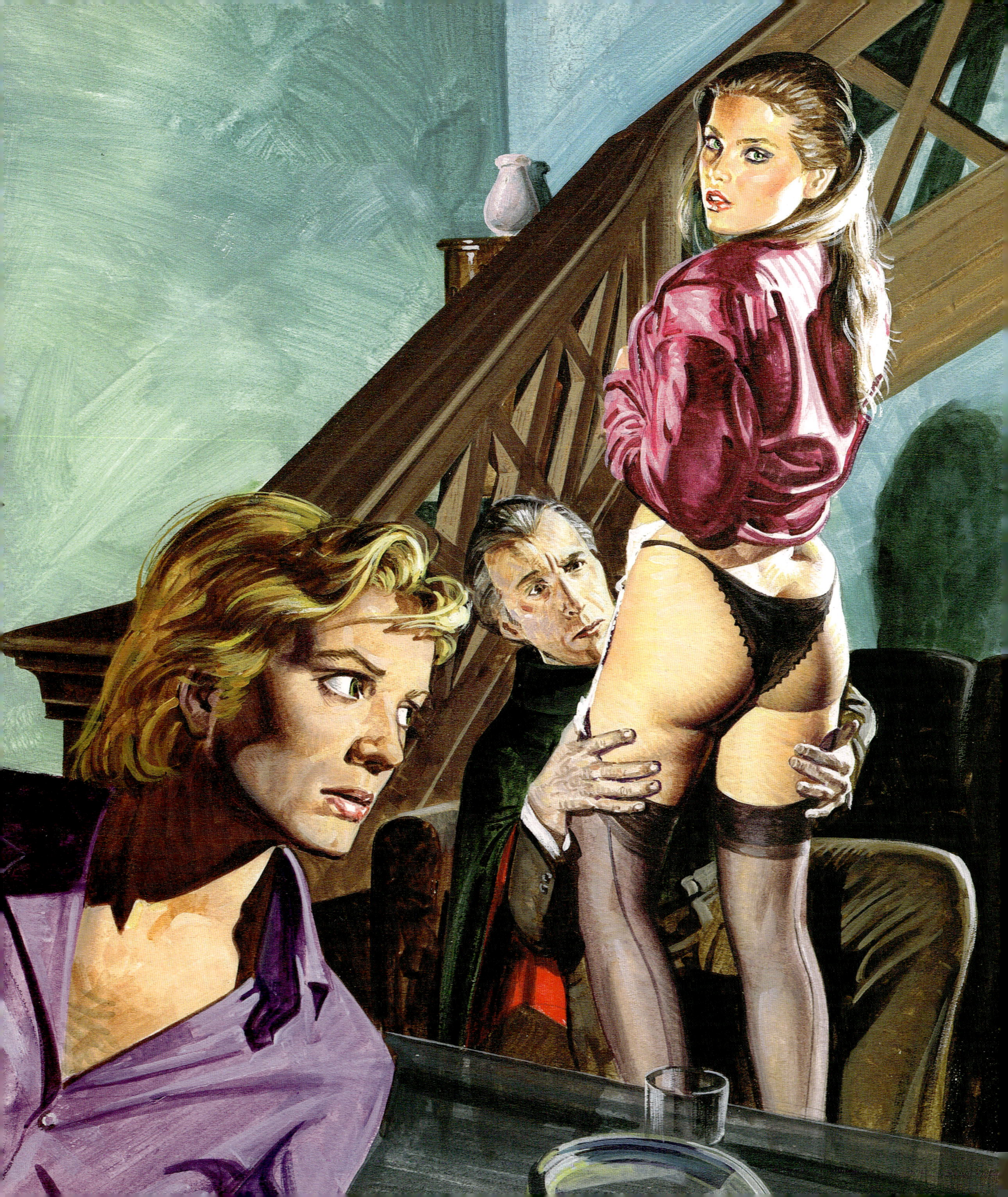

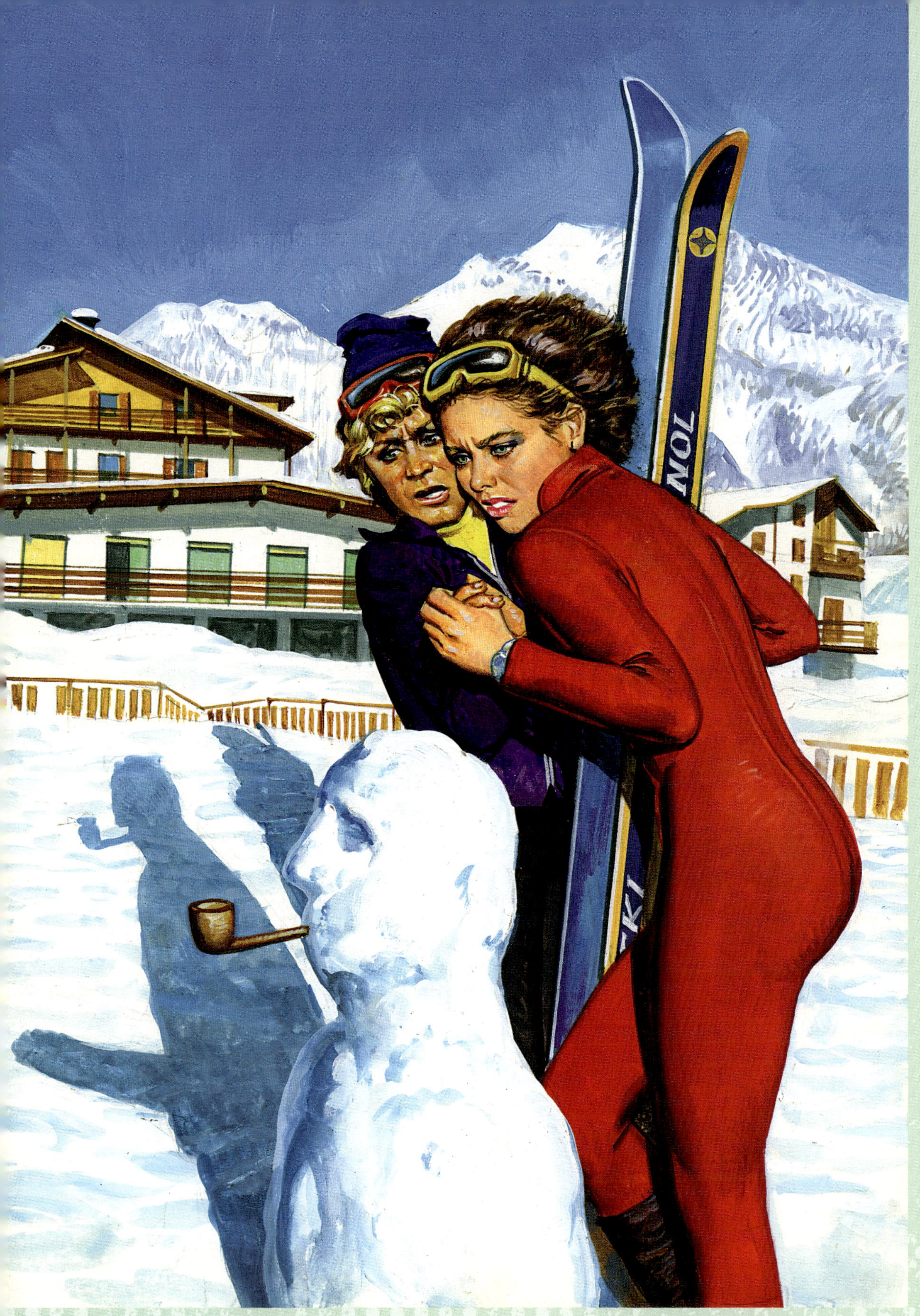

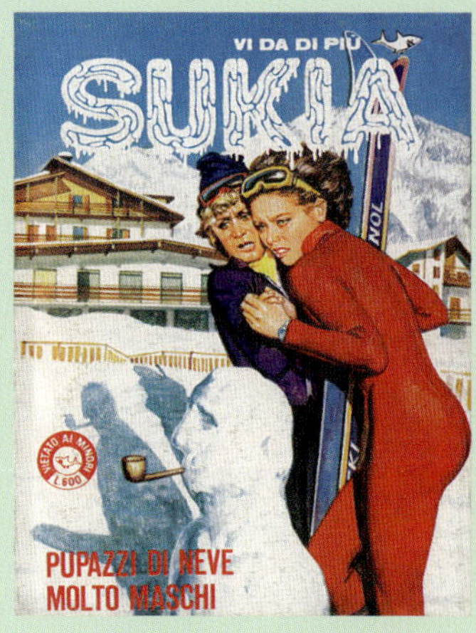

Left: Sukia, n. 98,
Pupazzi di Neve Molto Maschi,
The Very Male Snowman,
April 1982.

Right: Sukia, n. 114,
Una Femmina per l'Emiro,
A Female for the Emir,
December 1982.

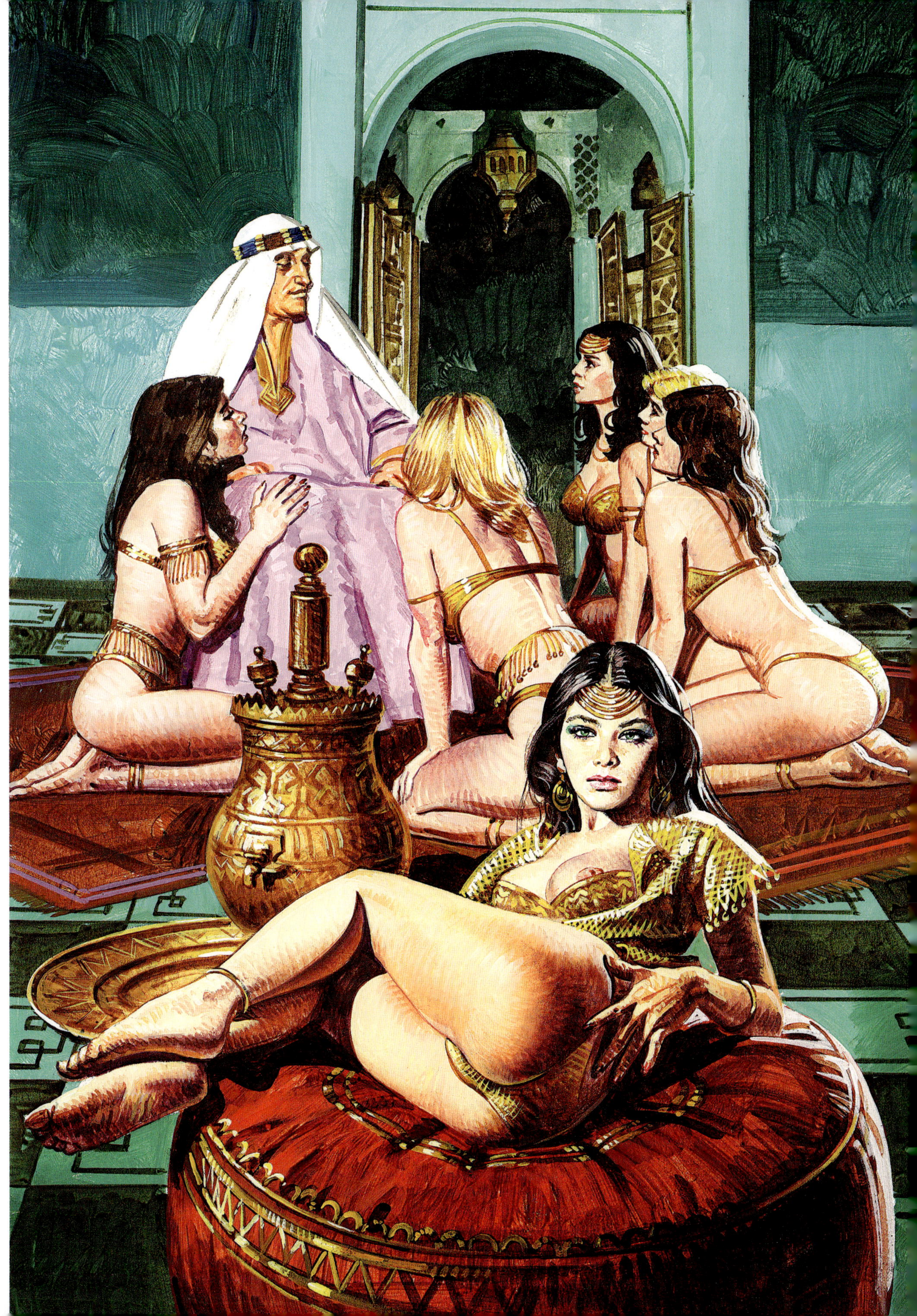

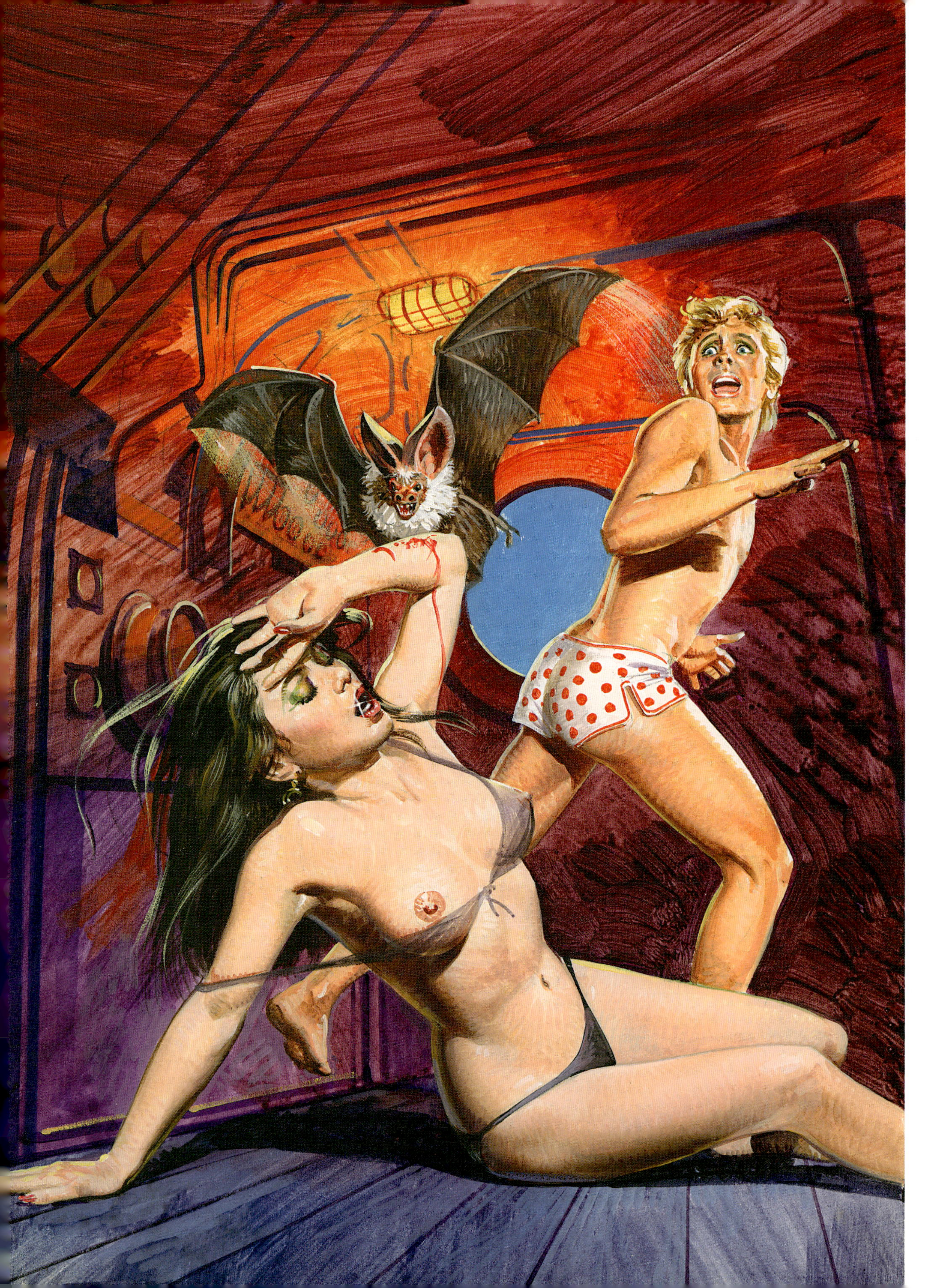

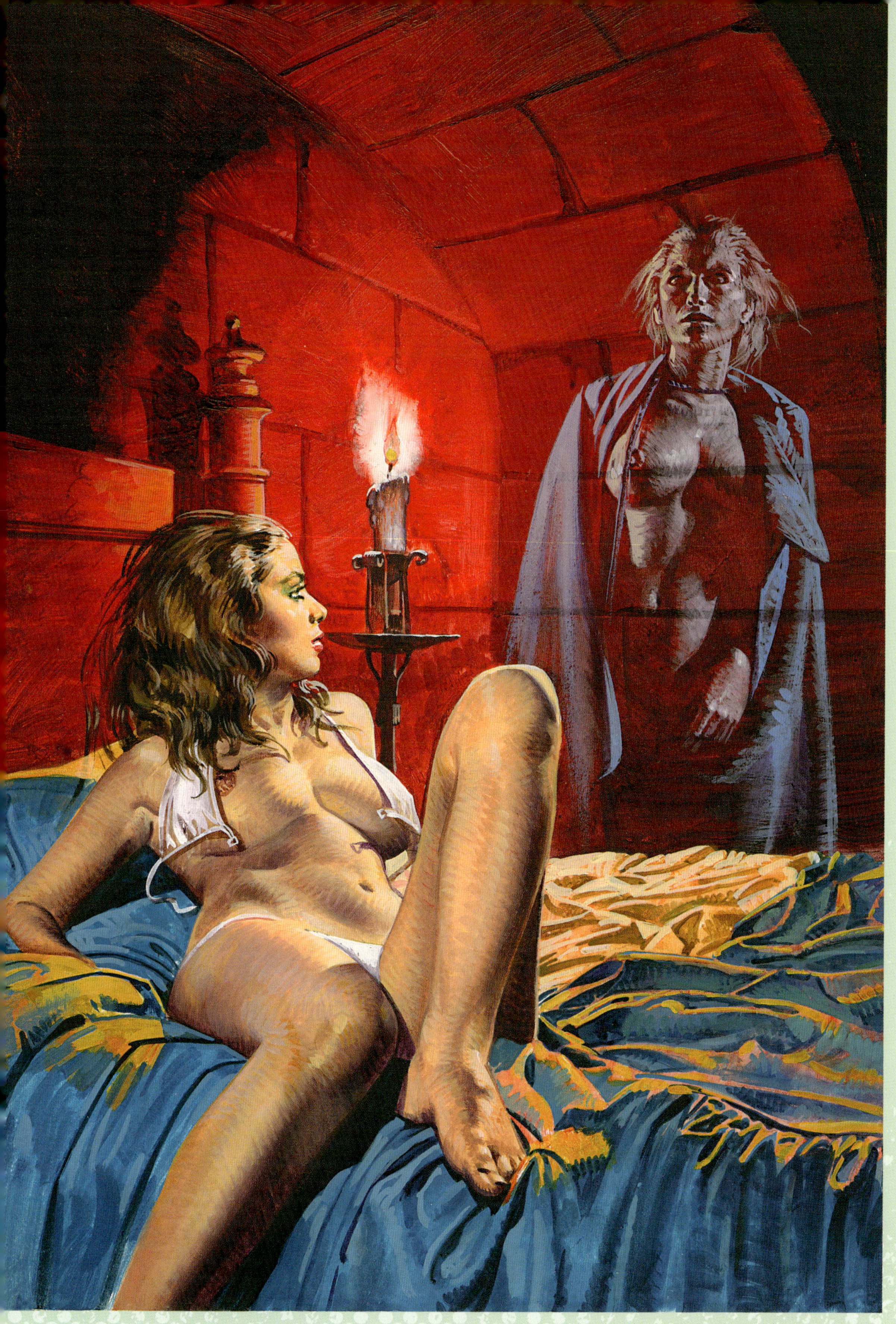

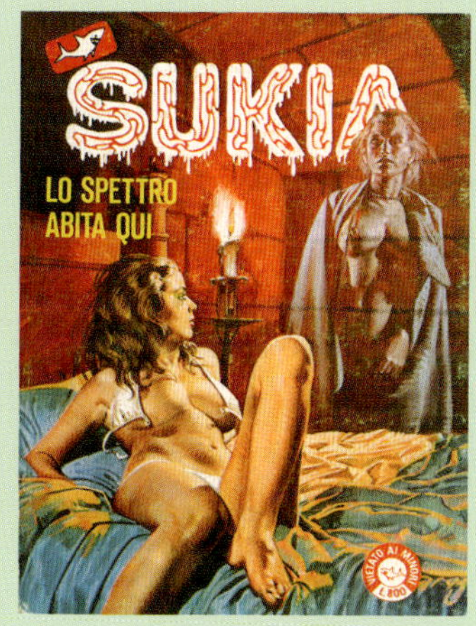

Left: Sukia, n. 125,
Lo Spettro Abita Qui,
The Ghost Lives Here,
November 1983.

Far left: Sukia, n. 120,
Il Vampiro del Transatlantico,
The Transatlantic Vampire,
June 1983.

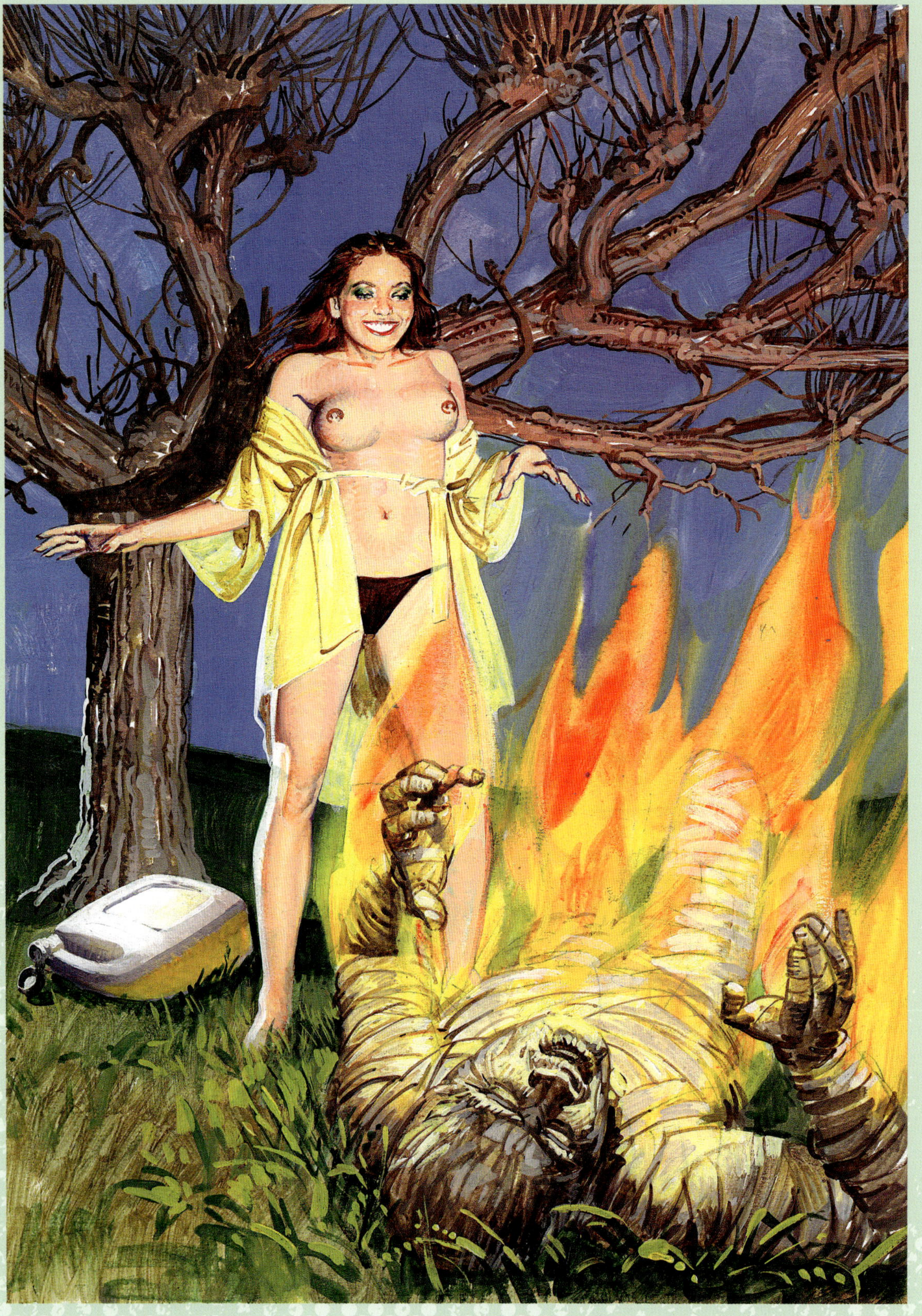

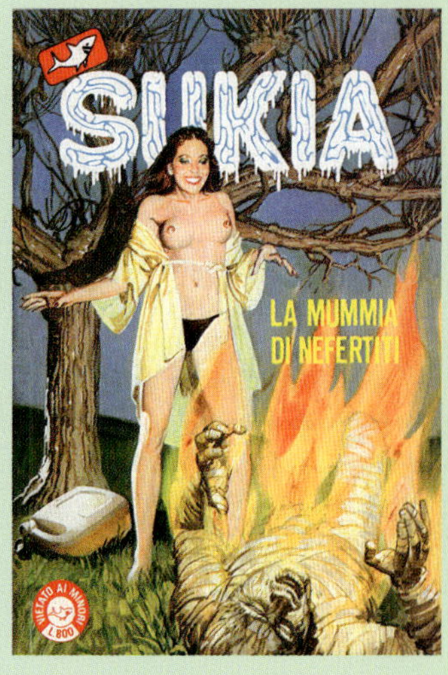

Left: Sukia, n. 132,
La Mummia di Nefertiti,
The Mummy of Nefertiti,
June 1984.

Right: Sukia, n. 135,
L'Occhio Intimo,
An Intimate Eye,
September 1984.

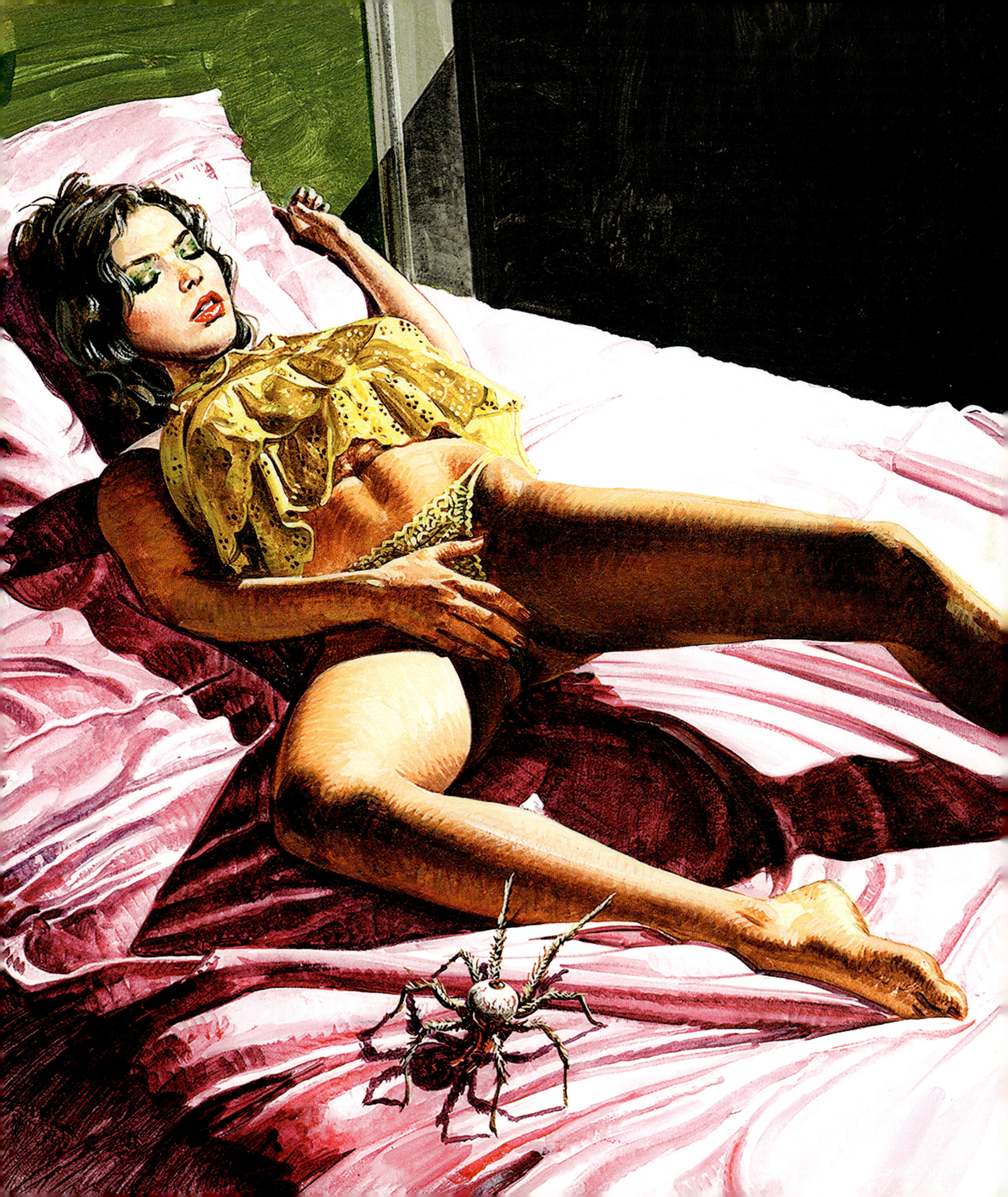

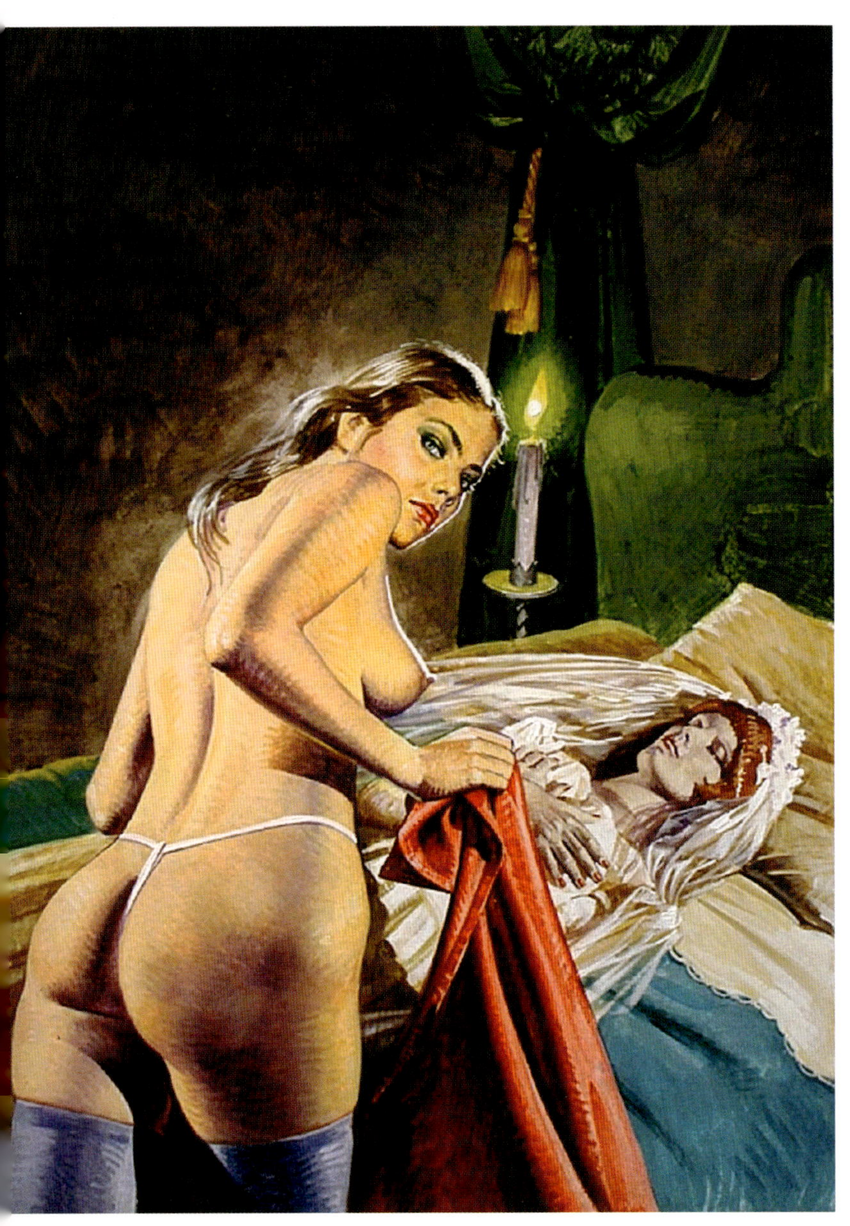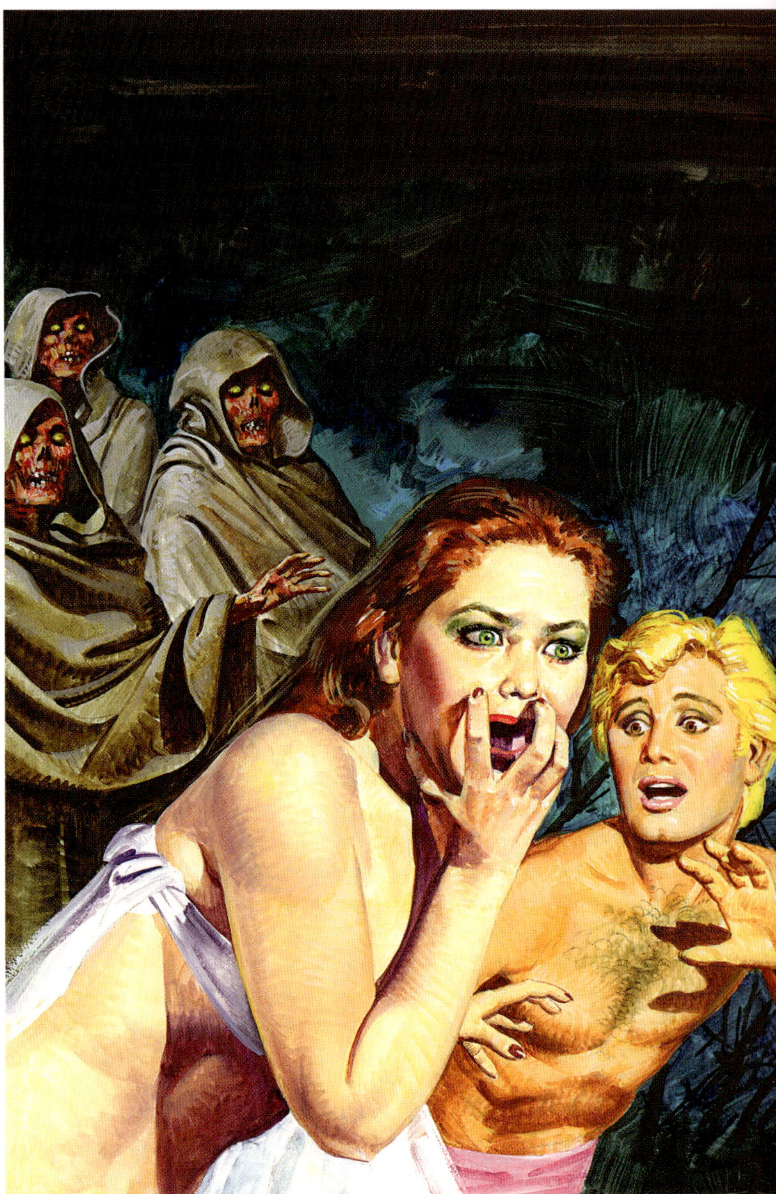

Above: Sukia, n. 136, *Forbici,* Scissors, October 1984.

Above: Sukia, n. 137, *La Lunga Notte,* The Long Night, November 1984.

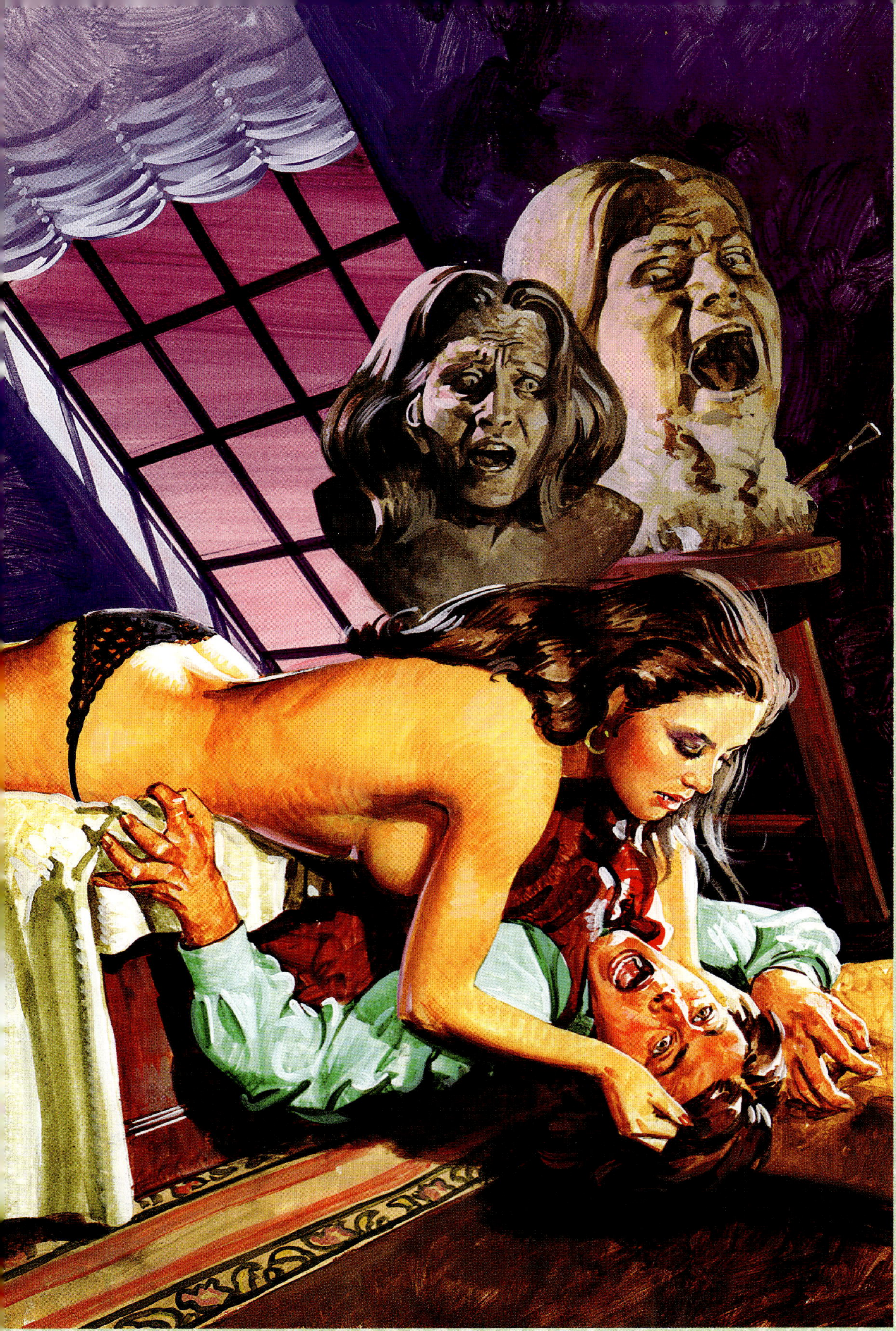

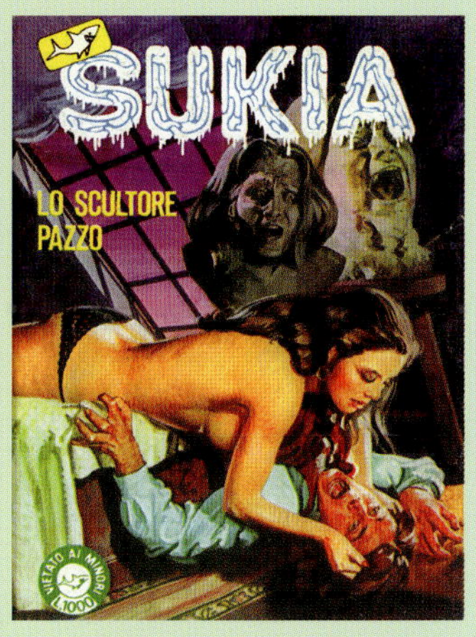

Left: Sukia, n. 149,
Lo Scultore Pazzo,
The Mad Sculptor,
November 1985.

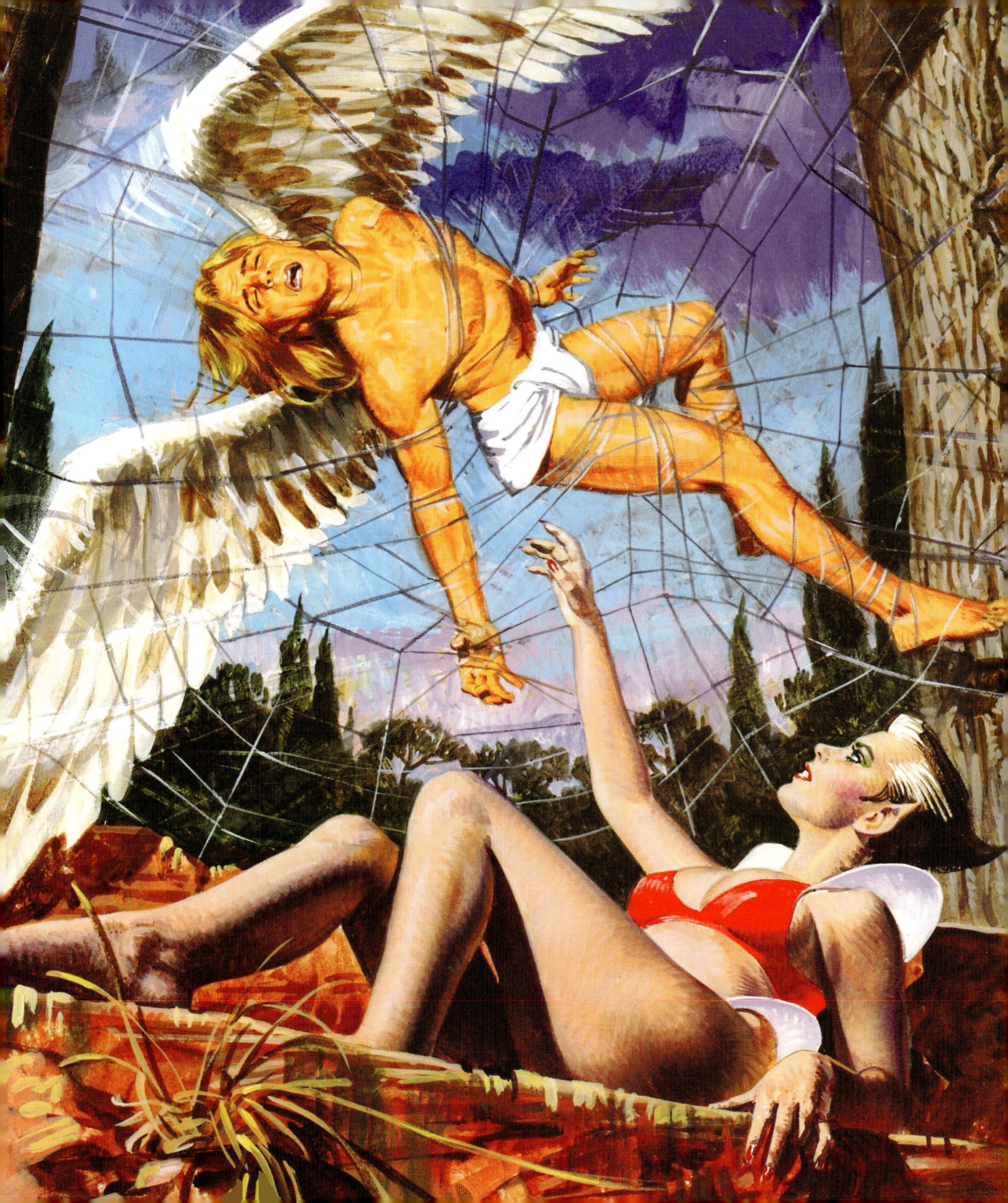

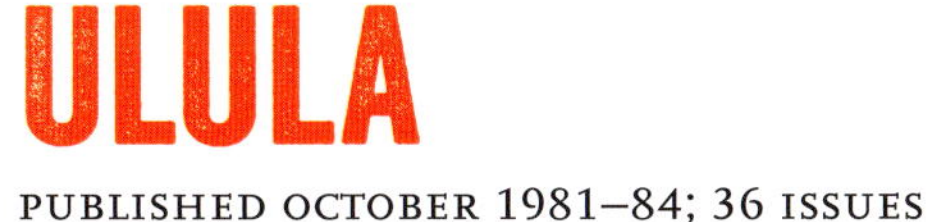

ULULA

PUBLISHED OCTOBER 1981–84; 36 ISSUES

Ulla von Hagen is a model who has been placed under a terrible curse – one that she reveals only to her gay friend Joe. In the first issue, Ulla is on her way to a party at the home of her uncle, Count Von Wilfrend Gagen, a specialist in diseases of the blood, when she's involved in a horrific car accident. Badly injured, she is transported to her uncle's huge castle in the Black Forest, and unless she gets a blood transfusion, she'll die. In the absence of any human blood, her uncle injects her with the blood of a wolf. Ulla survives her ordeal and recovers, but from that day on, during a full moon she turns into a hideous creature: a female werewolf called Ulula ("Howls"). In later issues, as Ulula's exploits take her around the world, several classic horror and sci-fi creatures pop up in the stories, including zombies, vampires and mummies and the Invisible Man. In the last issue a Romanian lesbian scientist returns Ulula to the state of a normal woman.

Left: Ulula, n. 26, *Dove Volano gli Uccelli*, Where Birds Fly, November 1983.

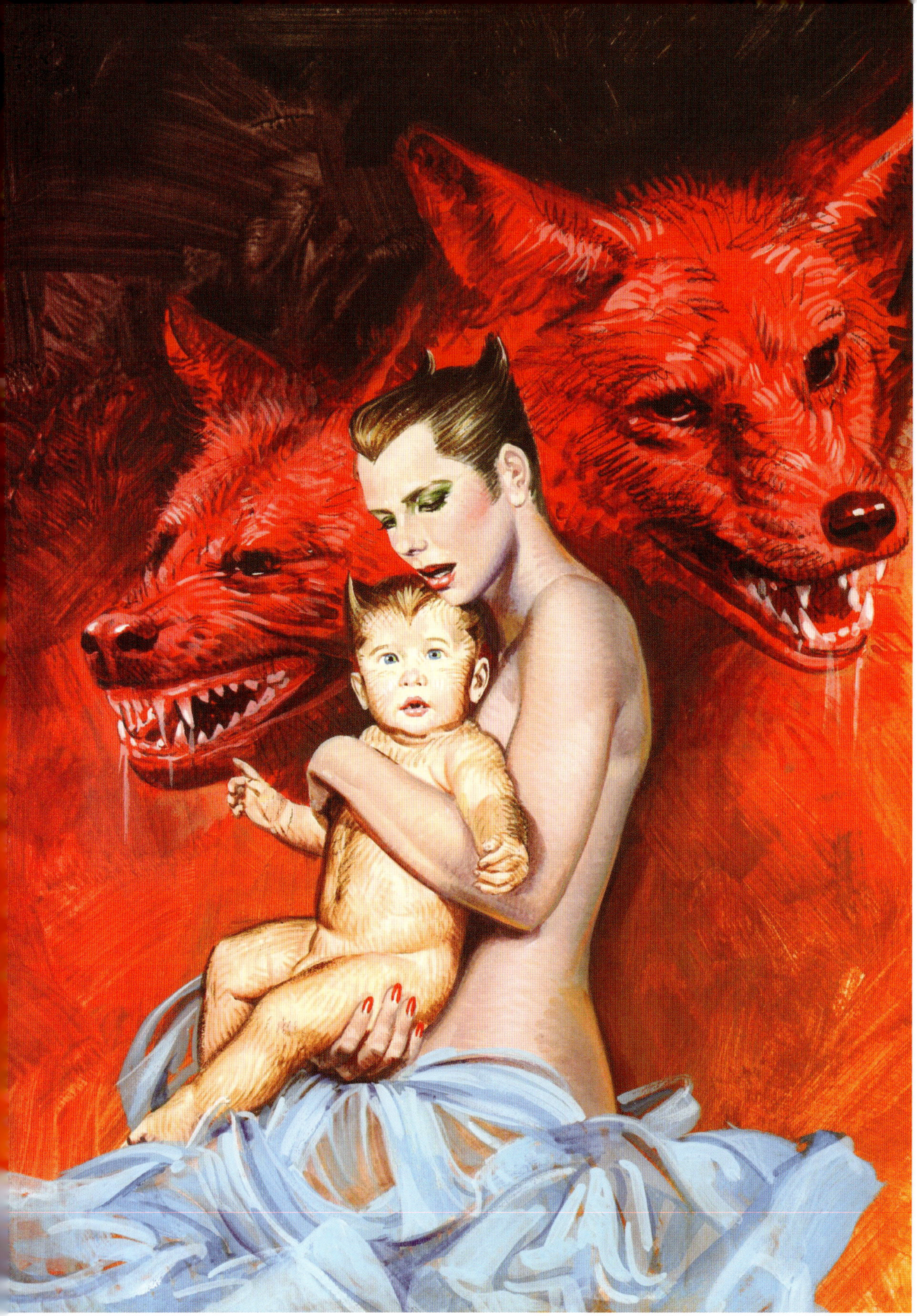

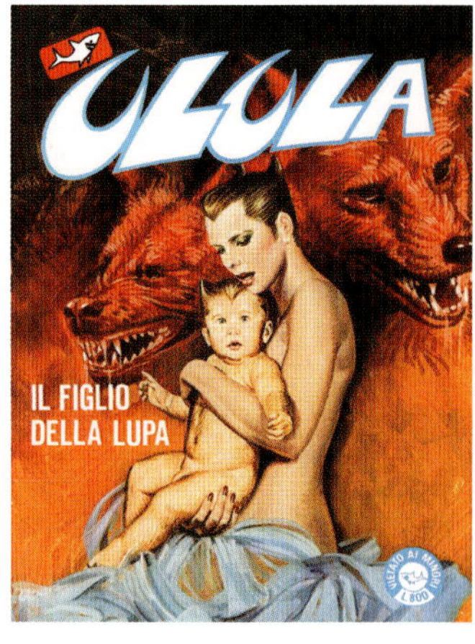

Left: Ulula, n. 21,
Il Figlio della Lupa,
Son of the Wolf,
June 1983.

Right: Ulula, n. 25,
Schiavo del Sesso,
Sex Slave,
October 1983.

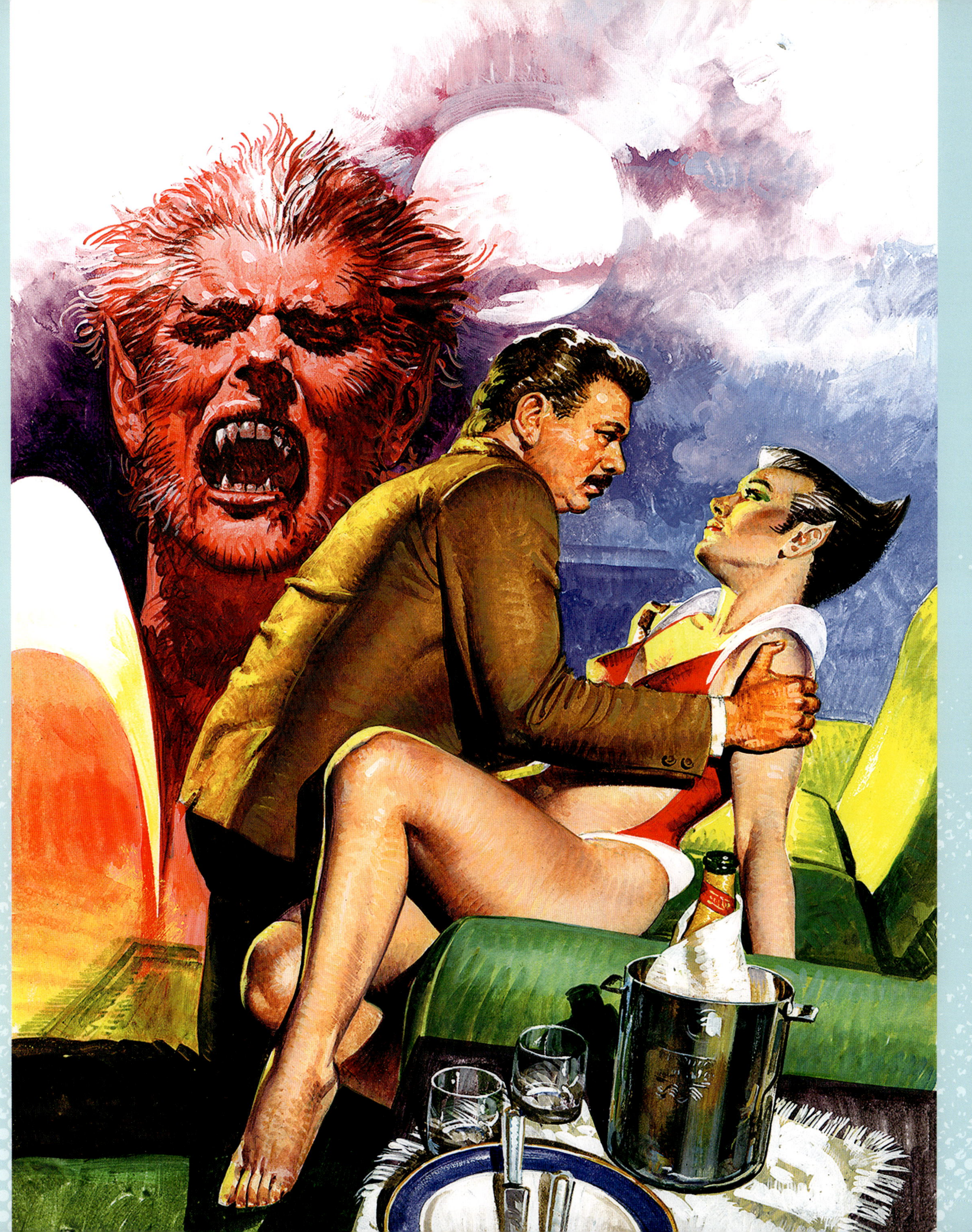

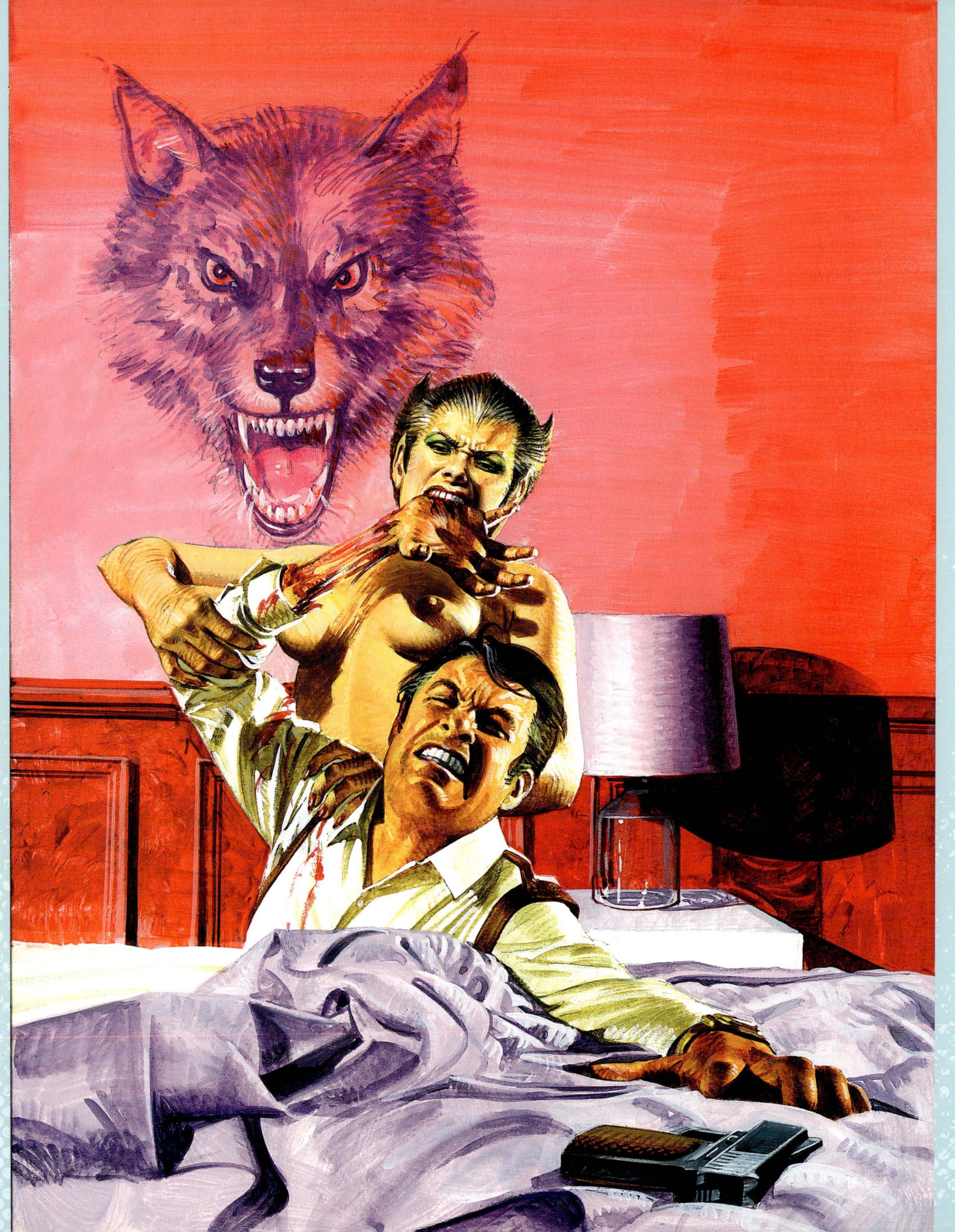

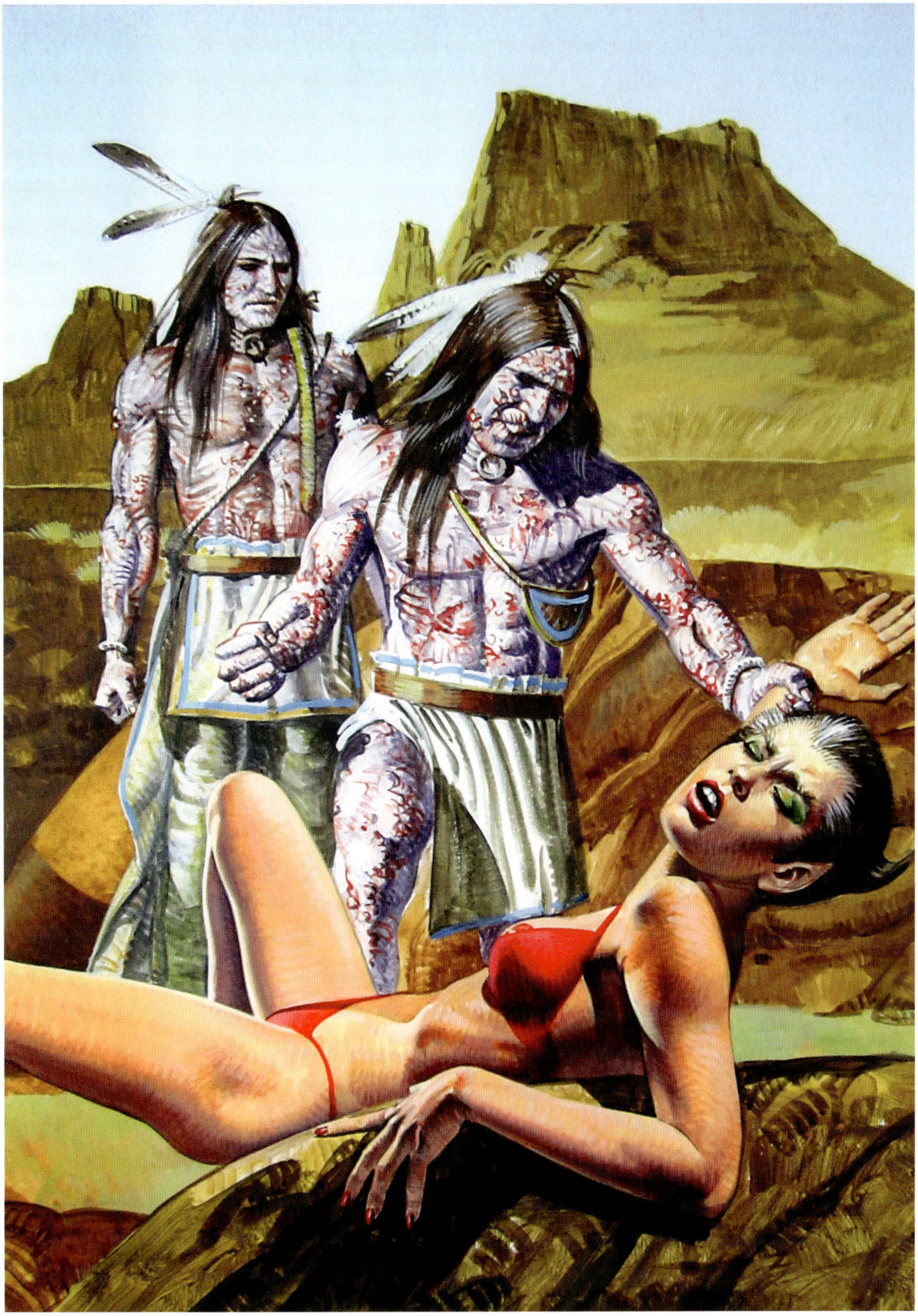

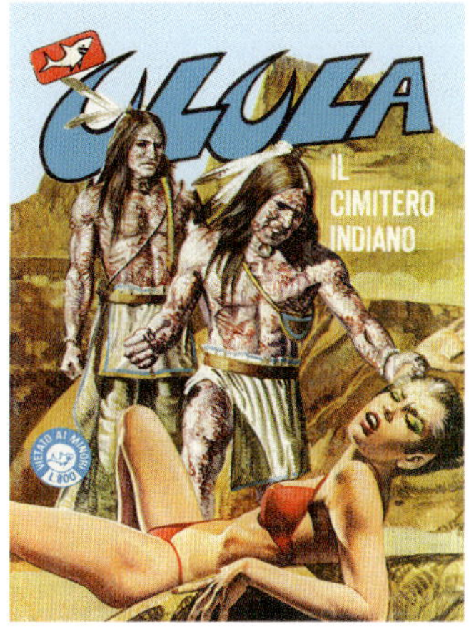

Left Ulula, n. 31,
Il Cimitero Indiano,
The Indian Cemetery,
April 1984.

Far left: Ulula, n. 30,
La Controfigura,
The Stunt,
March 1984.

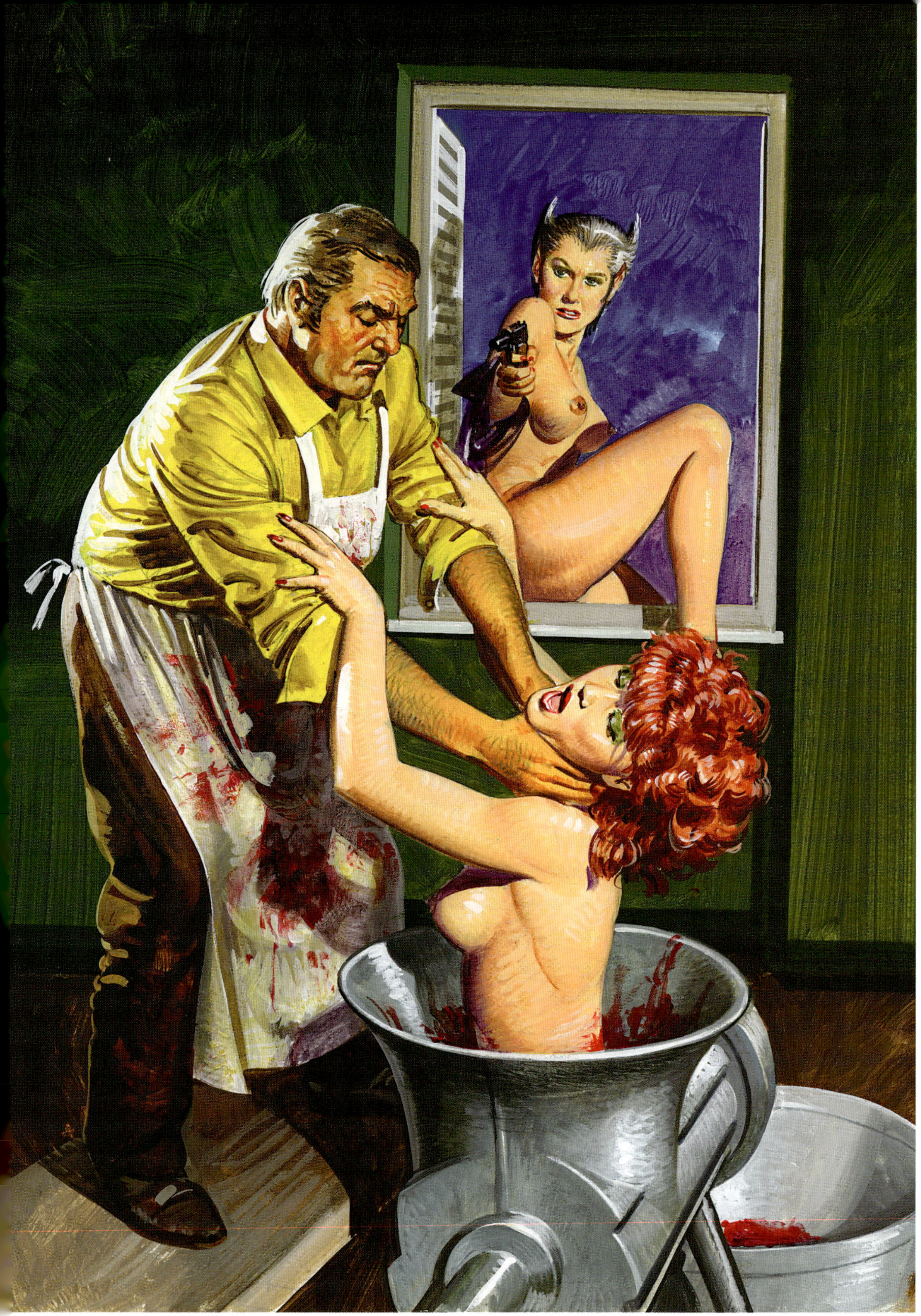

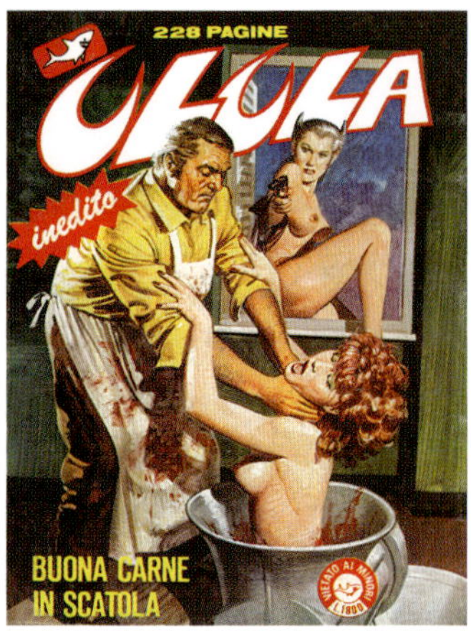

Left: Ulula Supplemento,
n. 33, *Buona Carne in Scatola*,
Good Canned Meat,
May 1984.

Right: Ulula, n. 35,
L'Isola del Terrore,
The Island Of Terror,
July 1984.

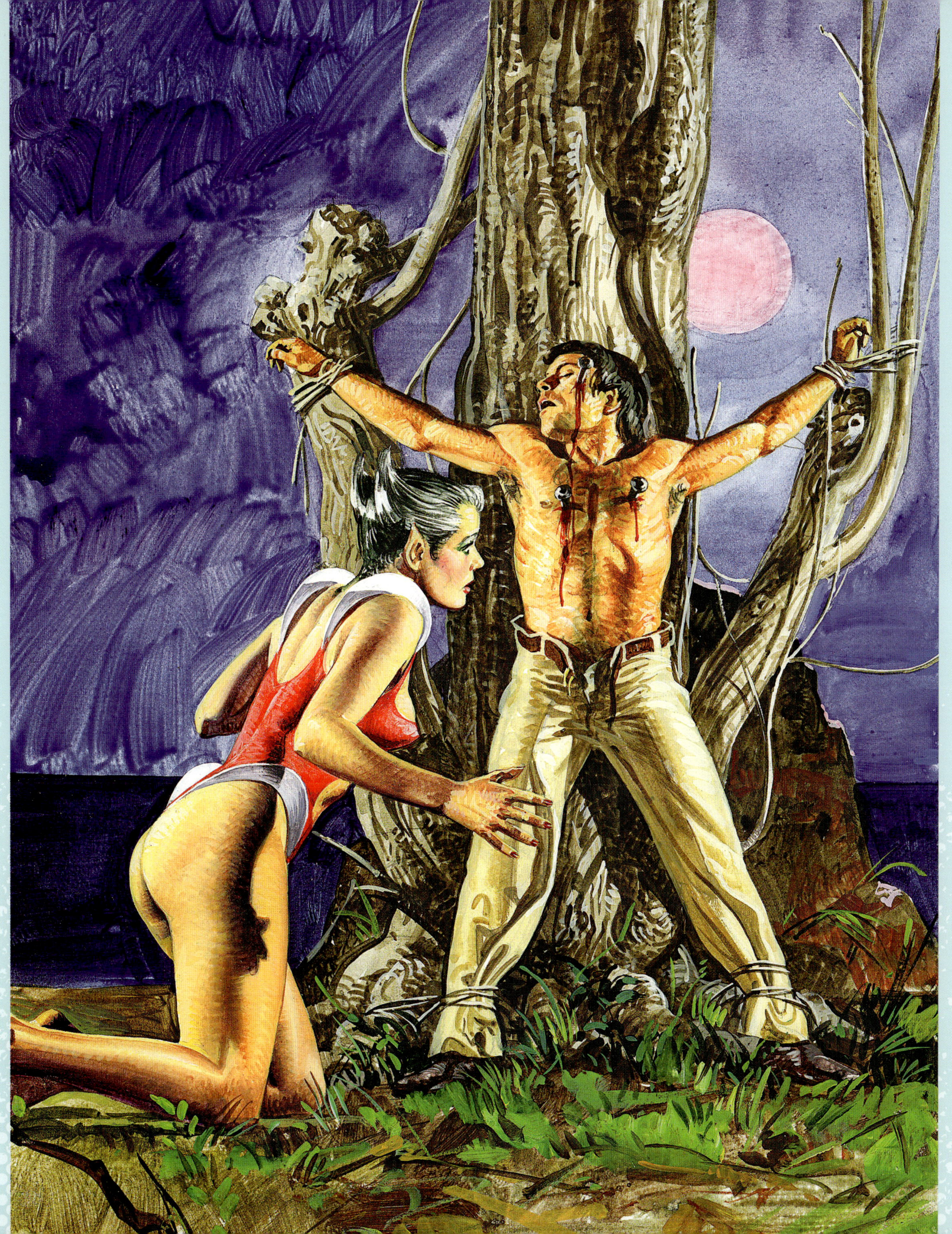

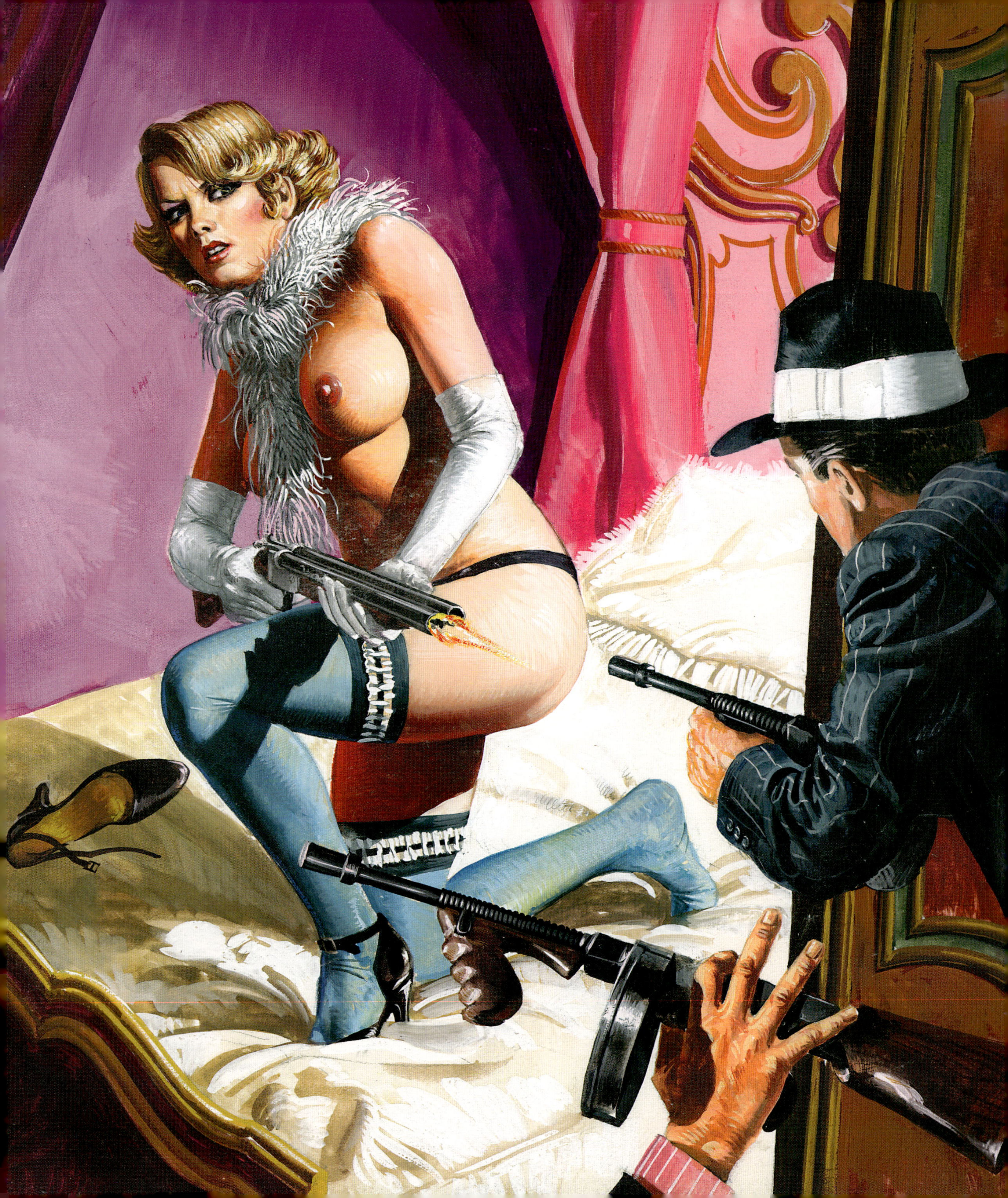

VIPERA BIONDA

PUBLISHED 1977–1980; 34 ISSUES

This series features one of Edifumetto's strong and sexually independent female protagonists. The setting is 1930s America, the era of the Great Depression, gangsters and Prohibition, and the Golden Age of Hollywood, and the stories evoke the period well. In the first issue the protagonist appears under the name "Cat Sparrow", but later her nickname, "Viper Blonde", becomes apparent. She's tough and daring, handy with a gun, a lover of luxury and the good life. When we meet her, Cat is working as a prostitute in a brothel, but she ends up, in later episodes, seeing off gangs of Mafia mobsters, cannibals, satanists, organ traffickers and the hooded Ku Klux Klan. In some of the covers it's possible to make out the features of famous American actors, such as Humphrey Bogart and James Cagney. The cover of number 16 features a reworking of one of the victims in the 1970 film *Mark of the Devil*, while the background of number 17 borrows imagery from the 1978 film *Coma*.

Left: Vipera Bionda, n. 1, *Le Belve della Citta'*, Beast of the City, July 1977.

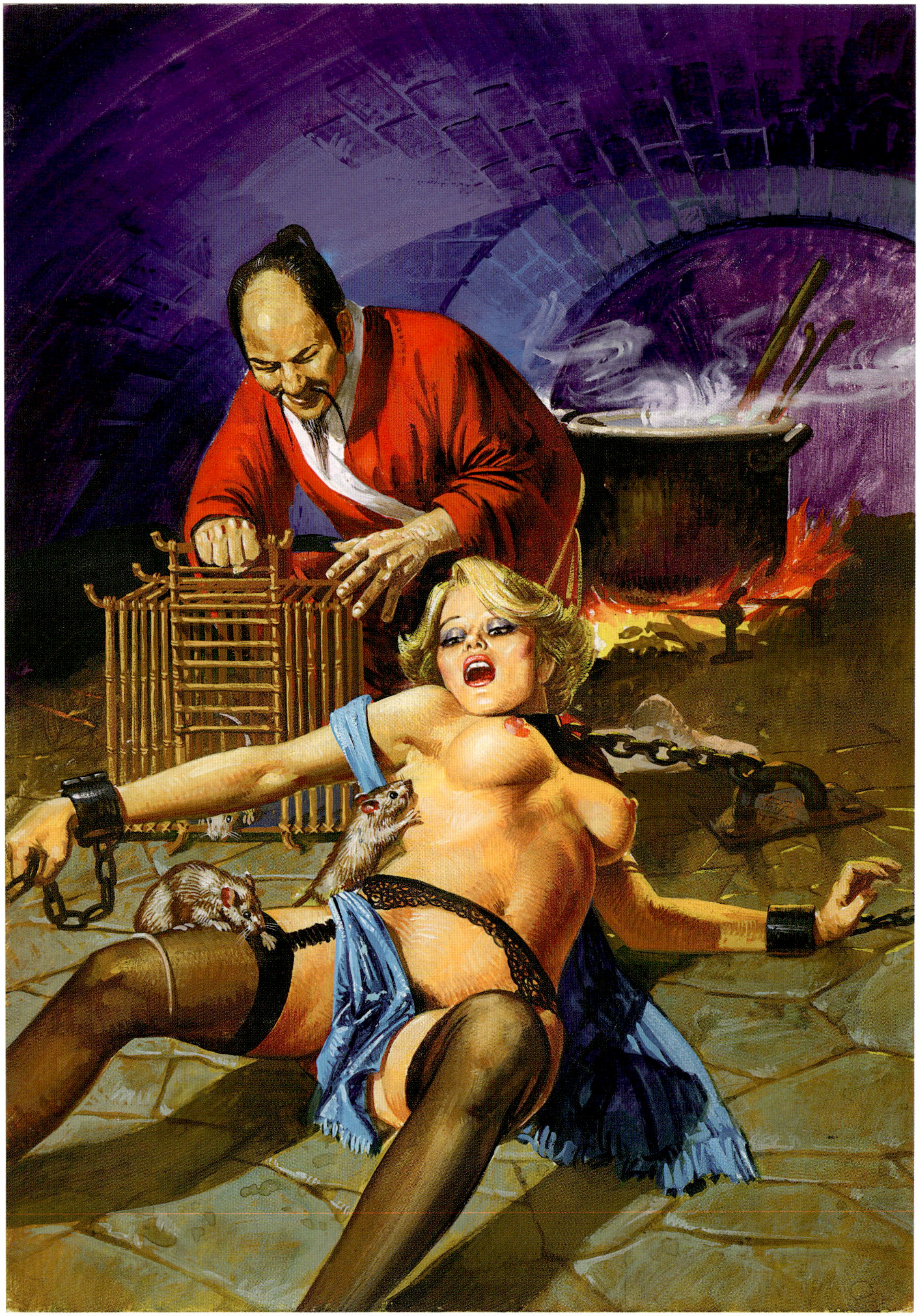

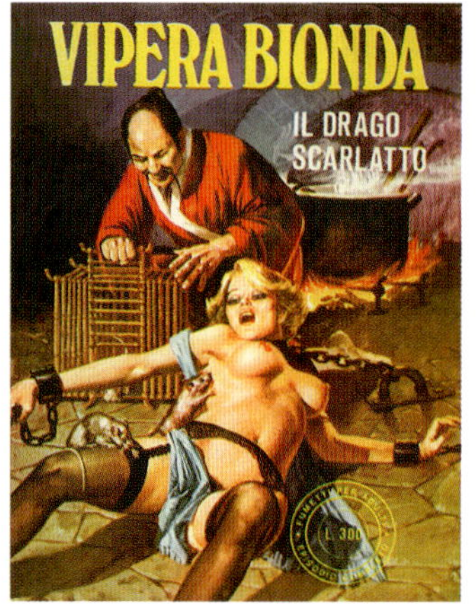

Left: Vipera Bionda, n. 5,
Il Drago Scarlatto,
The Scarlet Dragon,
November 1977.

Right: Vipera Bionda, n. 7,
I Tagliatori di Teste,
The Head Cutters,
January 1978.

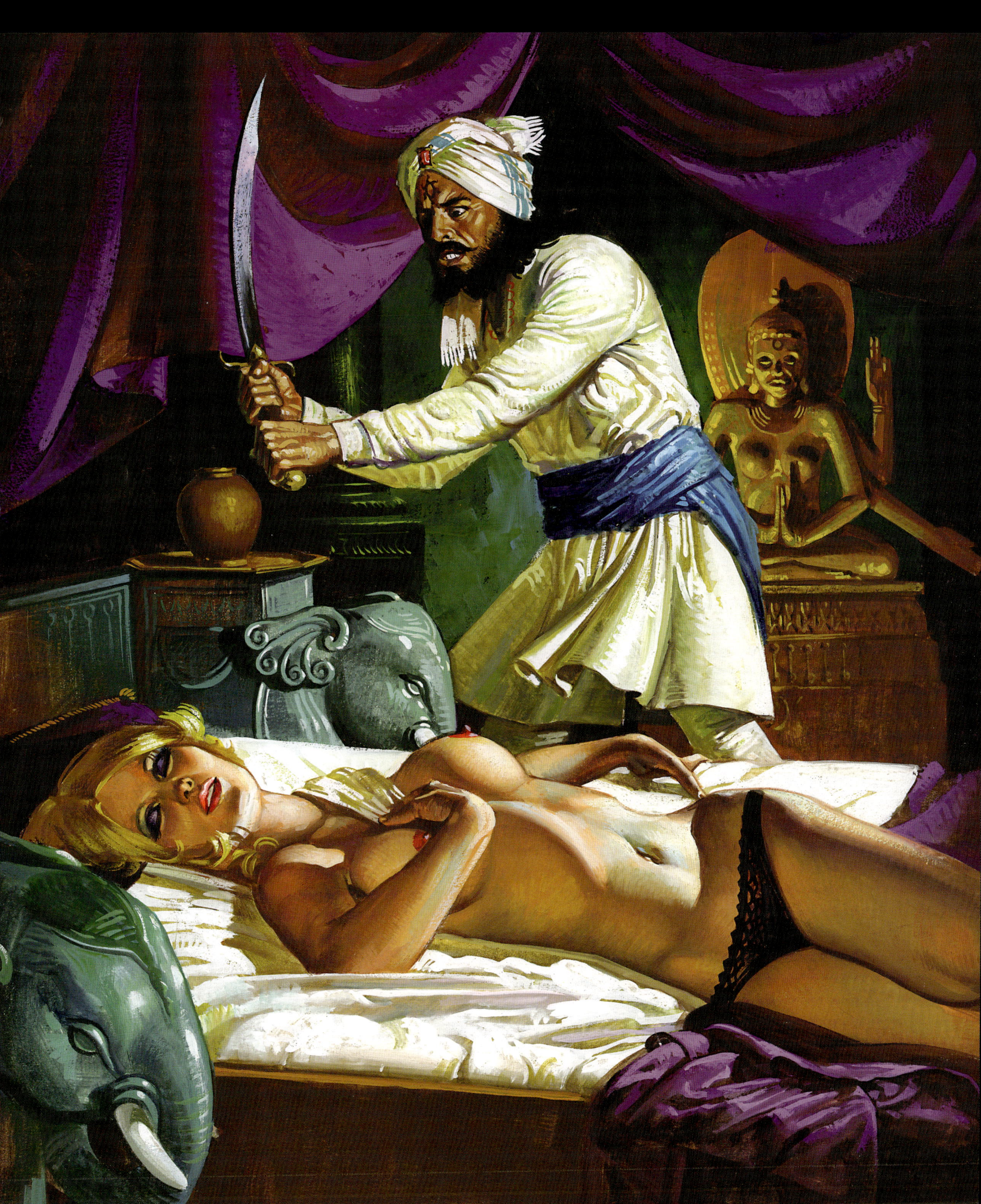

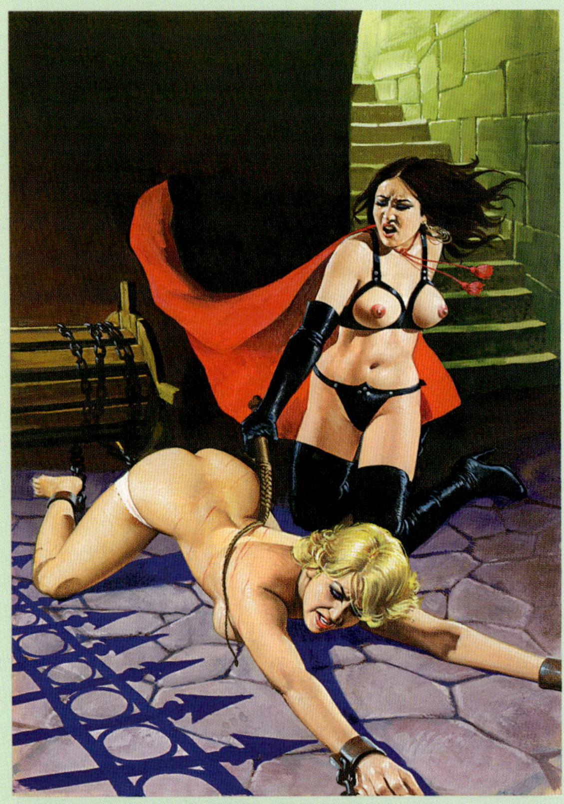

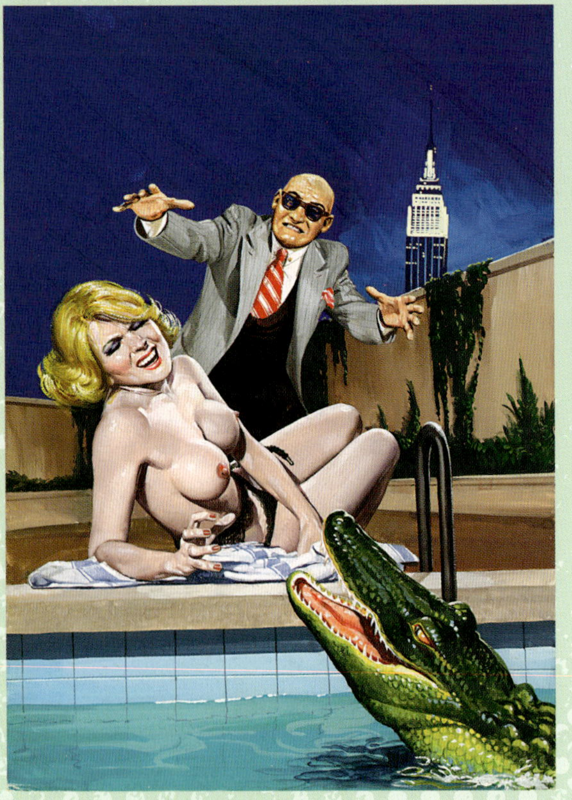

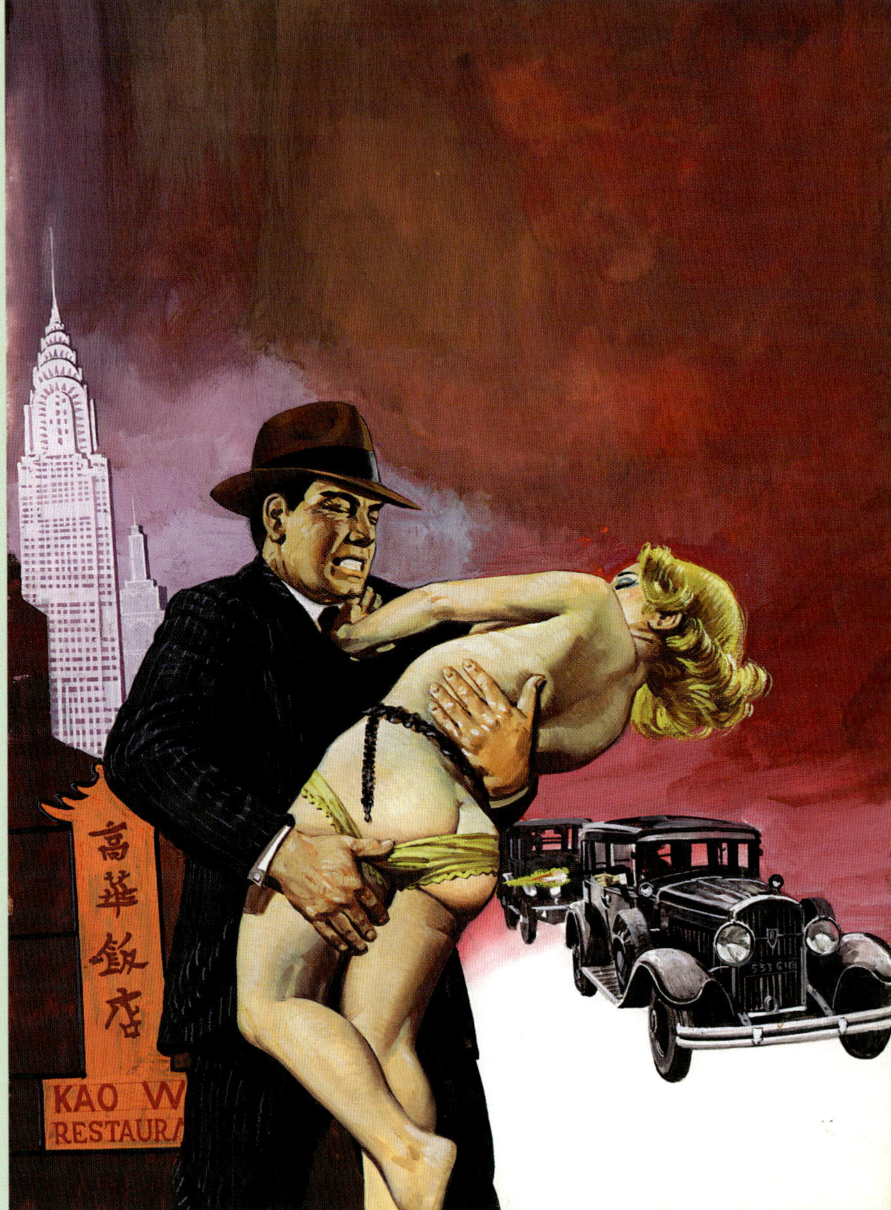

Above: Vipera Bionda, n. 10, *Massacro a New York*,
Massacre In New York, April 1978.

Top left: Vipera Bionda, n. 8, *I Killer di Parigi*,
The Killer of Paris, February 1978.

Left: Vipera Bionda, n. 9, *L'uomo dal Cranio D'argento*,
The Man with the Silver Skull, March 1978.

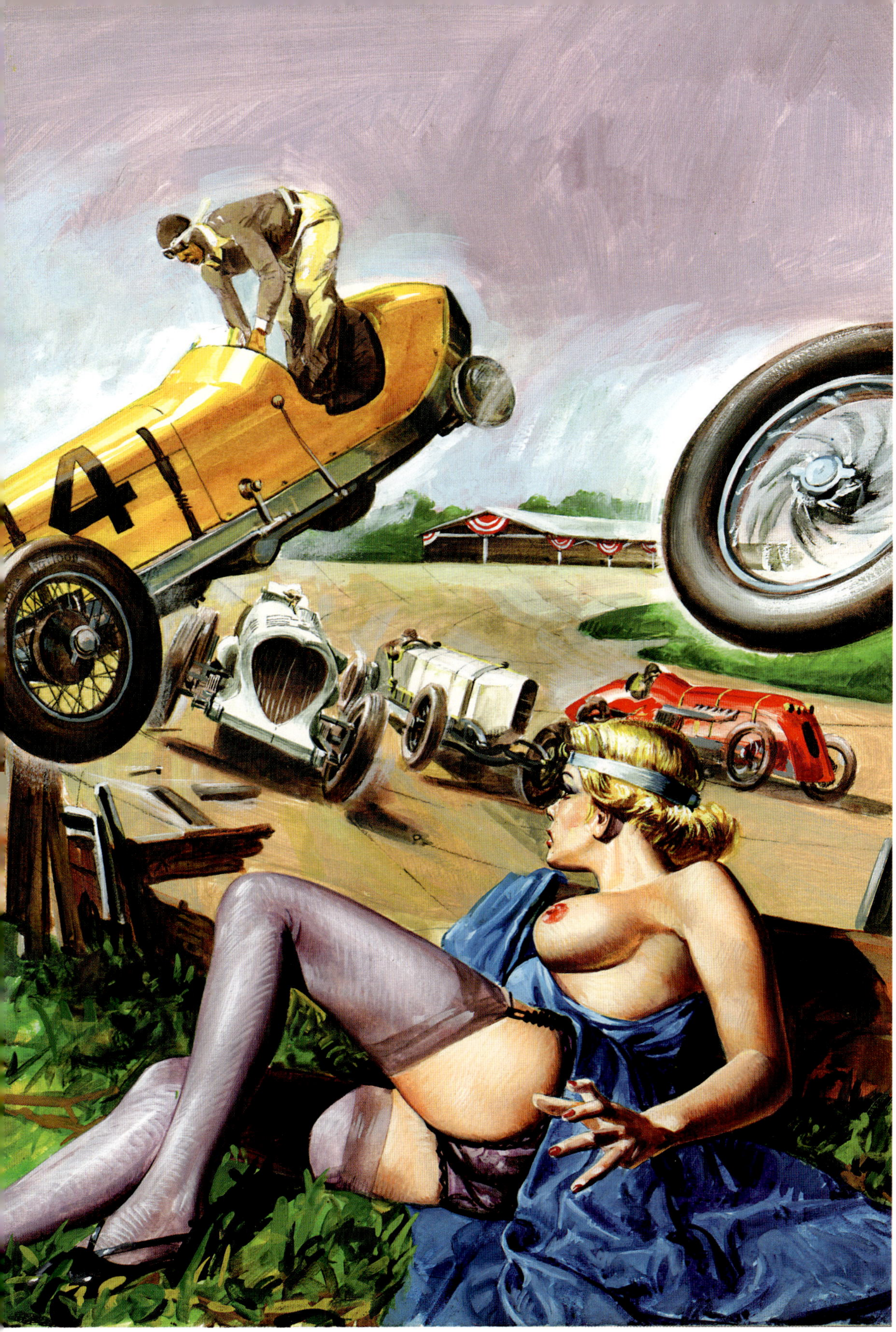

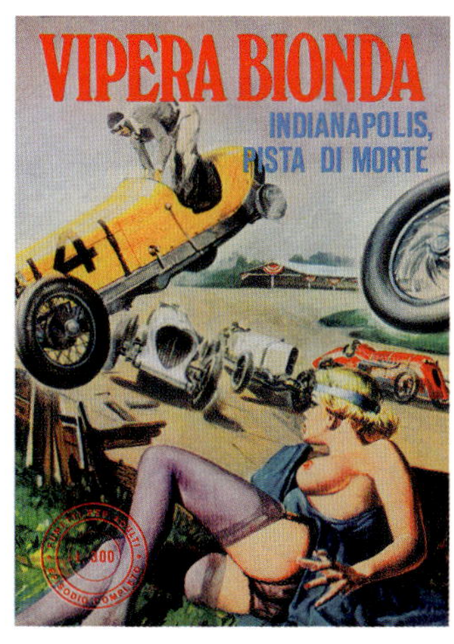

Left: Vipera Bionda, n. 11,
Indianapolis Pista di Morte,
Indianapolis Track of Death,
May 1978.

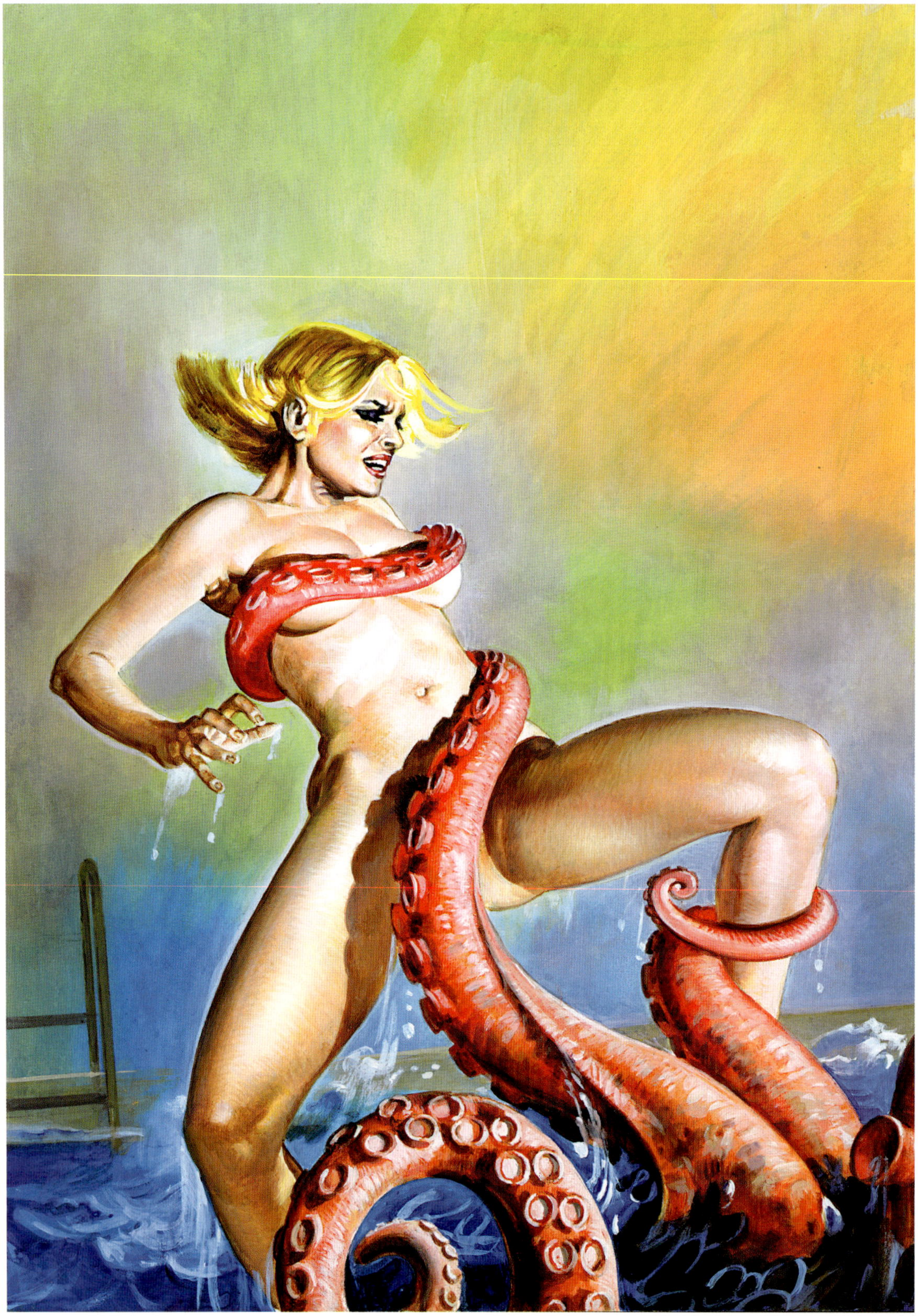

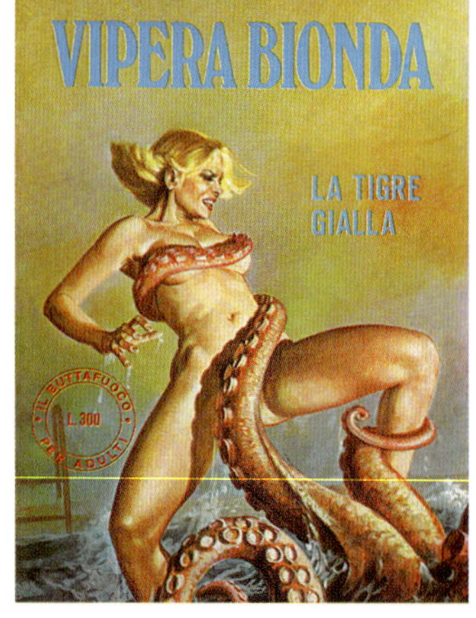

Left: Emanuele's 2012 re-creation of his original artwork for Vipera Bionda, n. 12, *La Tigre Gialla,* The Yellow Tiger, June 1978.

Right: Vipera Bionda, n. 15, *La Chiesa di Satana,* The Church of Satan, September 1978.

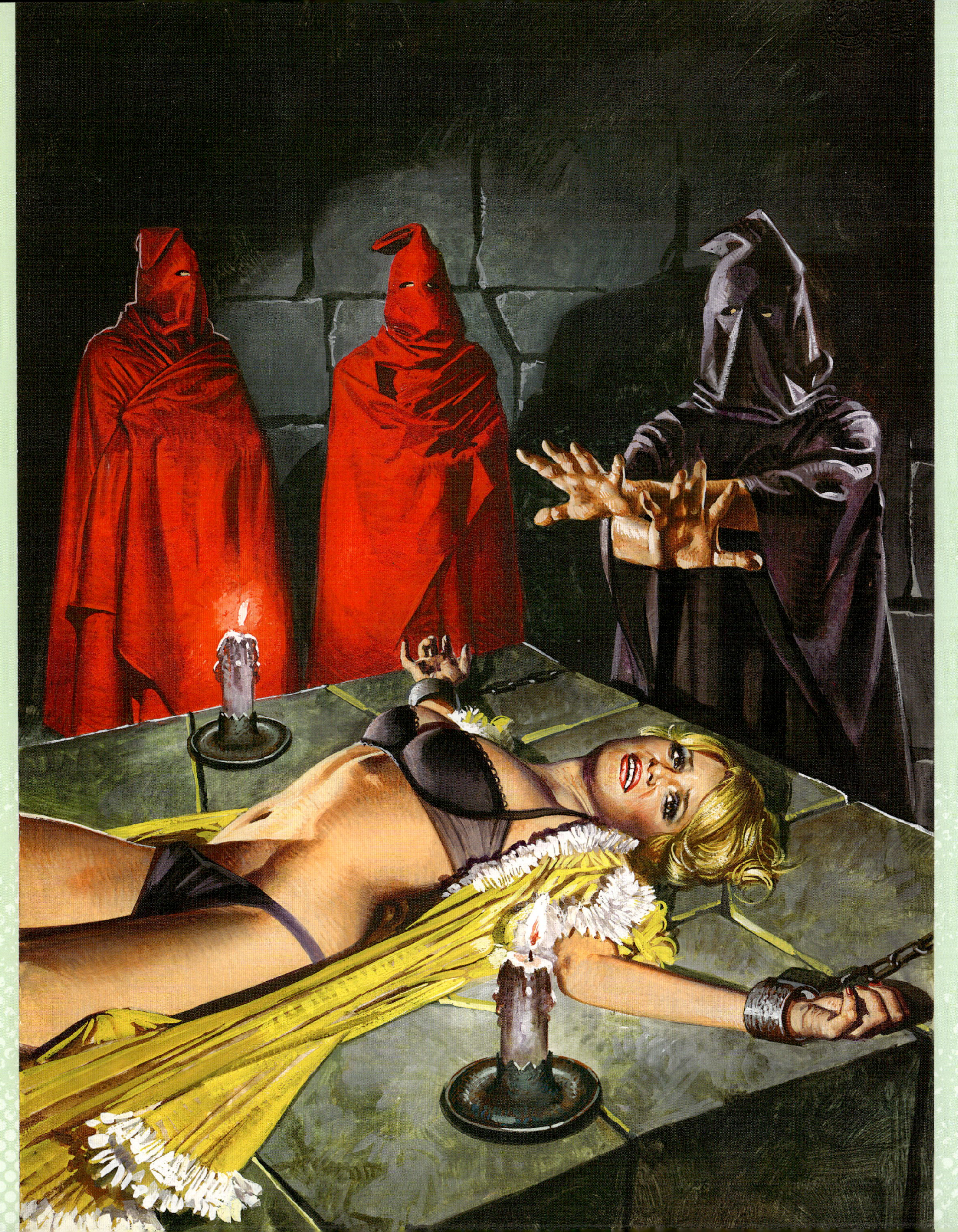

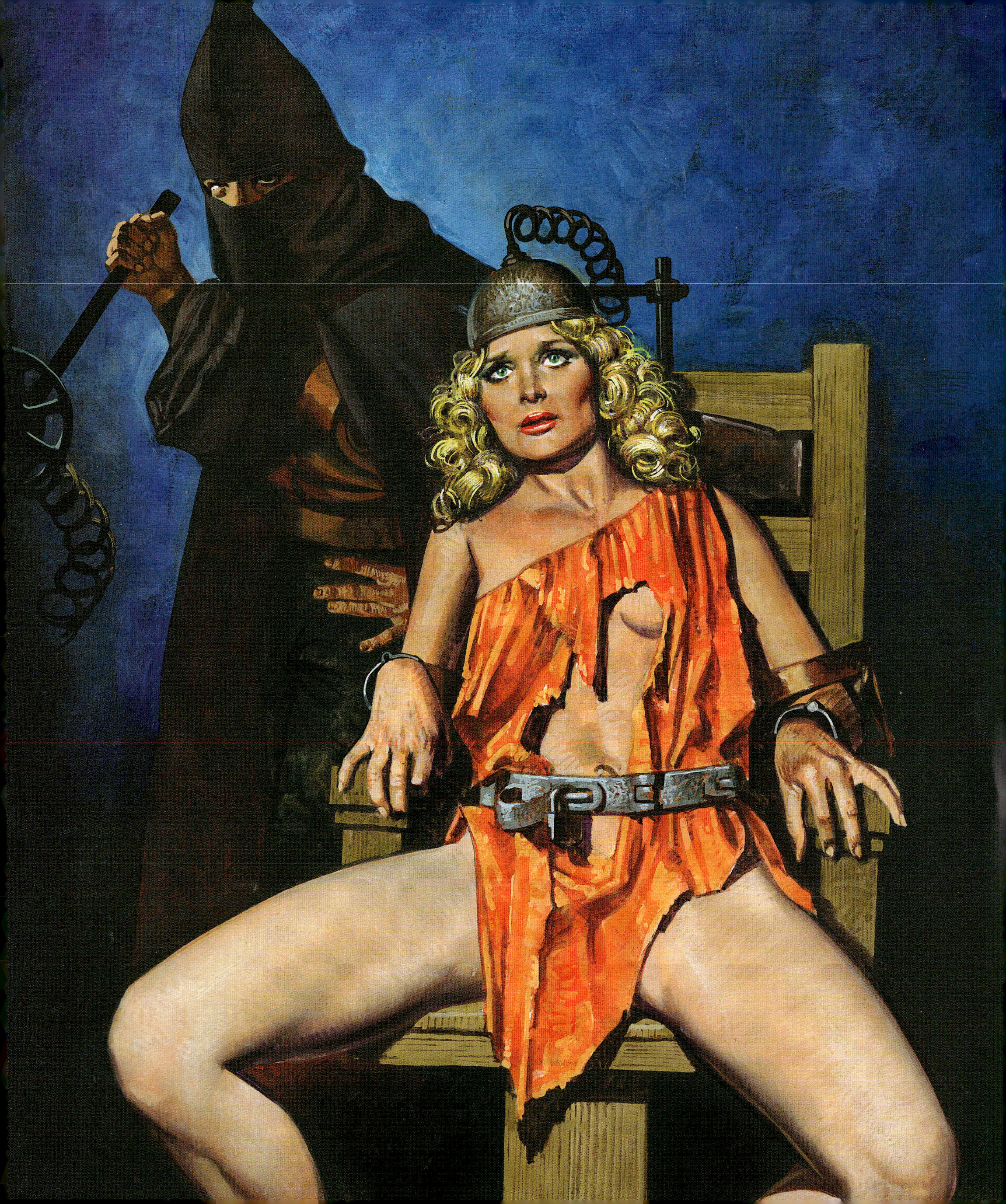

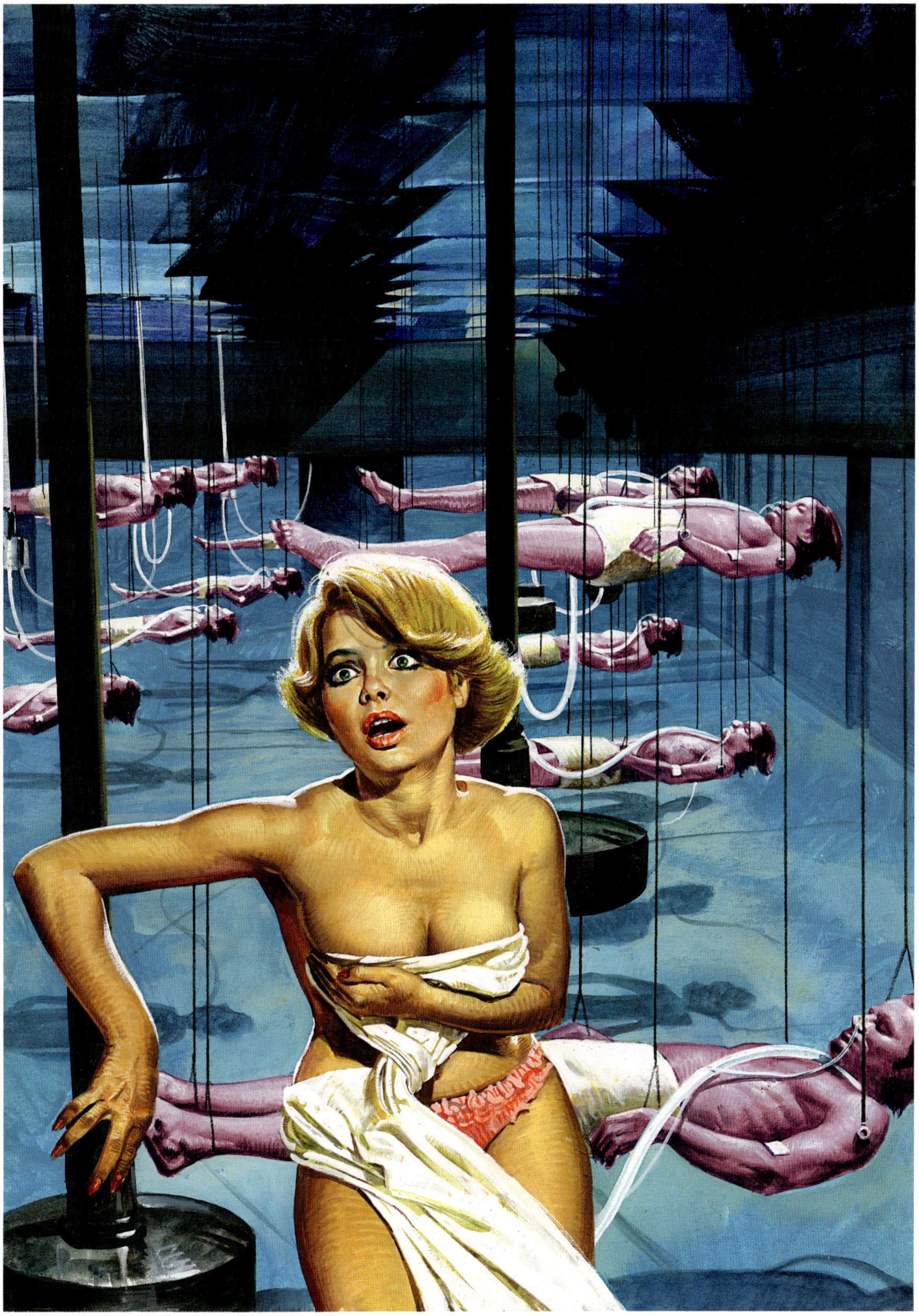

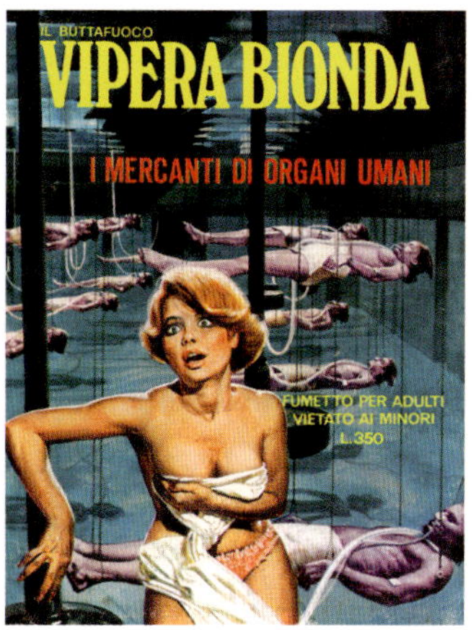

Left: Vipera Bionda, n. 17, *I Mercanti di Organi Umani*, The Merchants of Human Organs, November 1978.

Far left: Vipera Bionda, n. 16, *Sedia Electrica*, The Electric Chair, October 1978.

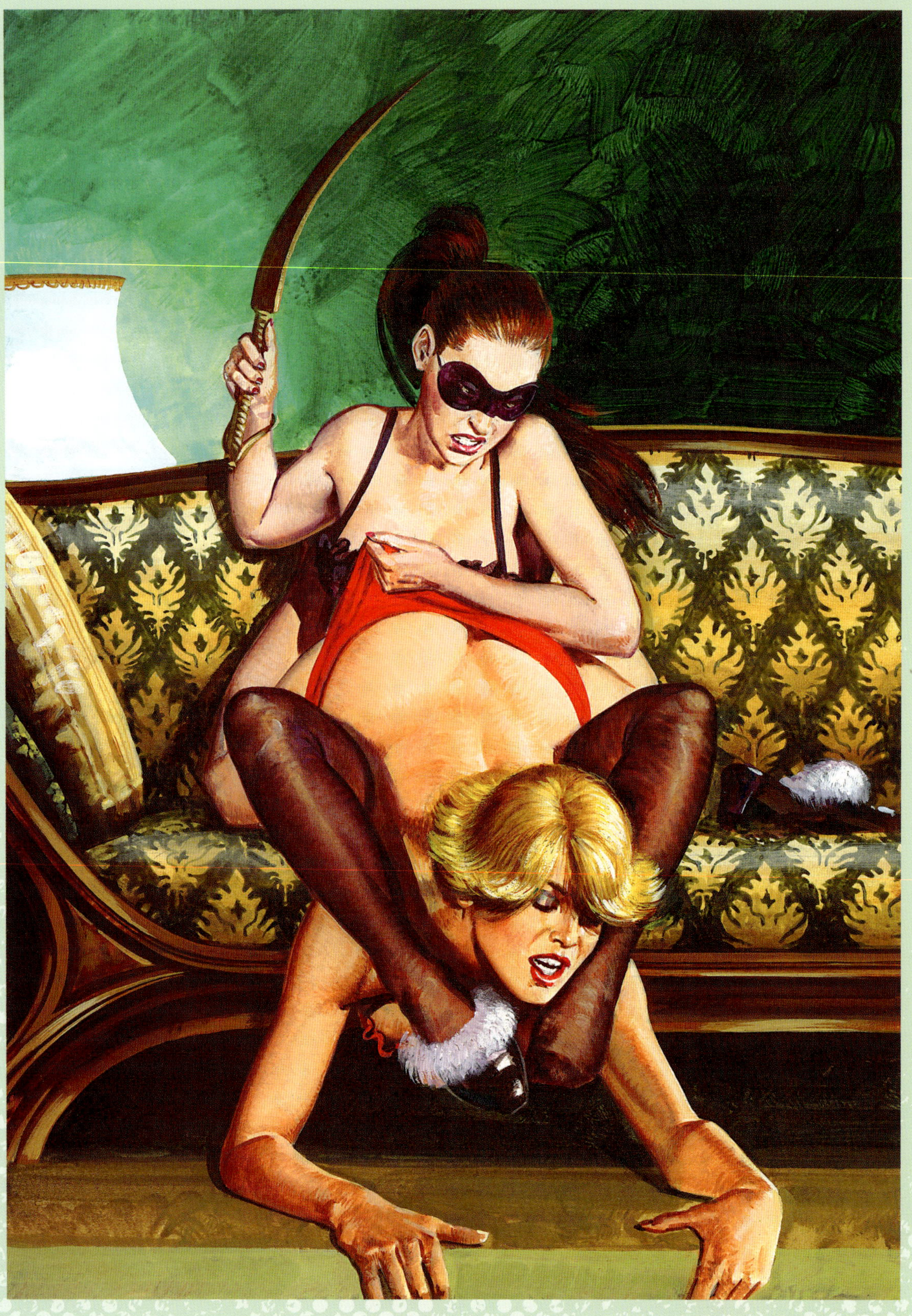

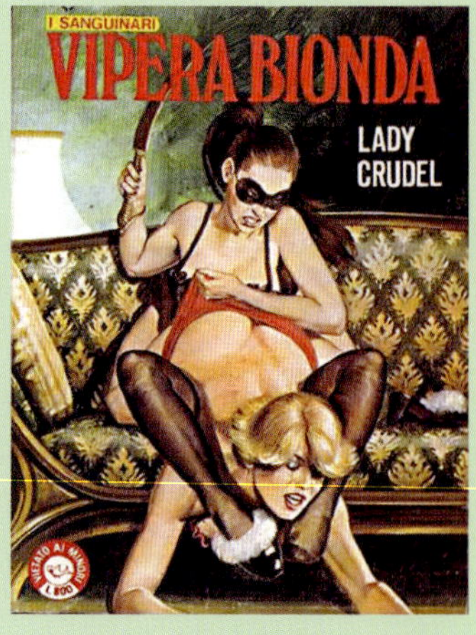

Left: Vipera Bionda, n. 2, *Lady Crudel,* Lady Cruel, August 1982.

Right: Vipera Bionda, n. 12, *Colpo da un Milione di Dollari,* Blow a Million Dollars, June 1981.

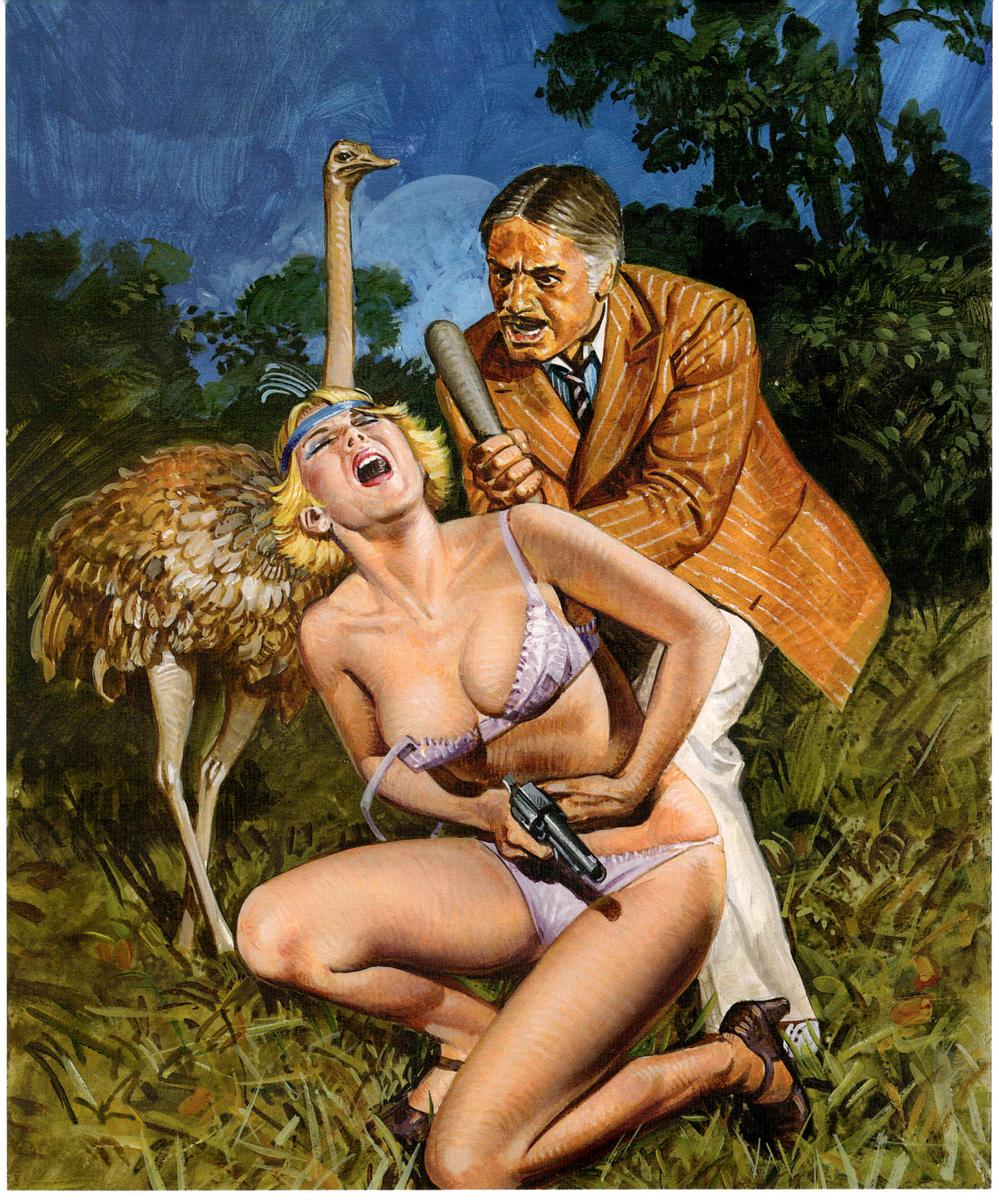

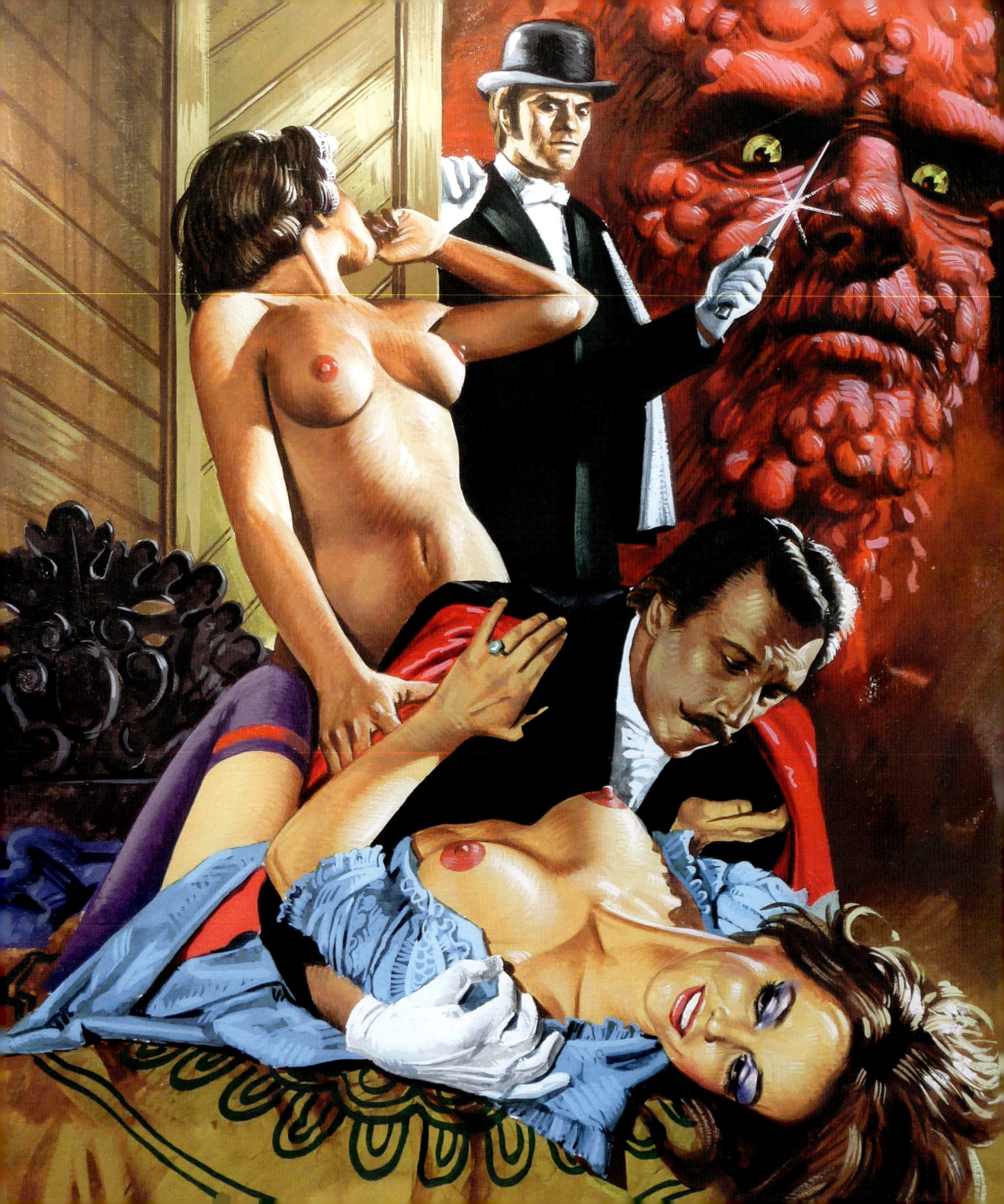

WALLESTEIN IL MOSTRO

PUBLISHED 1972–1982; 133 ISSUES

The protagonist of this horror series is Jimmy Wallestein, a hideous monster who is made up of formless matter that can spontaneously regenerate, making him virtually immortal. The story begins when the wealthy Count Wallestein is killed by his sister and her husband, who want to cash in their inheritance early. The count's son, playboy Jimmy Wallestein, hides his terribly deformed face behind a mask and gains possession of his father's castle, from where he launches a mission of vengeance against those who killed the count. Wallenstein's girlfriend discovers his secret, but agrees to help him. Wallestein dispatches his father's murderers before turning his eye to criminal organizations and other individuals, who are massacred in a gore fest that is so horrendously violent it borders on parody.

Left: Wallestein il Mostro, n. 5, *Il Mulatto*, The Mulatto, May 1975.

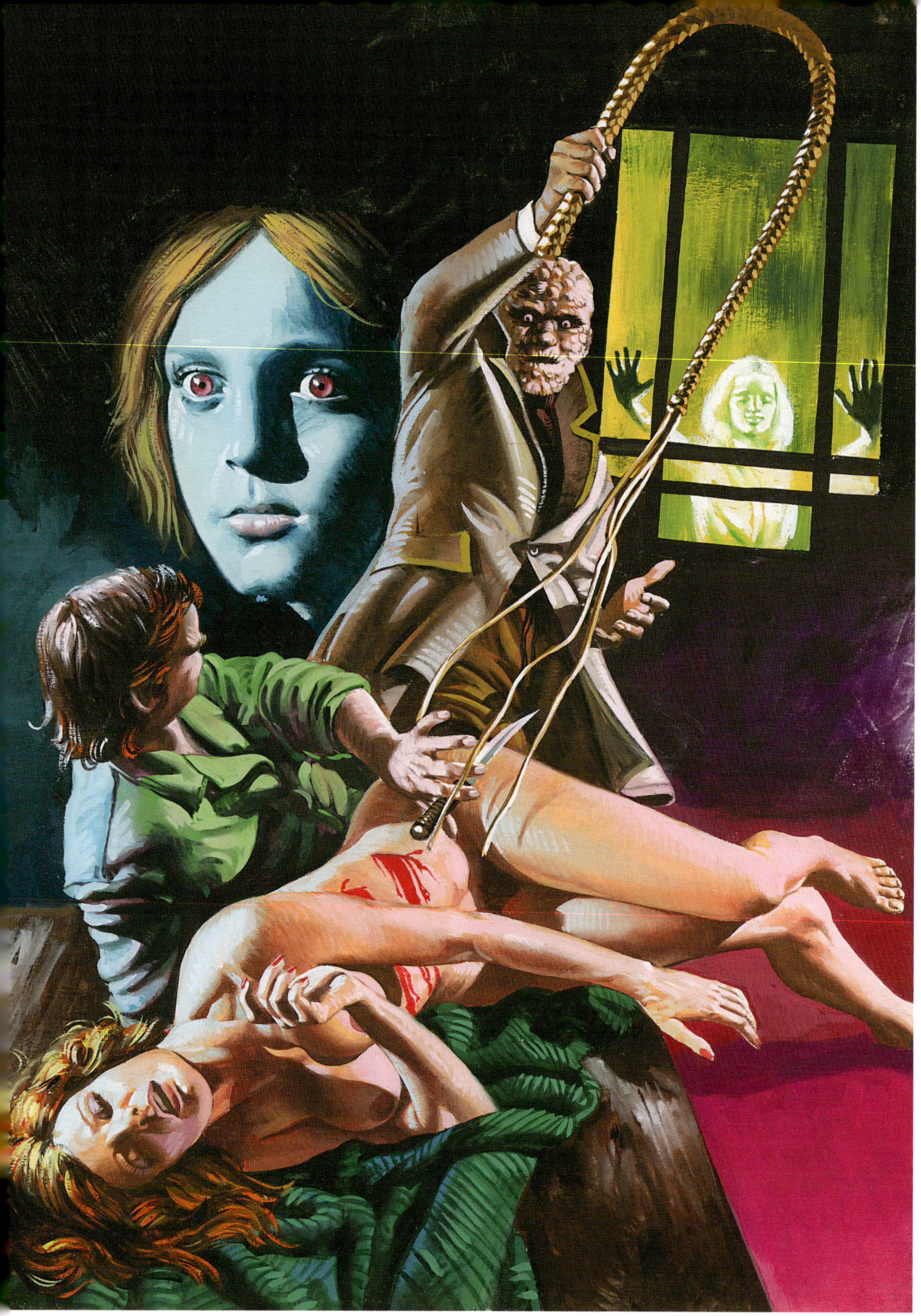

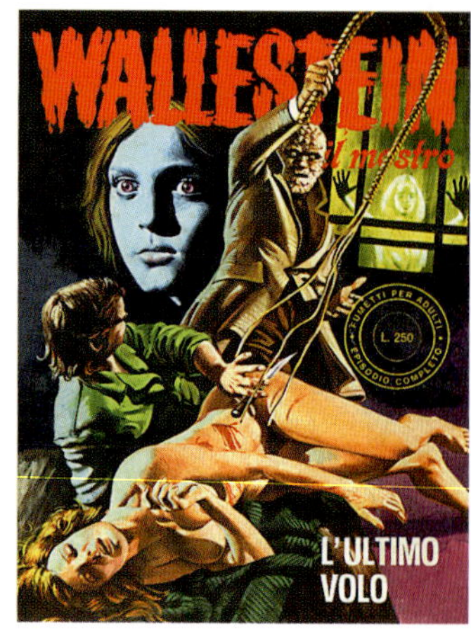

Left: Wallestein il Mostro,
n. 2, *L'Ultimo Volo*,
The Last Flight,
February 1975.

Right: Wallestein il Mostro,
n. 8, *La Spirale della Paura*,
The Spiral of Fear,
May 1974.

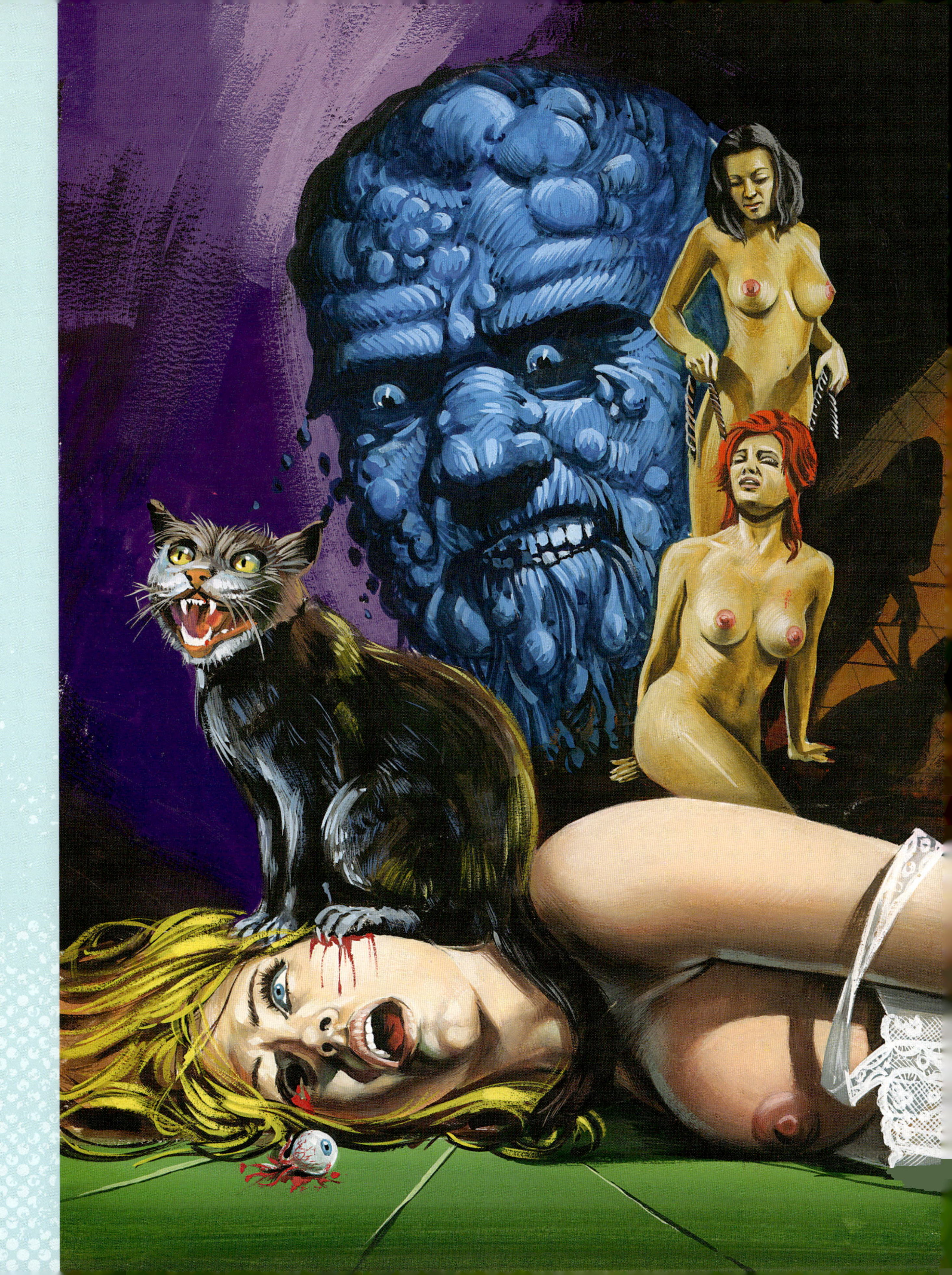

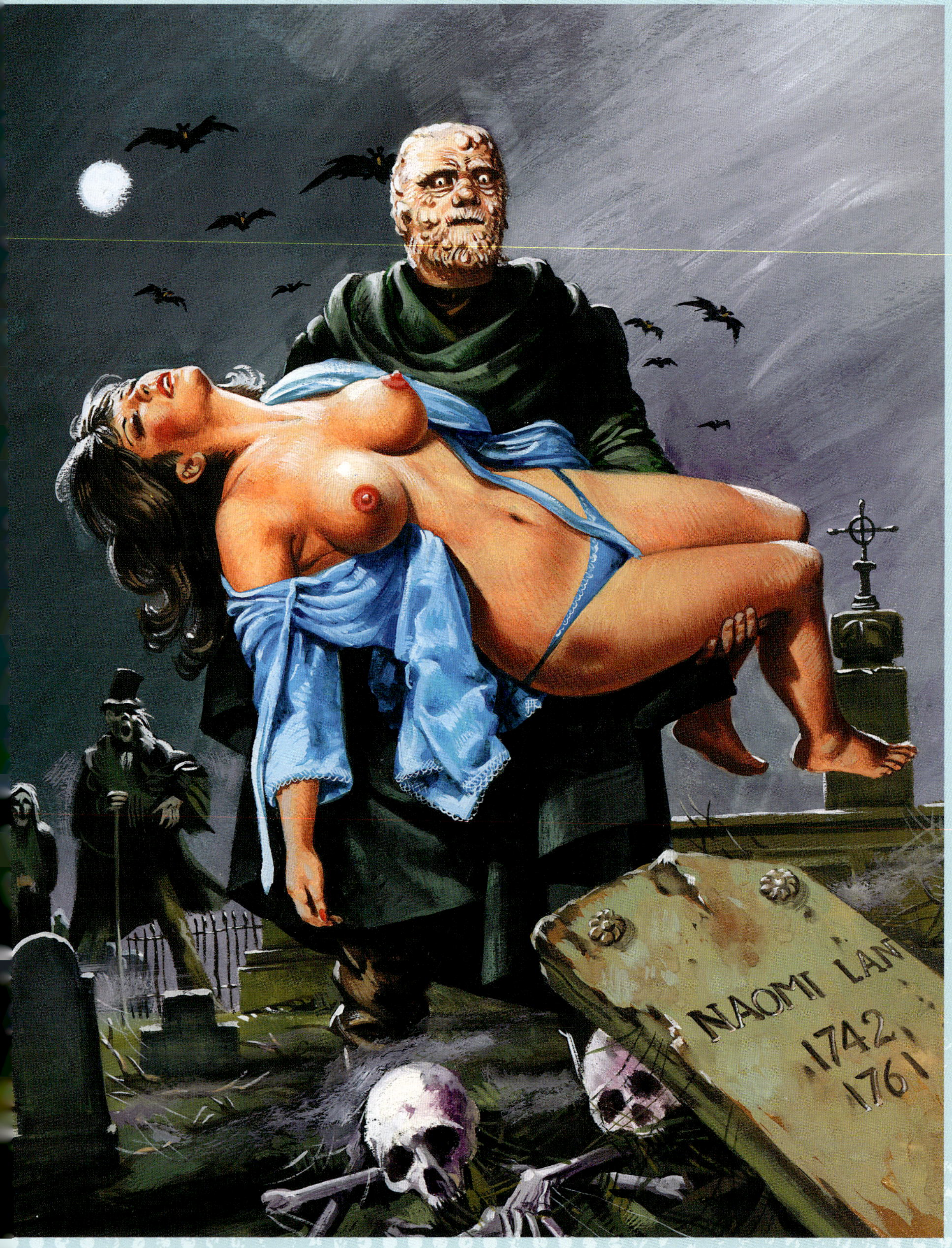

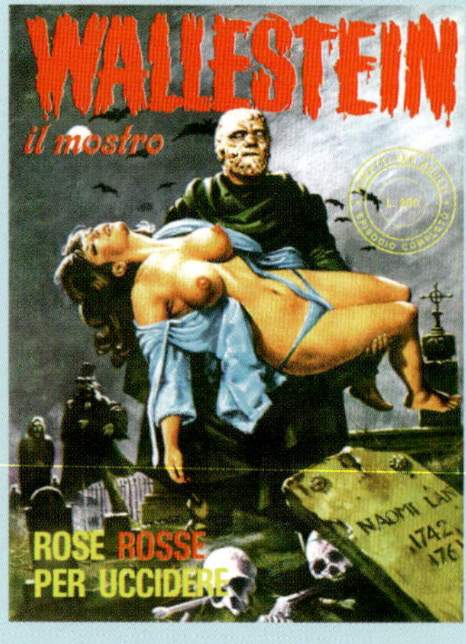

Left: Wallestein il Mostro, n. 8, *Rose Rosse per Uccidere*, Red Roses for Killing, August 1975.

Right: Wallestein il Mostro, n. 40, *Brividi di Orrore*, Horror Chills, August 1977.

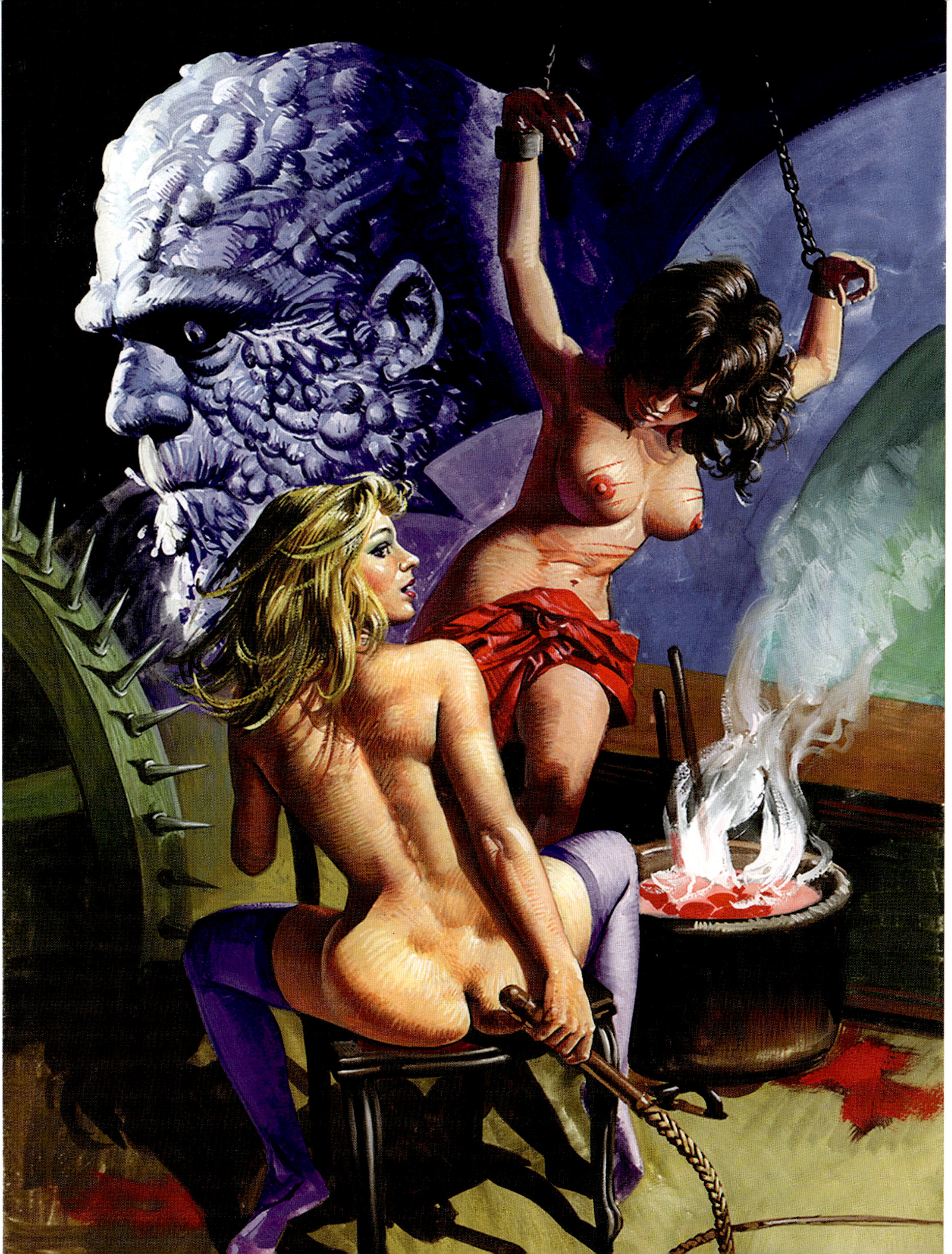

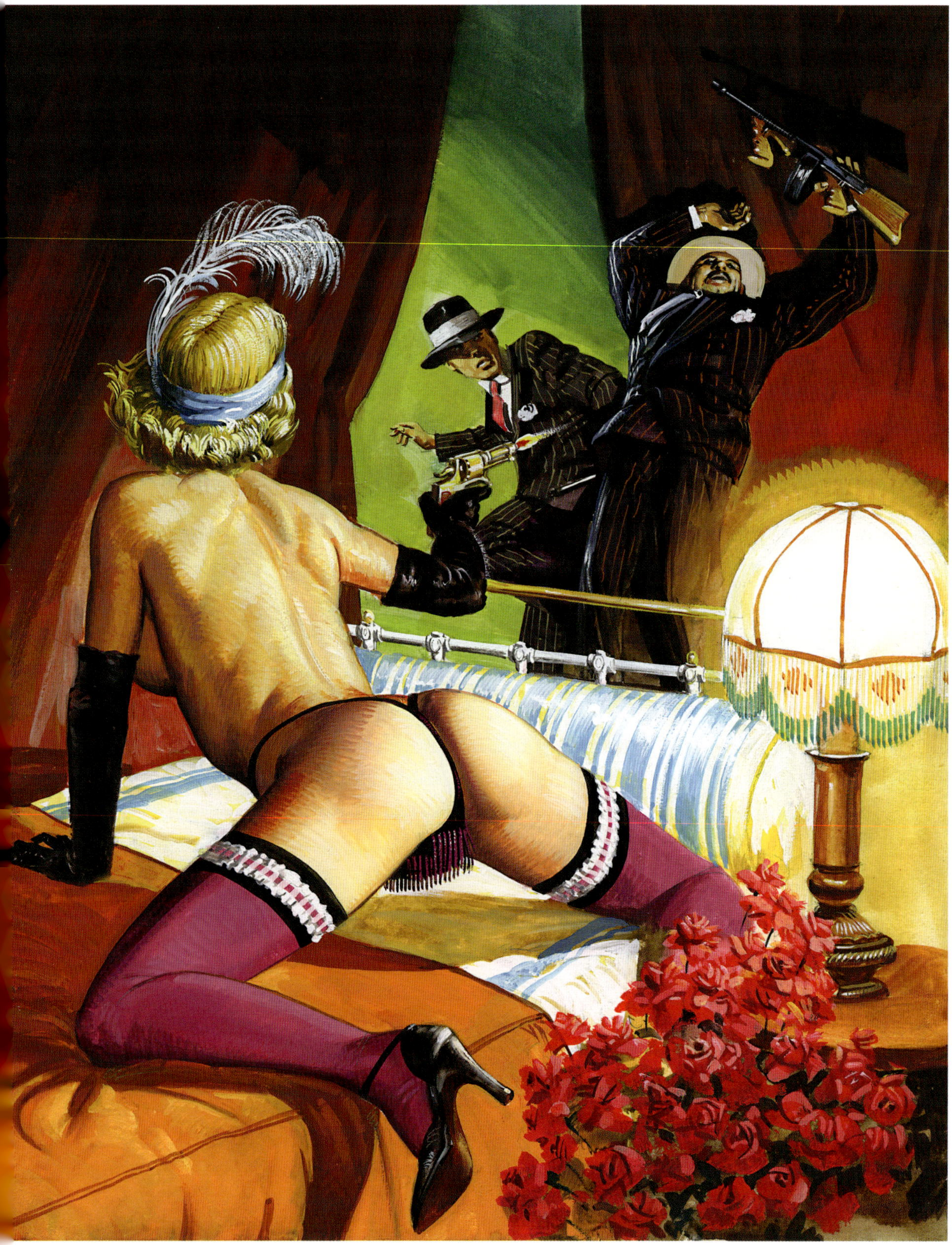

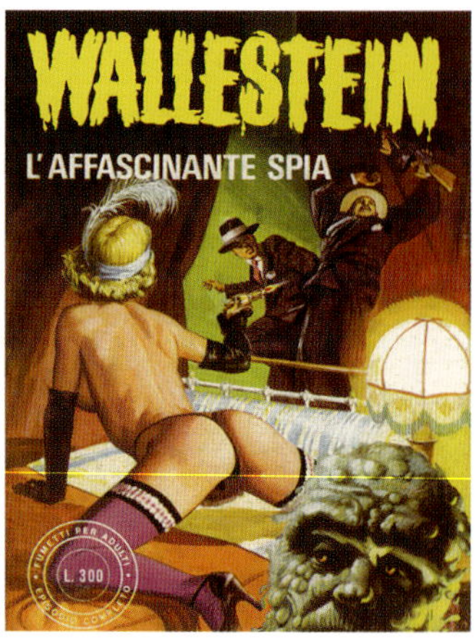

Left: Wallestein il Mostro,
n. 41, *L'Affascinante Spia*,
The Fascinating Spy,
August 1977.

Right: Wallestein il Mostro,
n. 45, *Il Segreto della Contessa*,
The Countess's Secret,
October 1977.

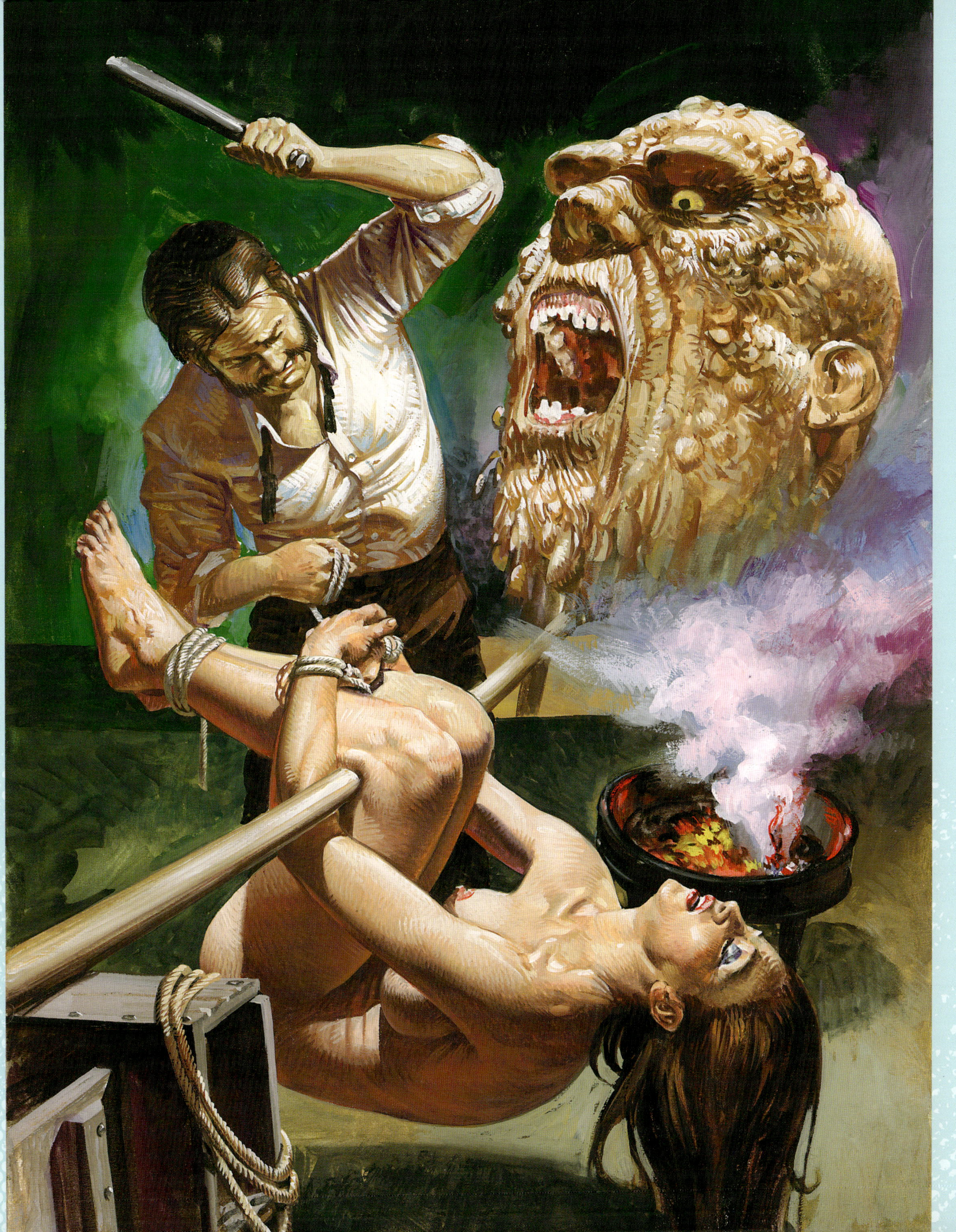

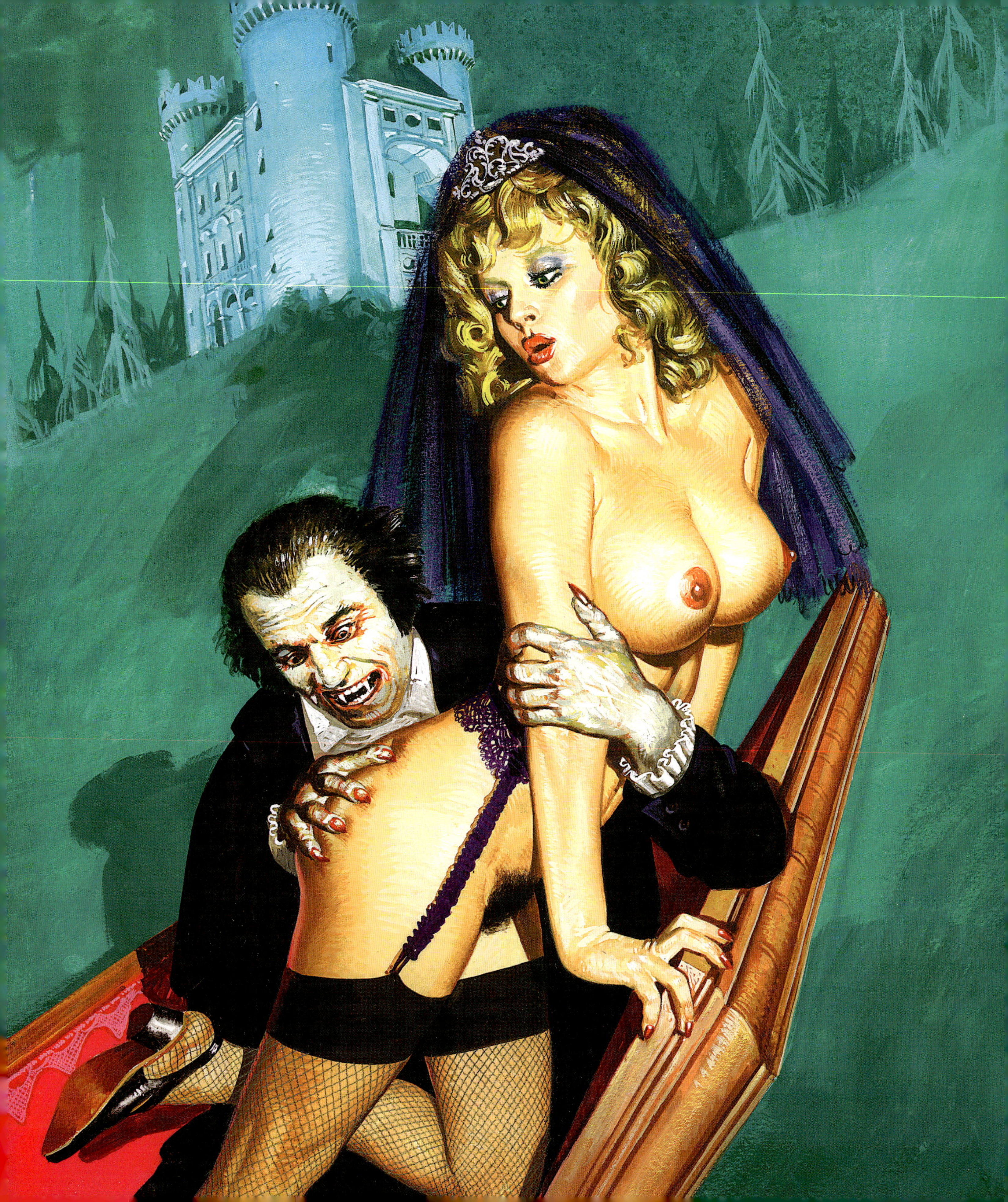

ZORA LA VAMPIRA

PUBLISHED 1972–1985; 288 ISSUES

"Zora the Vampire" is one of several voluptuous heroines to feature in '70s and '80s *fumetti*. The covers and stories usually show them being terrorized by all kinds of predatory and malevolent ghosts, killers and monsters. But few covers captured the iconic imagery of the horror genre as well as Emanuele's. Zora Pabst, a 19th-century aristocrat who has been possessed by the spirit of Dracula, sucks her way around the world, and even into outer space, satisfying both her sexual desires and her lust for blood. Her appearance is partly inspired by that of French actress Catherine Deneuve.

Left: Zora la Vampira, n. 62, *Ce l'Aveva coi Denti*, He had it with his Teeth, May 1977.

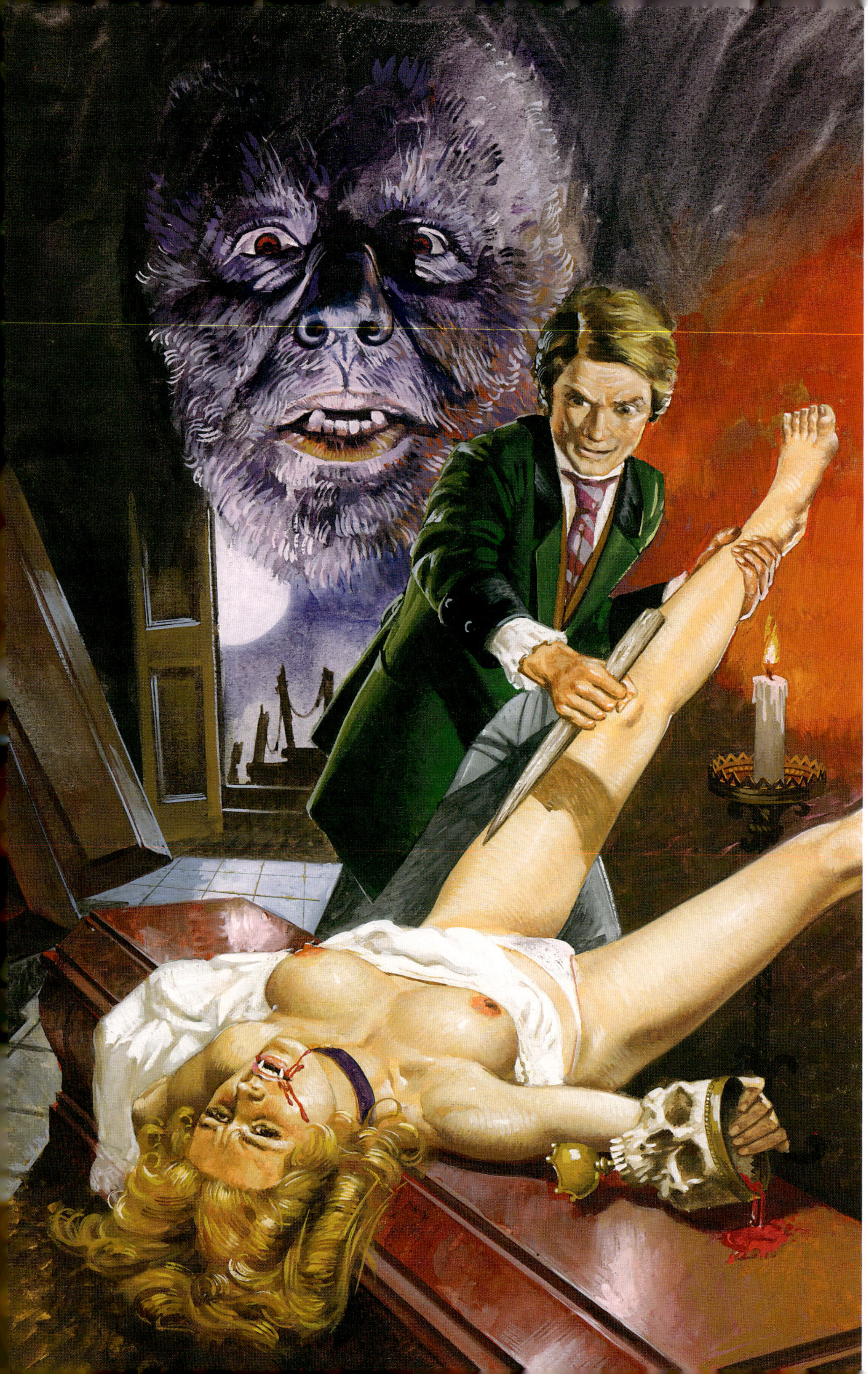

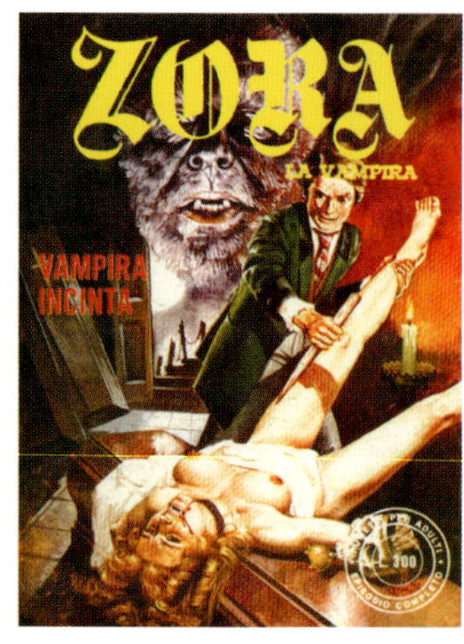

Left: Zora la Vampira, n. 59, *Vampira Incinta*, The Pregnant Vampire, April 1977.

Right: Zora la Vampira, n. 68, *Fig Kong,* Fig Kong, August 1977.

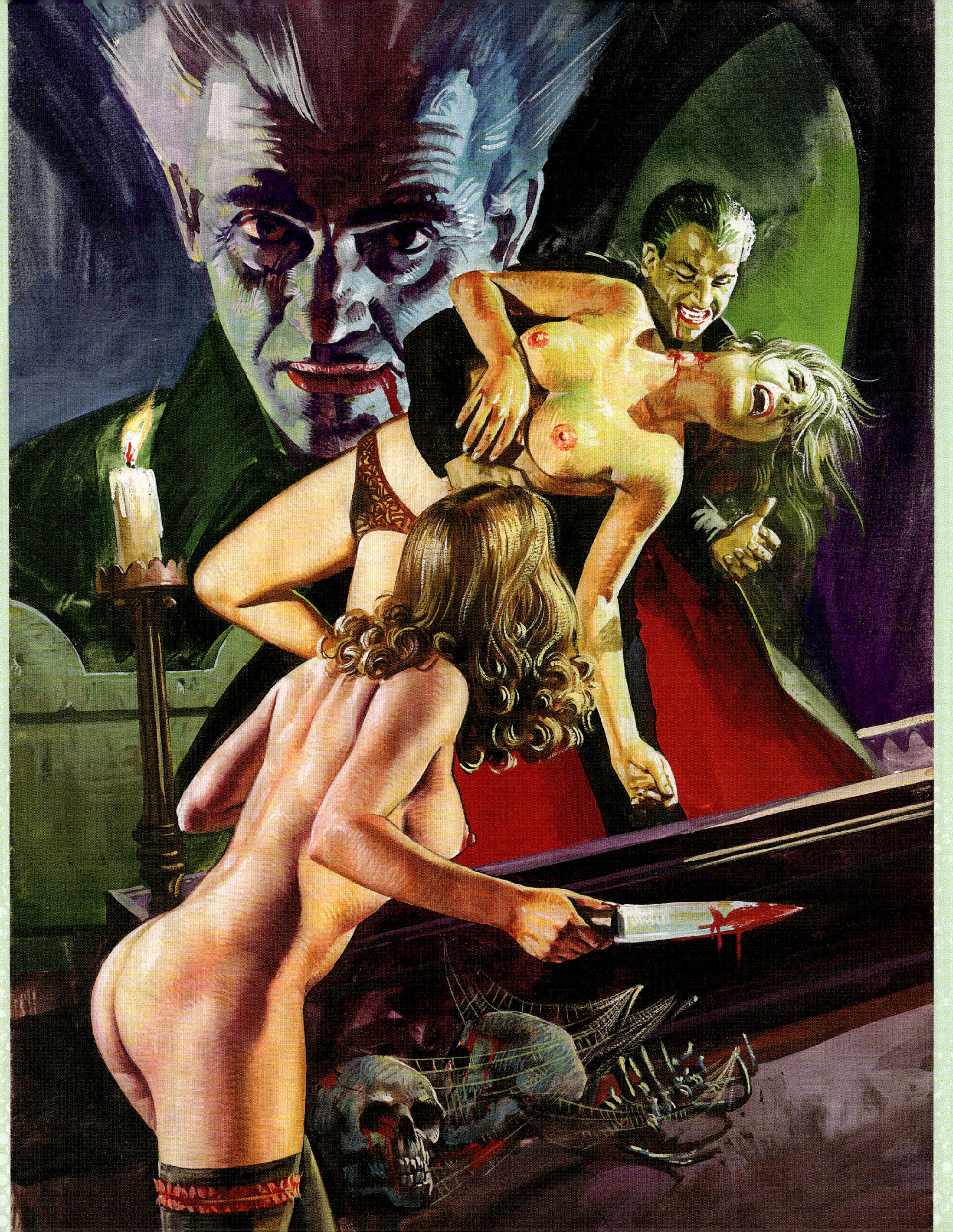

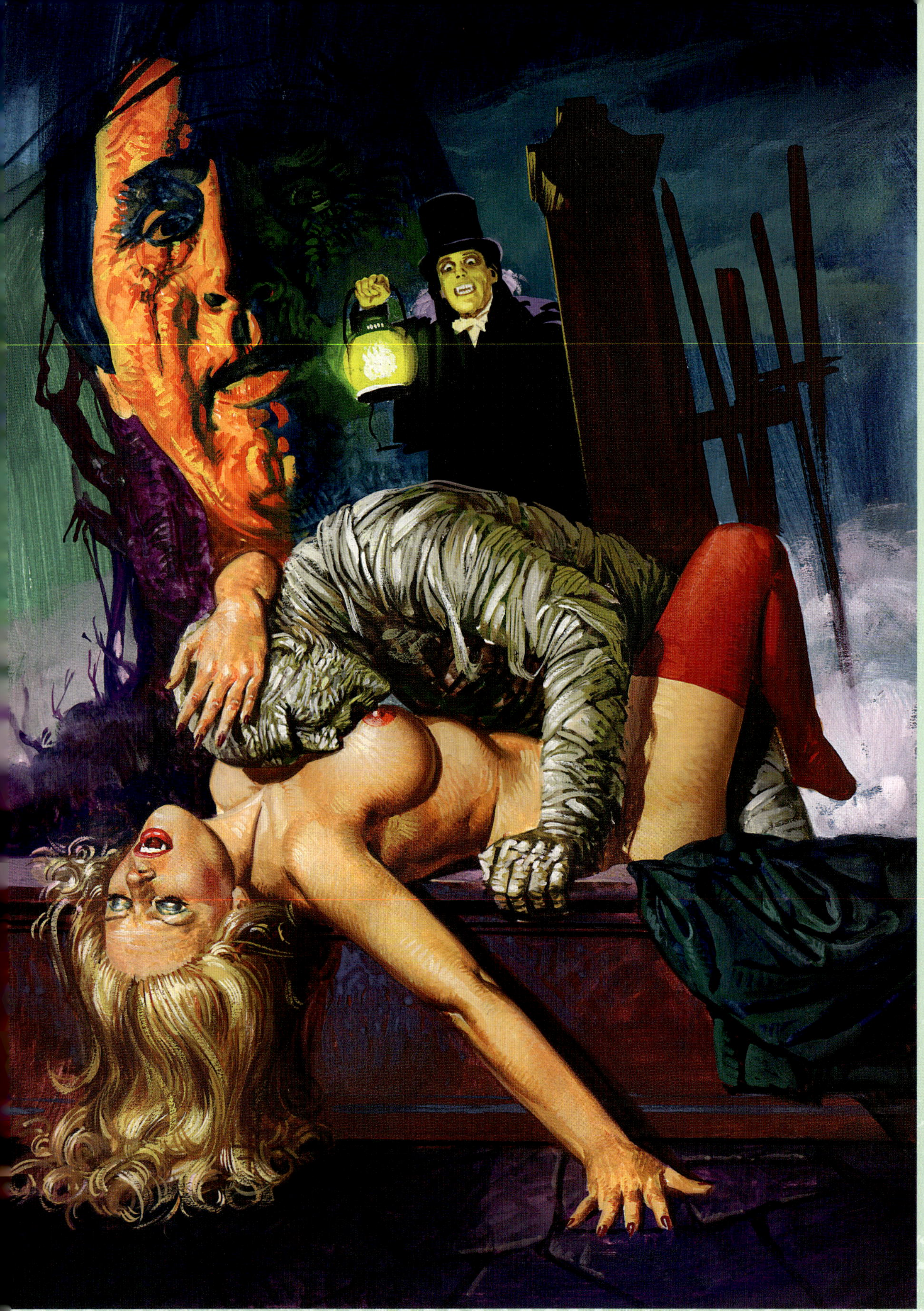

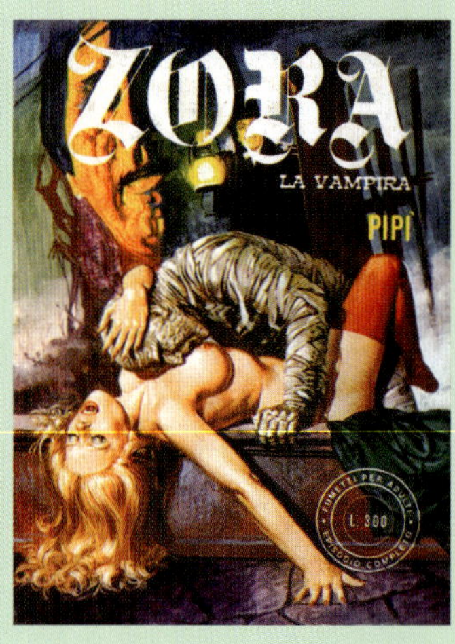

Left: Zora la Vampira, n. 74, *Pipi*, Pipi, October 1977.

Right: Zora la Vampira, n. 75, *Zora Bambina*, Baby Zora, November 1977.

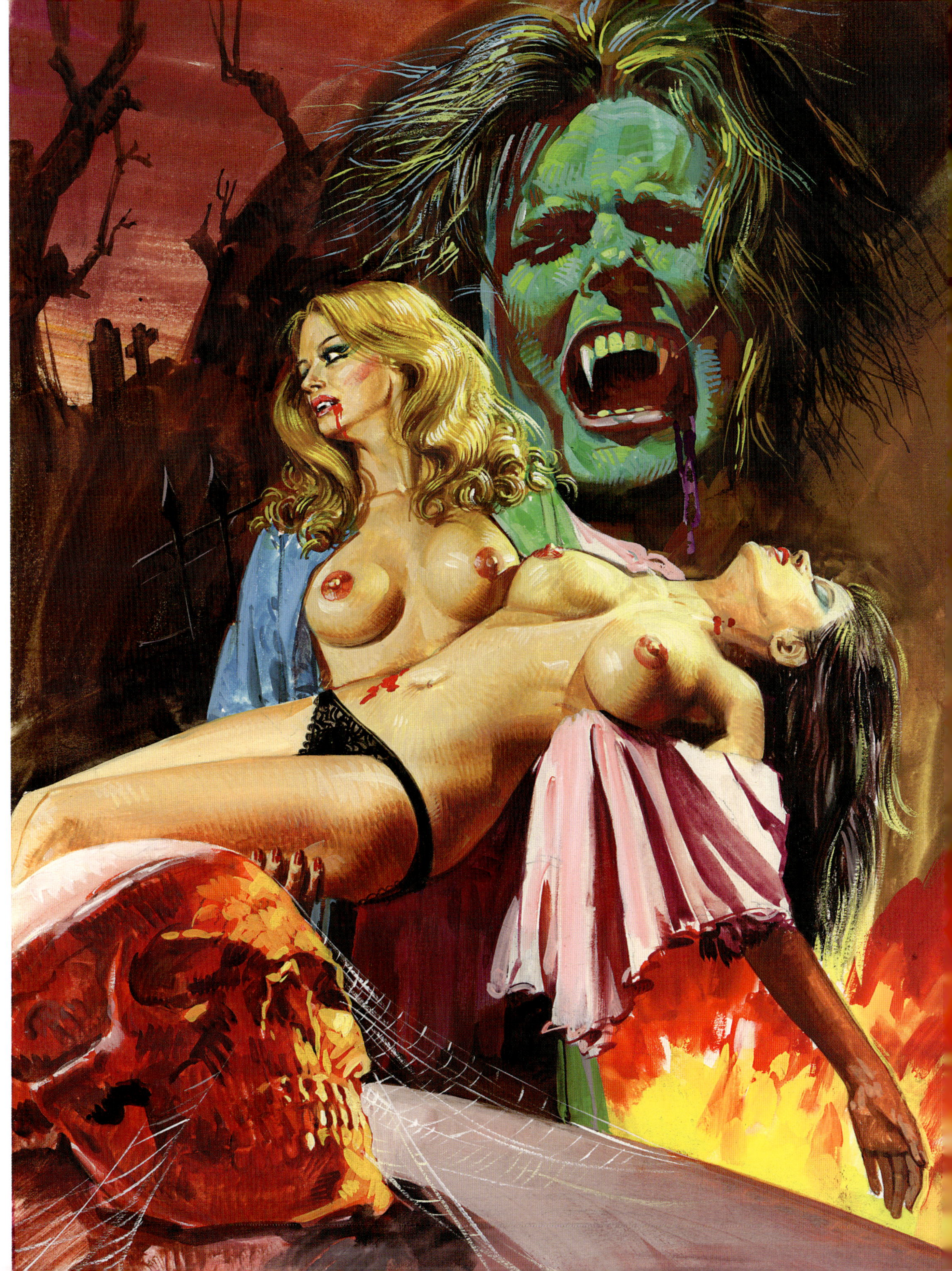

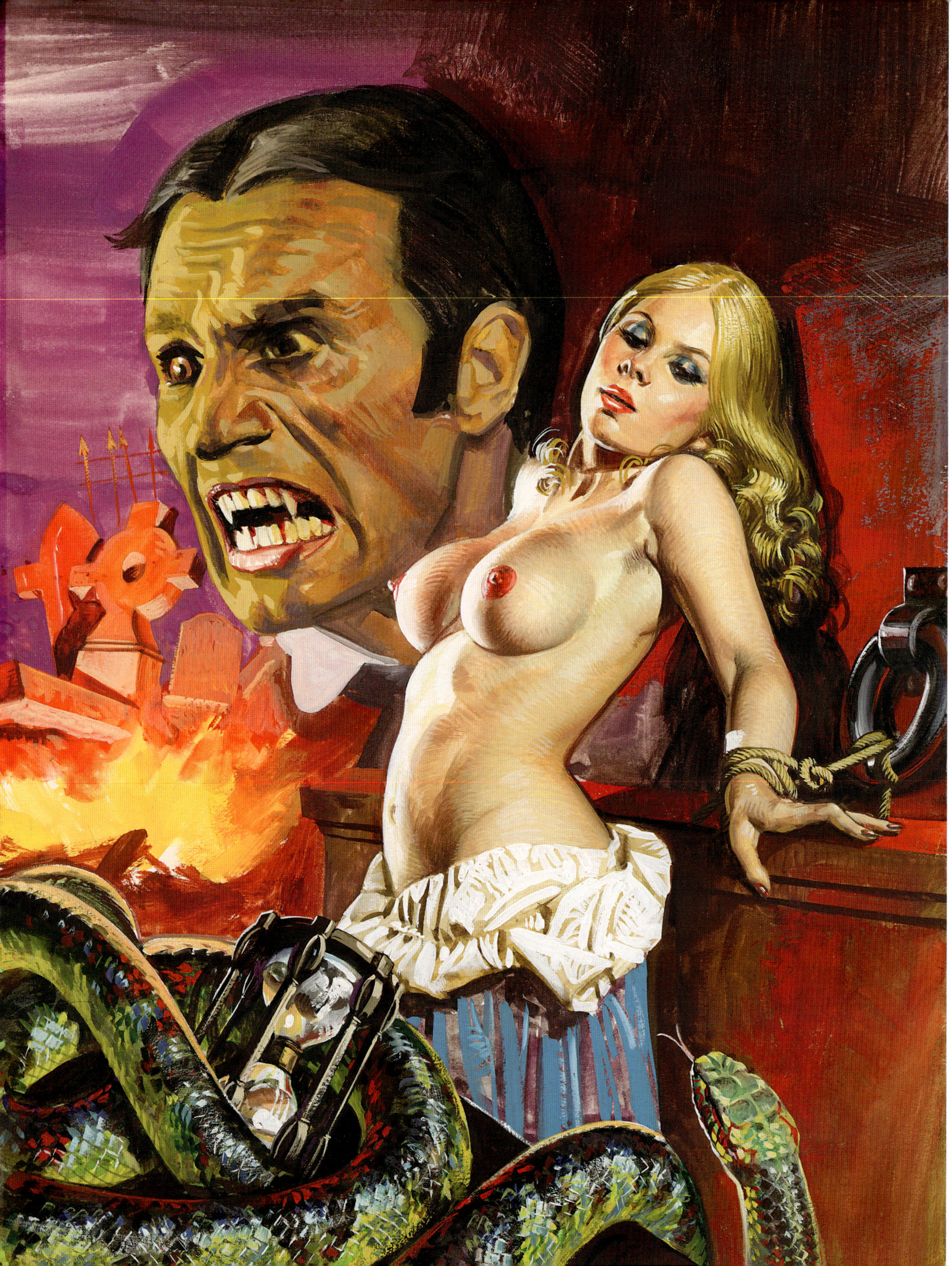

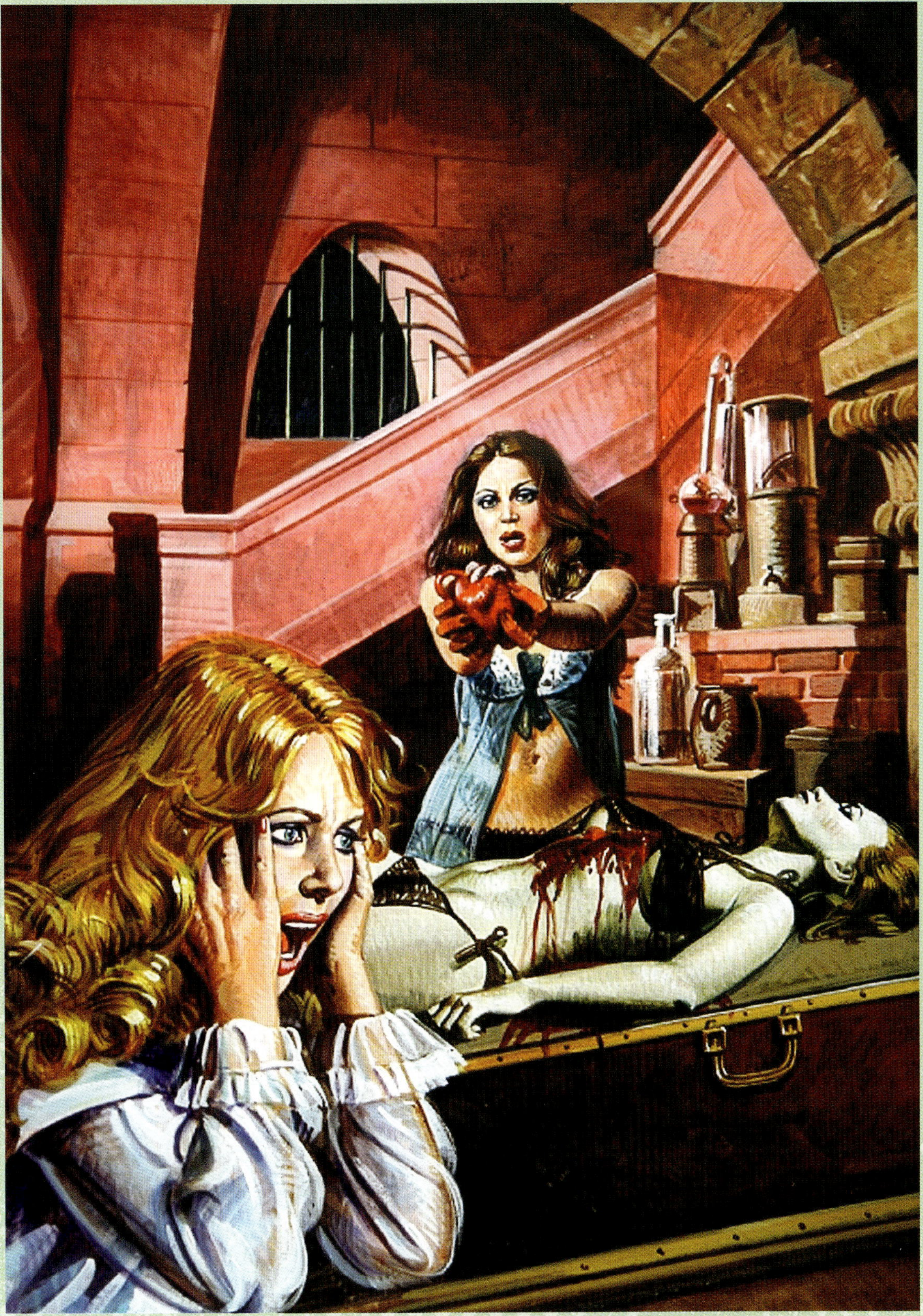

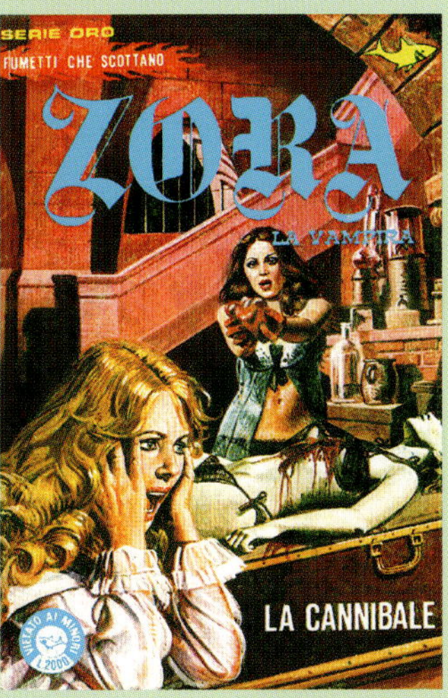

Left: Zora Serie Oro, n. 3,
La Cannibale, The Cannibal,
July 1982.

Far left: Zora la Vampira, n. 77,
Lo Schiavo di Dracula,
The Slave of Dracula,
December 1977.

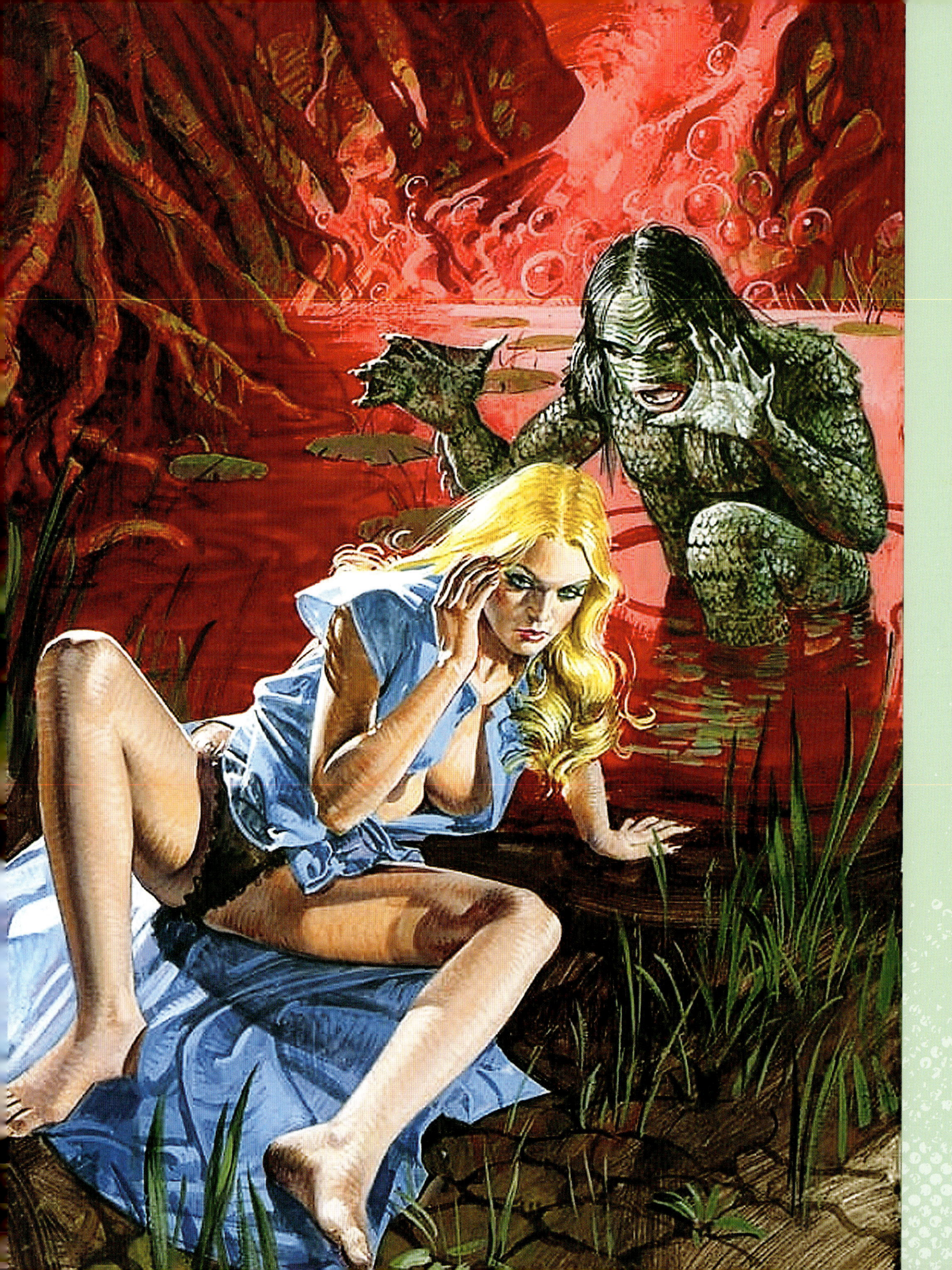

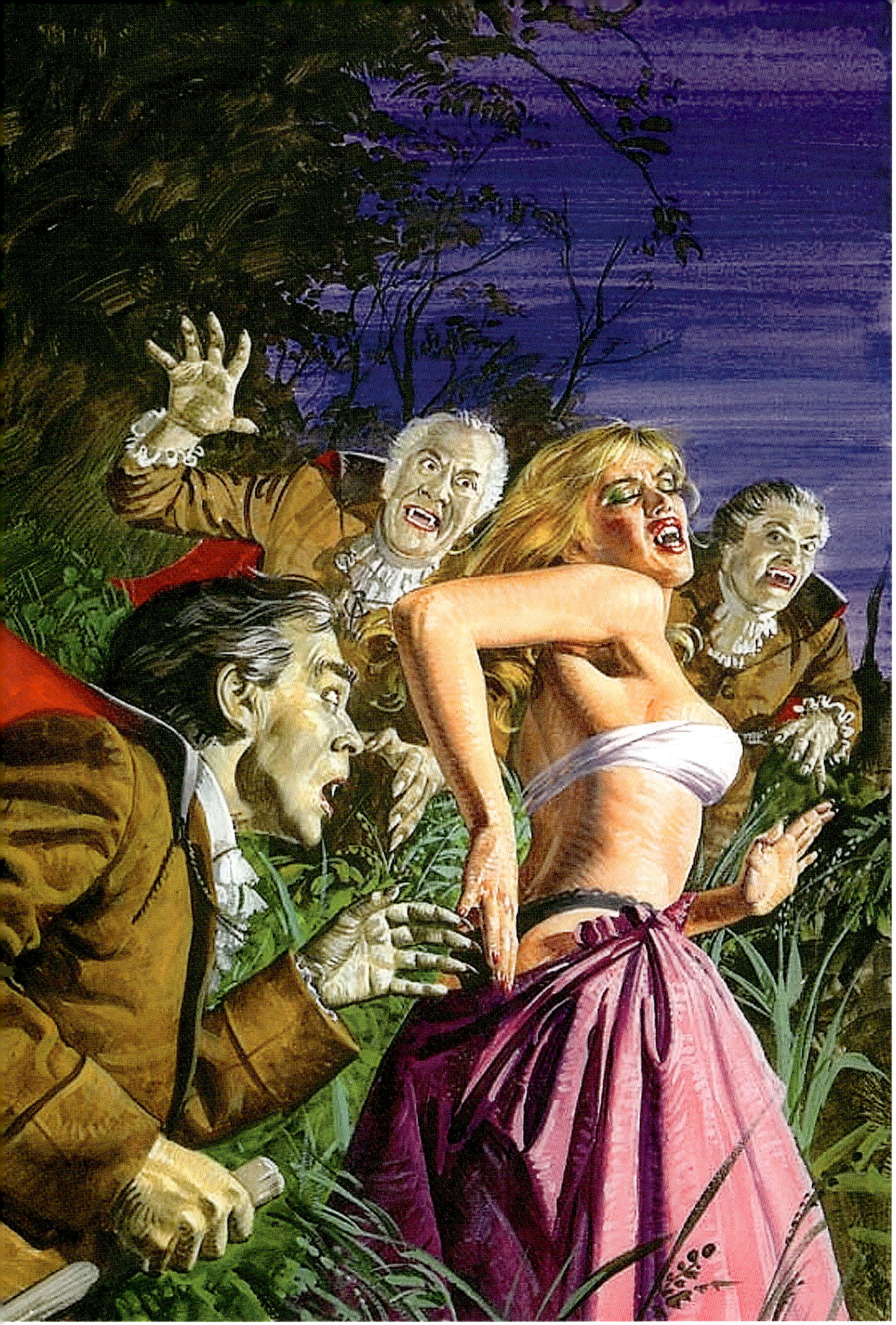

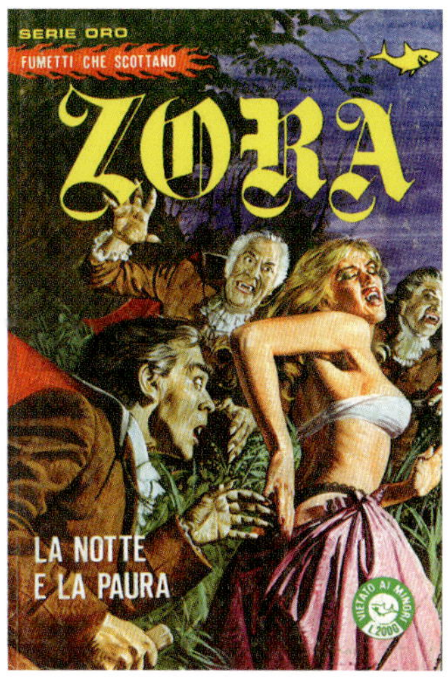

Left: Zora Serie Oro, n. 6,
La Notte e la Paura,
The Night and the Fear,
September 1982.

Far left: Zora Serie Oro, n. 5,
Lo Sguardo che Uccide,
The Look that Kills,
September 1982.

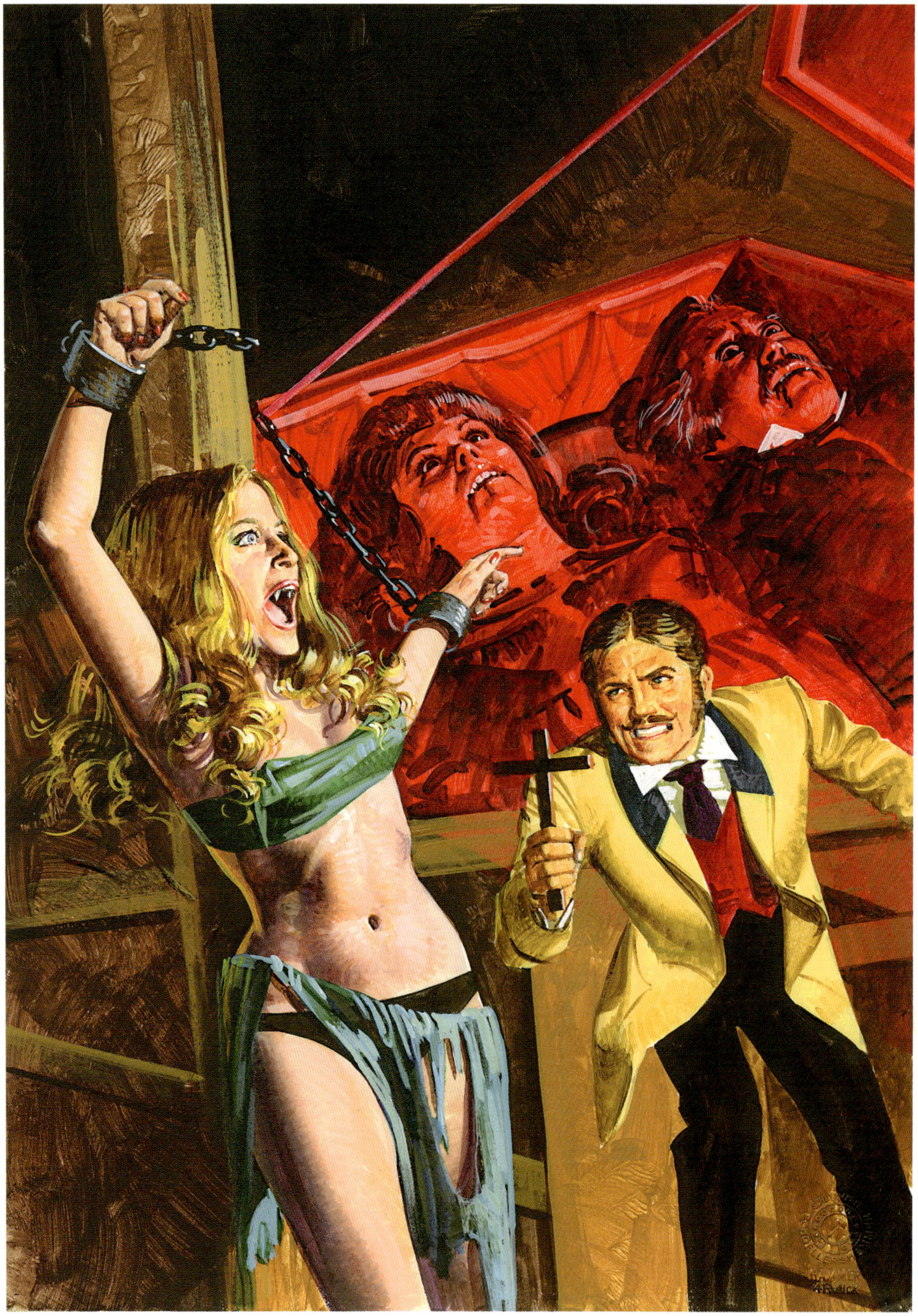

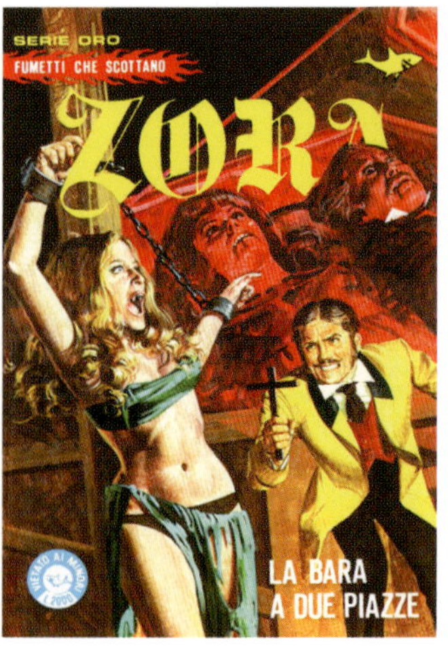

Left: Zora Serie Oro, n. 7,
La Bara a Due Piazze,
The Coffin on Two Squares,
November 1982.

Right: Zora Serie Oro, n. 8,
La Corruttrice, The Corrupter,
December 1982.

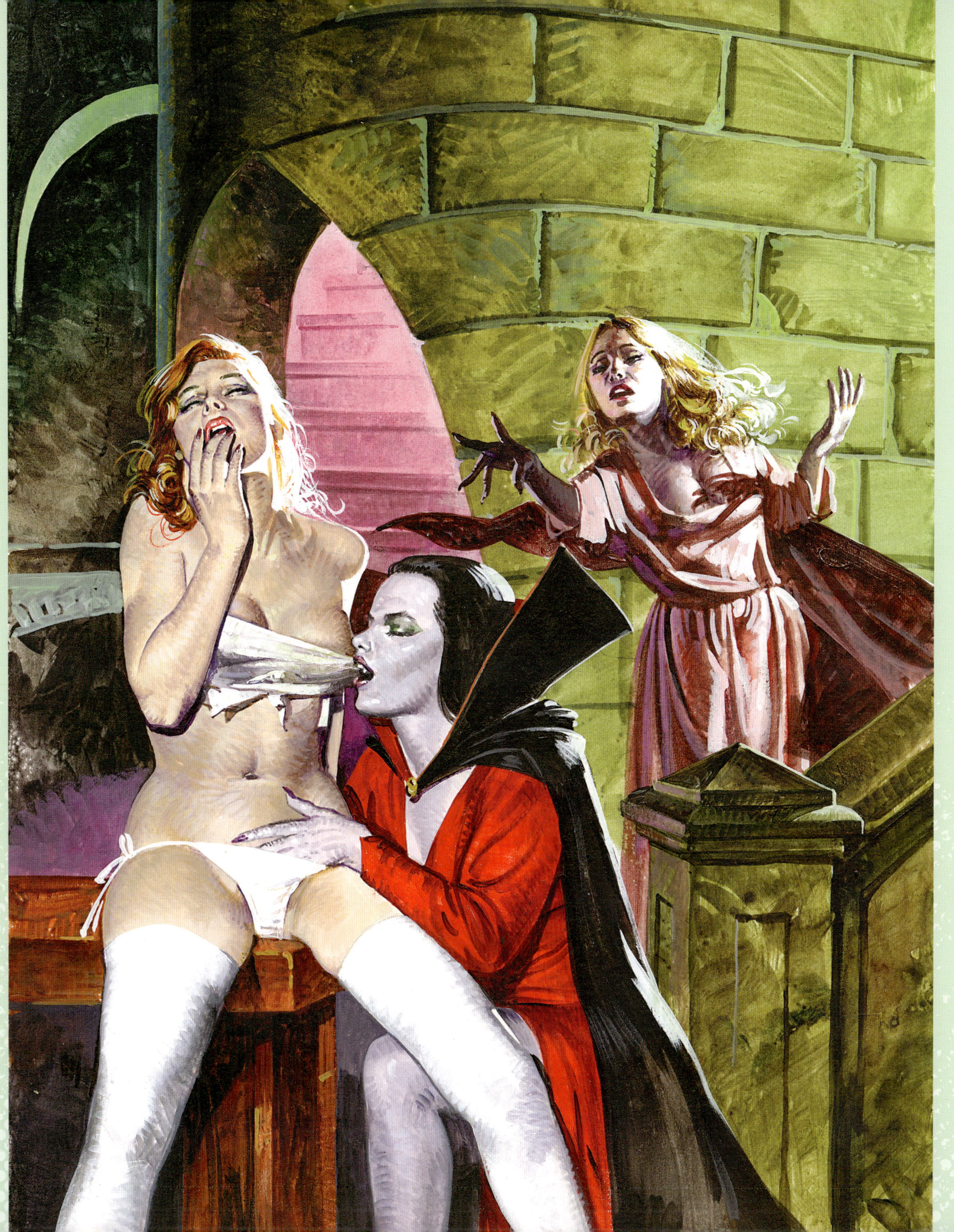

ACKNOWLEDGEMENTS

Korero Press and Emanuele Taglietti would like to thank the following people, without whose help this book would not have been possible: Gianni Bono, Giada Barbieri, Katia Petronelli, Gianluca Pellegrini, Vinicio D'Intino, Steve Silvester, Luciano Visani (Muller), Diego Torrini (Squitty) and all those below who provided images.

PICTURE CREDITS

aelhra: 64, 84, 115, 129

Bruno & Carlo Parrillo: 113, 119

Diego Torrini (Squitty) – vintageroticomics.forumcommunity.net: 34, 83

Emanuele Taglietti: 2, 9, 12, 14, 15, 16, 17, 18, 19, 160

Francesco Lo Presti: 106

Marcello Di Graci (Il Doge): 21, 40, 55, 62, 70, 77, 90, 95, 109, 134, 136

Mark Alfrey – spaghettifumetti.com: 4, 6, 11, 27, 32, 33, 48, 58, 72, 76, 78, 92, 98, 99, 108, 122, 127, 128, 130, 133, 142, 148, 149, 154, 155, 158, 159

Marco Boffi: 80, 103, 144, 157

Paperissima123: 20, 53, 54, 56, 57, 59, 60, 61, 63, 64, 67, 68, 70, 104, 107, 123

Private collection: 10, 28, 44, 52, 91, 105, 112, 114, 116, 123, 141, 151, 152, 153

Rhasko: 121

Ritorno al Fumetto di Claudio Felici: 116, 118

Rich Oberg – mensadventure.com: 24, 26, 30, 35, 36, 38, 39, 42, 45, 46, 49, 50, 65, 66, 68, 69, 70, 71, 74, 75, 79, 82, 83, 86, 87, 88, 90, 94, 97, 100, 101, 102, 110, 111, 124, 126, 128, 131, 132, 135, 138, 139, 140, 143 146, 147, 150

Segni and Disegni di Claudia Salmin: 90

Tiziano Baratella: 96, 120

Right: La Poliziotta and Frankenstein, 2014.

FOLLOWING SPREAD

Left: Orrornero, n. 6, *Nelle fauci del coccodrillo, Telecinesi, Caccia alla Vampira,*
In the Jaws of the Crocodile, Telekinesis, Vampire Hunt, March 1, 1985.

Right: Sbarre, n. 30, *Povero Sbirro,* Poor Cop, June 1986.

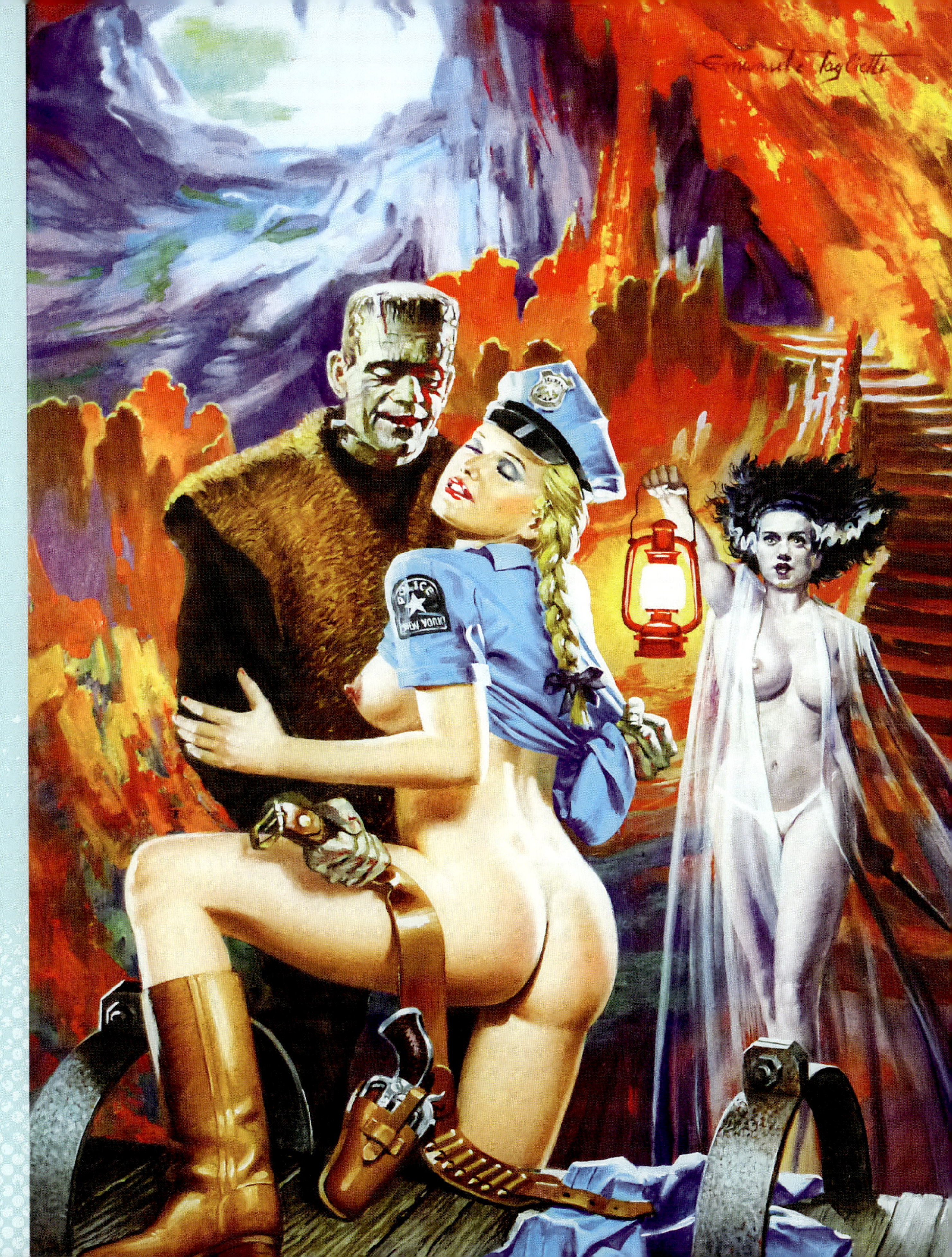

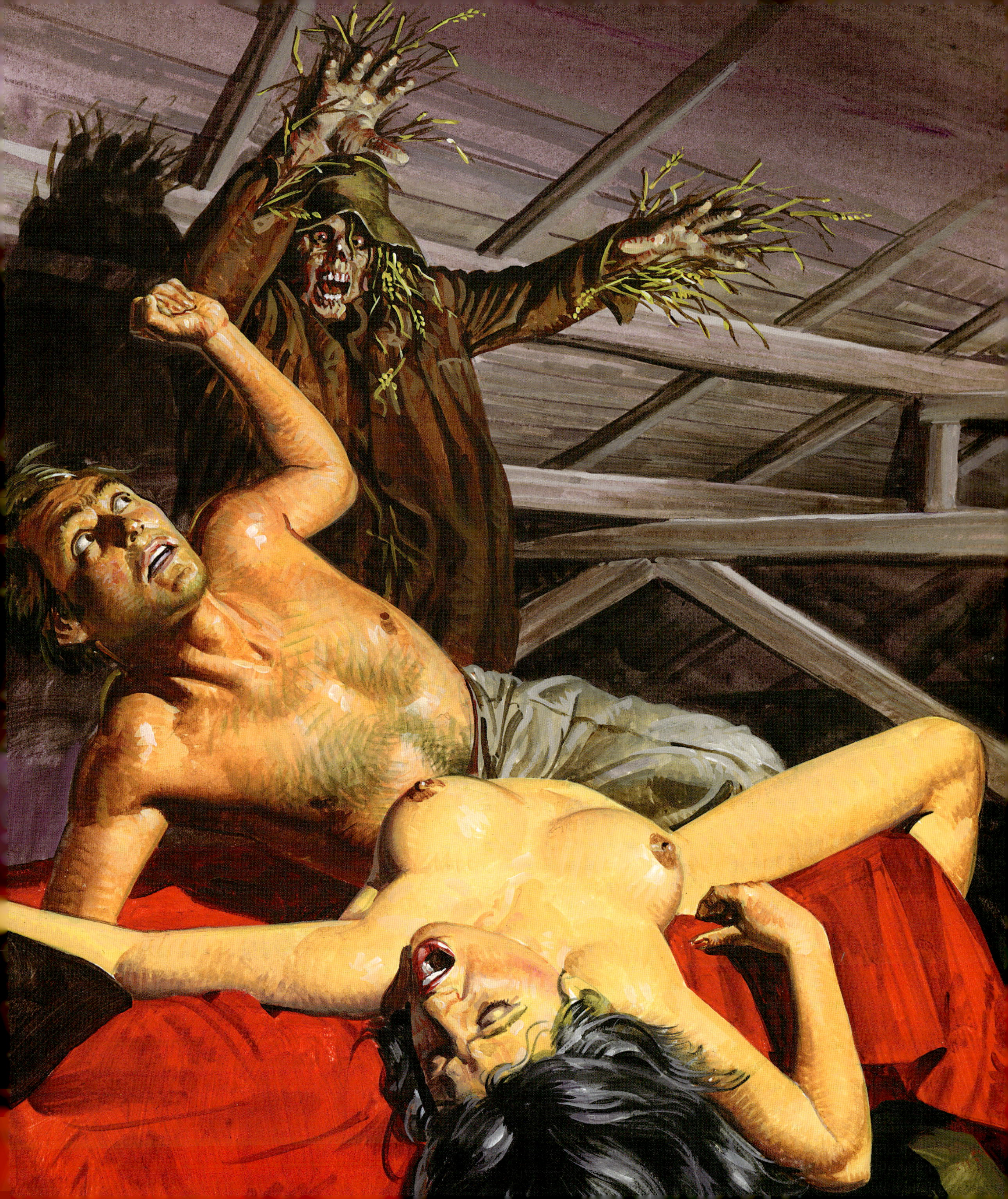

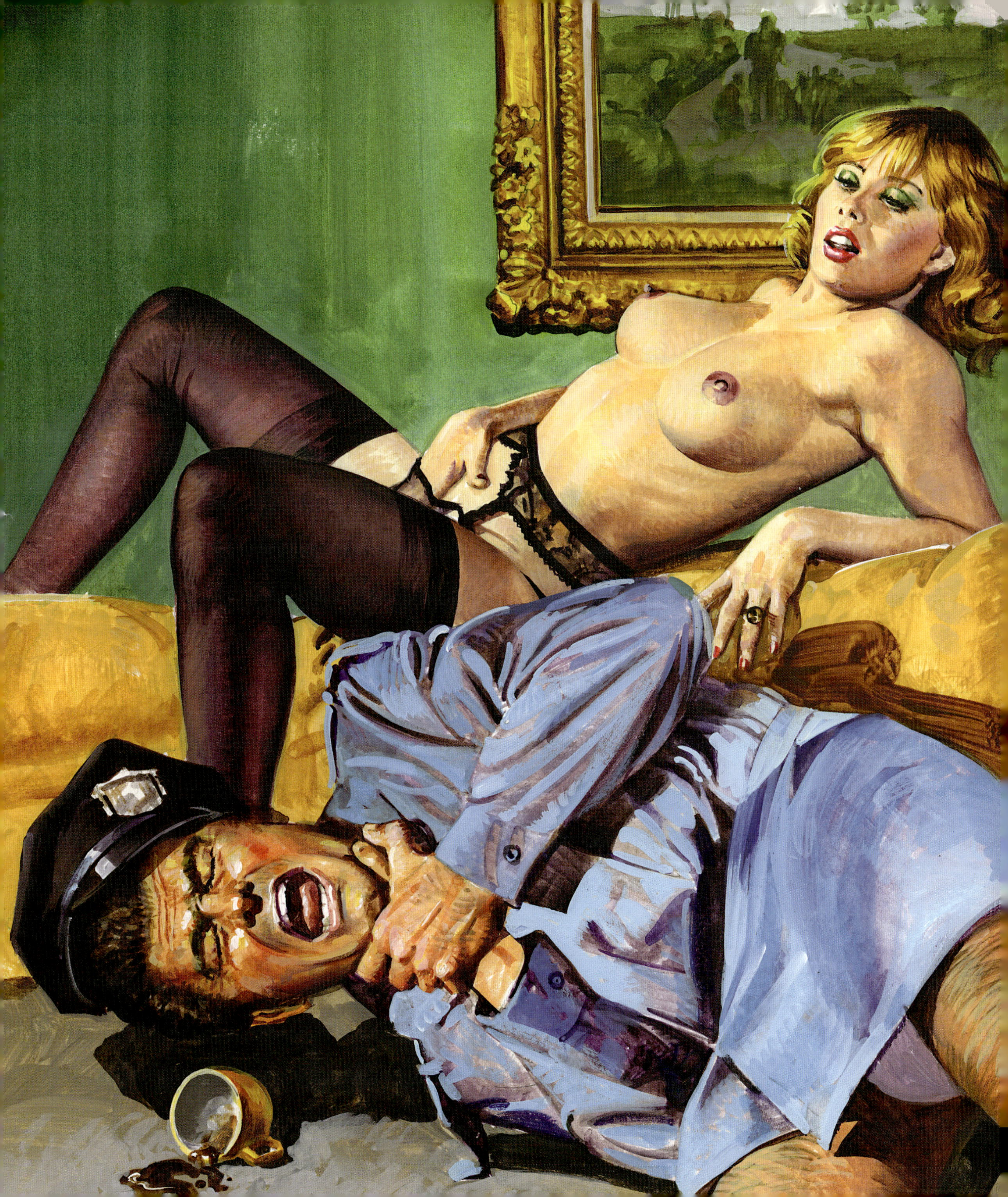

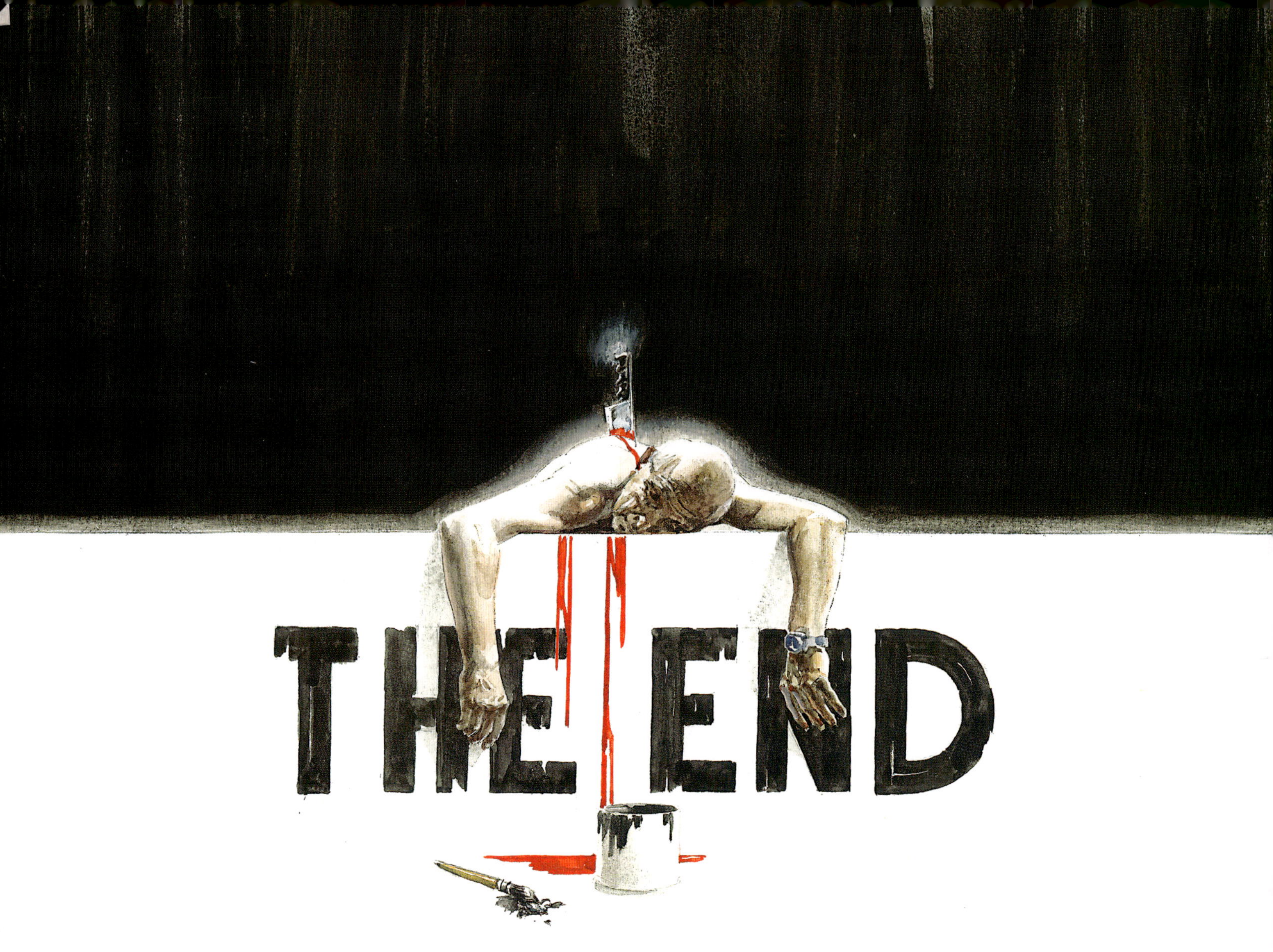
THE END